THE
POLITICS OF PICTURES

The creation of the public
in the age of popular media

John Hartley

London and New York

First published 1992
by Routledge
11 New Fetter Lane, London EC4P 4EE

Simultaneously published in the USA and Canada
by Routledge
a division of Routledge, Chapman and Hall Inc.
29 West 35th Street, New York, NY 10001

© 1992 John Hartley

Typeset in 10/12 pt Linotron Times by
J&L Composition Ltd, Filey, North Yorkshire

Printed in Great Britain by
Butler & Tanner Ltd, Frome and London

British Library Cataloguing in Publication Data
Hartley, John
The politics of pictures: the creation of the public
in the age of popular media.
I. Title
302.234

Library of Congress Cataloging-in-Publication Data
Hartley, John
The politics of pictures: the creation of the public in the age
of popular media / John Hartley.
p.   cm.
Includes bibliographical references and index.
1. Mass media – Audiences.   2. Mass media – Political aspects.
3. Politics – Social aspects.   4. Pictures.   I. Title.
P96.A83H37   1992
302.23–dc20   91–47601

ISBN 0–415–01541–3 (hb)
ISBN 0–415–01542–1 (pb)

To T.H.
(for/on/and the beach)

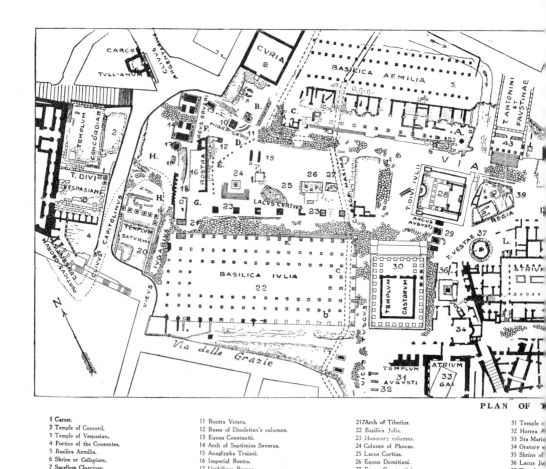

PLAN OF T

Plan of the Roman Forum: the public domain as forensic ambiguity

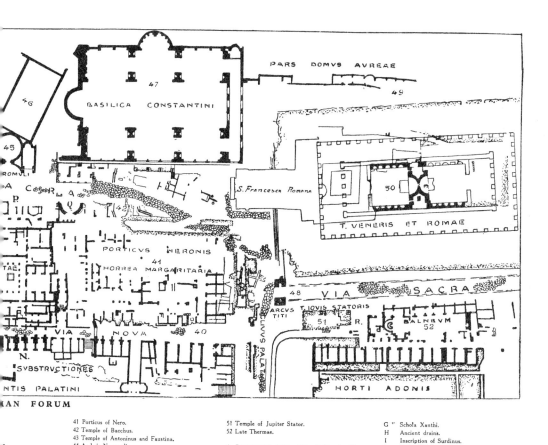

PARS DOMVS AVREAE

49

BASILICA CONSTANTINI

47

46

45

ROMVLI

A CO...R A

P

42

TAE.

PORTICVS NERONIS
41
HORREA MARGARITARIA

N.

SVBSTRVCTIONES

NTIS PALATINI

VIA NOVA 40

ARCVS TITI

CLIVVS PALAT...

S. Francesca Romana

T. VENERIS ET ROMAE

50

48 VIA SACRA

T. IOVIS STATORIS
51 R. BALNEVM 52

HORTI ADONIS

...AN FORUM

CONTENTS

LIST OF FIGURES

ACKNOWLEDGEMENTS

I'd like to thank Tina Horton, Anna Patterson, Frances O'Brien, Rose Barnecut, Ien Ang, Meaghan Morris. By accident and good fortune, the book was completed while I was travelling, so I've had the benefit of the company and conversation of these exceptional people, globally dispersed but collectively an inspiration, which I think shows in the book, and I thank them for it as well as for their friendship. I'd also like to thank my best-ever editor, Rebecca Barden, for much the same reasons. Two other exceptional but not very big people, my daughters Karri and Rhiannon, made me want to write something worthwhile, and I thank them for that incentive; also, given that they were between 0 and 3 years old while all this was afoot, I thank them for staying asleep long enough in the mornings for me to get on with it.

Part of Chapter 4 was originally given as a paper to the 'Toward a Comprehensive Theory of the Audience' conference at the University of Illinois in 1990, and I thank Lawrence Grossberg, Ellen Wartella and James Hay for the invitation and for letting me use the material here. The same applies to the organizers of the fourth International Television Studies Conference at the University of London in 1991, where part of Chapter 5 was given as a paper. Thanks to Deborah Chambers and Graeme Turner, who gave me a forum at the Inaugural Australian Cultural Studies Conference at the University of Western Sydney in 1990, to raise the issues that have resulted in Chapter 1. Thanks, too, to Steve Mickler for his research at the Royal Commission into Aboriginal Deaths in Custody, which I have drawn on in Chapter 8.

The publishers and I would also like to acknowledge gratefully the use of copyright material in the illustrations from the following people and organizations:

3.1 New Age Nature: 'For All Flesh is as Grass' Carol Lewis, Marketing Manager, Innoxa Cosmetics, and Omon Advertising Agency, Australia;
3.2. Our Family Picnic: Eastman Kodak Consumer Markets Division, Rochester, New York;

3.5. Set Table: Maureen Swanage, Managing Editor, Australian Academy of Science, Canberra;

3.6 Cubism/Postmodernism: Alan Tobin, Lintas Advertising Agency, Melbourne;

3.7. Album: Bruno Giagu, Publisher, Brugi Design Pty. Ltd., and Tom Sullivan, Sydney;

3.8. Picnic at Ayers Rock: David Arthur-Simons, Sydney, 1984, 154 × 110 mm, collage. From the series 'Historic Australian Moments';

3.10. 3.11. See Jungle: RCA Ltd. London, Nick Egan and Andy Earl;

3.12. Art: The Face, London;

4.1. Washingtoon: The Village Voice, Mark Alan Stamaty and The Washington Post Writers' Group, New York (and Greg Seigworth of the University of Illinois);

4.2. Sophie Lee: John Hall, Editor-in-Chief, *TV Week*, Melbourne;

4.3–4.17. (pix of TVs): Denise Corrigan, Museum of Contemporary Art, Sydney and Jim Mayne, W. Anderson, Noel Blundell, Susan and Tracey Lloyd, Jan Pukallus, Jean Grice, Doreen Gilbert, V. Shephard and Bouncer, Dawn Livingstone, Alison Muir, Renée Stacey, Ron and Joyce Elbourn, Joy Ferrie, Allan Mitchell and the Ali-Kurang Community, Freda Thur;

7.1. The Great Chartist Crowd: The Royal Archive, Windsor Castle, *The Sunday Times*, London and Harold Evans;

8.13. 'Two Darwinites': Andrew Cowell, Editorial Director, Mason Stewart Publications;

8.14–8.17. (West Australian): West Australian Newspapers, Perth;

8.18–8.22. (Truth): Owen Thomson. Publisher, Truth Newspapers, Melbourne.

Every attempt has been made to obtain permission to reproduce copyright material. If there are any omissions, please contact Rebecca Barden at Routledge's London office.

PUBLIC-ITY
(Introduction)

This book is about the search for something which, from one point of view, does not exist. Looked at another way, it is something so obvious that its existence is usually taken for granted. It cannot be interrogated, inspected, observed or investigated directly, but it completely surrounds us socially and it permeates our personal identity. It has no bodily form, but it is powerful; by some reckonings it is the ultimate power, being the source of sovereignty. It is a place, but you can't walk into it, and it is a group of people – a vast group of people – but they never meet. The place and the people are familiar figures, but although you know them well, you have never seen them and you never will, even though you're one of them.

What is it? Who are they? The place is the public domain, and the people are the public. The public domain has not, since classical city states, existed as a place you can literally enter, while the public in its entirety has never met at all, for even in classical times those who gathered in the agora or forum to legislate and adjudicate their own and each other's affairs in the name of democracy were a small, unrepresentative minority of the people of the city states so governed, well outnumbered by slaves, women, and so on.

Neither the public domain nor the public itself can be found in contemporary states; they've literally disappeared. However, both of them are very familiar figures, figures of speech, in which everyone spends quite a bit of time. So while they don't exist as spaces and assemblies, the public realm and the public are still to be found, large as life, in media. Television, popular newspapers, magazines and photography, the popular media of the modern period, are the public domain, the place where and the means by which the public is created and has its being. The clue to its whereabouts is not to look for citizens in the city centre (that will only produce paradox and sore feet), but to look for the public in publicity.

If the public can nowadays only be encountered in mediated form, it becomes necessary to look at these mediations to discover the state of the contemporary public domain. This entails a new kind of political analysis – not the study of government, nor of constitutional and electoral

1

arrangements, nor of the way a sovereign power executes its will. Instead, it is necessary to ask what institutions and what discourses are engaged in making the mediated representations of the public domain, what the resulting picture of the public looks like, and who speaks for – and to – the public so created.

There is also the question of the relationship, if any, between these representations and any people who may be looking in at the time. This becomes a riddle too, for when you look beyond the media for a more accurate view of the real public, you only come across more media, and more institutions which produce and peddle their own visualization of the public for their own purposes. So there is ultimately no real public which can be appealed to by the analyst in search of the truth, no reality to oppose to or compare with media publics. However, it is at this point that traditional political analysis falters; it cannot get past a Platonic opposition between image and reality, an opposition which has, incidentally, never unduly troubled the popular media.

Instead of dismissing media images or discourses as unreal 'shadows in the cave', it is necessary to recognize that images, discourses, texts, media and so on are themselves quite real. They can be observed and investigated empirically (which is more than you can say for the public as such), and they are all too real in their modes of industrial production, their social force, political effects and cultural power. So it is not a question of contrasting a real public with the illusory media (almost vice versa, in fact); it is a matter of showing how pervasive the textualization of public life has become, and how it works. This new kind of political analysis is easily named; it is the politics of pictures.

The politics of pictures is part of cultural studies, which in turn is concerned with a large area of civil life whose myriad practices are now widely seen as political. But this isn't traditional politics; in the politics of pictures there's no party organization, no manifesto, no institutional apparatus for formulating policy, no legislature, no executive, no administration, no leadership cadre, no campaigning, no polling, no electoral victory and no defeat, though there are certainly winners and losers. In the politics of pictures, it would be intolerable to have to toe the party line, to compromise principles on a daily basis for the sake of unity, to display loyalty to a leader, to fiddle about with constituency problems and to lie convincingly in public in order to win support. This kind of discipline, collective responsibility and compromise is not what the cultural sphere is for. On the contrary, culture is for the expansion of difference, the expression of identity, individuality, imagination. It's the last place you'd look for politics. In cultural politics people are more like Groucho than Karl Marx – they wouldn't want to belong to any party that would have them as a member.

But the cultural sphere is nonetheless political, and so are pictures. They are the place where collective social action, individual identity and symbolic imagination meet – the nexus between culture and politics. Pictures, including the 'talking pictures' of electronic media and the word-pictures of the press, are much more socially pervasive, commonplace components of everyday life than straightforward politics is, or ever has been, for most people. Their public, political aspects are real, and engagement with them is personal and practical, so they are more directly participatory than representative politics ever could be. They are also the form in which democracy is diffused and disciplined; not only do pictures dramatize and teach the democratic process, but also, for vast readerships, they are the very form in which that process is performed, and the means by which traditional political issues and activists are tested, sometimes to destruction.

Something to confess

If the public domain of today is like any previous place, it isn't the classical forum in the city centre, but the much lonelier medieval confessional box. The modern popular media are, among other things, media of disclosure, of visualization – of confession. The traditional form of religious confession was a strictly private, personal affair for the sinner, but it was performed in and for a global institution, represented by the shriver. It was thus a means by which populations could keep a disciplinary eye on themselves, constantly checking that their actions, thoughts and relationships conformed with what their maker wanted of them. It was a technology of the self, even if the major beneficiaries were the forces of authority (including the church, the mediating institution between selves and salvation). Public confession, on the other hand, was much rarer, more ceremonial, and more a matter of political theatre; the confession on the scaffold, the show trial, the use of the body and words of the condemned to teach massed onlookers the truth of certain well-known political tenets. Pre-democratic societies tied public confession to penance, and made that virtually synonymous with punishment, usually capital. A visible cause/effect nexus between public confession and death naturally discouraged imitation on a wide scale; it was a technology of society.

Confession, both private and public, is still the province of a global, mediating institution, but it is no longer the church. When both private selves and public society were secularized, confession was disengaged from sin and punishment. Public confession retained the theatricality of exhibition of the self, but dropped the requirement for death and/or damnation. The result was television; public confession, the place where self and society meet, the means by which reader becomes citizen, the frame in which you show and tell and don't go to hell. The modern popular media are thoroughly confessional, with reward (in the shape of enhanced social visibility) for those who confess in public (in both actuality and drama formats), and a lesson in social selfhood for the massed onlookers. There's even a system for measuring the efficacy of public confessions which comprises the commissioning of private ones, on a mass scale, in the form of vox-pops, opinion polls, feedback shows, letters pages, agony columns, ratings and audience surveys. Now it's our civic duty to state, vote or tick our opinion of, preference for, or assent to scenarios, choices or questions to which we have been invited to respond in the media we read, see or hear. By such means various publics are created, circulated, adjusted and supplanted, in competition or coexistence with each other, available for media readers to slip on and off like a jacket as the need arises, or to wear simultaneously like layers of clothes: different, complementary, mutually enhancing, and each designed for its appropriate place and function, from top to toe, underwear to winter coat.

These media publics are produced (and endlessly reproduced) by institutions (broadcasting, publishing, etc.) and discourses (of nationhood, consumerism, citizenship, etc.); that is, by large-scale social forces, and by organized structures and practices over which the individual person has very little control. You don't make the coat you wear, even though it's *yours* from fit and style down to legal ownership; the number of people, professions, industries and transactions that do go into its making is scarcely credible, but they're hardly comparable with what's needed to make one media text. Similarly, you don't make the public of which you're a member. It is true that publics cannot be created from nothing, only from existing populations which already form complex communities, but nevertheless they are not made in their own image, whatever that may be. Competing institutions and discourses vie with each other to create very different publics, so not surprisingly each available version turns out to be the image of its maker, not, primarily, of its 'wearer'. Even so, it is a mutual process; the media are simultaneously creative and participatory. They create a picture of the public, but it goes live, as it were, only when people participate in its creation, not least by turning themselves into the audience. Participation takes the form, among others, of confession, even as we read and watch, requiring, in response to the public confessions on screen and page, constant private soul-searching, comparison, internal interrogation and realignment of the self, and in the process we participate in the creation of ourselves as social others; as 'the public'.

A history of looking

Just as clothes are good to look at as well as being useful to wear, so they are public as well as private. If you glance appraisingly at your reflection in shop windows as you walk down the street, you'll see your own public image through a stranger's eyes; you're a public picture. At a social rather than merely personal level of observation, public visibility, whether of pictures, clothes or selves, is part of what may be called the 'history of looking', a perspective on public politics and social change that foregrounds the relationships between media and their audiences.

Within this history of looking it is possible to see in different times and places, among disparate media and for different purposes, a recurring politicization of the readers and viewers of popular media, both within the textual fabric of media productions and in the relationships between media institutions and members of the public. In fact, and this is a general argument of *The Politics of Pictures*, the creation and politicization of readerships is a key feature of politics in contemporary society, while, at the same time, the public domain as traditionally understood has become increasingly mediated, transformed from a place on the ground into a space in the schedules. Two moves then: the textualization of politics, and the politicization of texts, accomplished within the ambiguous frames of public/private, secret/confessional, talkative pictures.

So in very general terms *The Politics of Pictures* is about the historical construction of media readerships, the building techniques employed in that symbolic construction process, and the political uses of the resulting media audiences. It traces changes in the notions of the public and the public domain from classical political theory to contemporary media practice, and it shows how visualization operates in the history of drama and journalism as creators of 'popular reality'. Part of the popular reality so created is the public itself.

If looks could kill

All this has clearly got something to do with politics, but perhaps the other term of the title needs some justification. Why pictures?

There is a fundamental reason for thinking about popular politics in terms of pictures. Ever since classical city states began the traditions that still underlie contemporary political organization, an integral component of political practice has been the faculty of sight. This has been exploited in different ways over the years, so there's a history of looking in which the *visualization* of the public, the public domain, and of political practice, has developed and changed. Visualization is the means by which direct or 'primitive' democracy can be enlarged and complicated to become representative democracy; it's the foundation of contemporary political process, and is therefore among the most important tasks that popular media have undertaken, a task made more rather than less crucial by the fact that representative and direct democracy are not the same thing, and that things have changed since the disappearance of a physical space in which the public could congregate, gaze upon, and so govern, its collective self.

5

So ingrained is the idea that public affairs are visible that metaphors of light and sight suffuse political rhetoric, acting as guarantors for the credibility of the representation. Politics and truth become inextricably bound up with notions of visualization, representation, pictorial power. In the end, which is now, visualization by rhetoric and representation becomes not just a convincing metaphor which stands for something going on elsewhere, but independently real, standing up for itself. Contemporary politics is the politics of pictures, and for the purposes of political effectivity, the public is a representation in the popular media. In the end, pictures achieve their own political status, never mind what actuality they seem to depict. And so the politics of pictures refers to the deletion of the public as an assembly of people and its reinvention as pictures which serve the same purpose.

Just as the public has become progressively more mediated, so political contestations have moved ever more decisively into the realm of visual representation. Campaigns on all issues, from 'political' issues like elections and the environment to 'cultural' ones like lifestyle and leisure, have become progressively more pictorial. In the process, the politicization of pictures pervades the whole media domain (the 'public domain'), so that traditional distinctions between public and private, political and cultural, are increasingly blurred, and pictures become public and political even in formerly private, personal, cultural spheres. A clear example of this process is in gender representations, where a long campaign by feminists and others has ensured the politicization of visual representations which had previously seemed ideologically inert, from paintings in art galleries to family photos on the mantelpiece, from what you keep in the wardrobe to what you see on the news-stands. And the purpose of these campaigns has been not only to politicize and change mediated visualizations of gender, but to change readers' behaviour in turn; using pictures, in short, to dramatize and teach private politics.

Meanwhile, the popular media have pictorialized. None of them is made entirely of pictures, but even the word-based press depends in the crucial area of readership appeal upon pictures. In fact, it might be argued that increasing pictoriality is a precondition for the popularity of every medium; success and survival depend on popularity and that depends on pictures. Thus, all of the popular media have, over the last two or three hundred years, tended to become ever more pictorial, with whole media declining in popularity when something apparently more visual comes along (print giving ground to cinema and TV), while within the press, those books and periodicals with large circulations are, without exception, the heavily illustrated ones.

Even on TV, a medium which is made of pictures, it is possible to see a similar historic tendency towards increasing pictorialization. Compared with its early days of static, wordy reliance upon definitions of story and substance borrowed from the press, TV news is now picture led, sport is ever more spectacularized, documentaries don't get commissioned unless there's a good visual angle to start with, and natural history shows are regularly promoted not for their fauna and flora but on the strength of their heroic camerawork. Even TV drama, which has an intrinsically visual component, is ·drifting inexorably towards pictoriality and away from dialogue (especially the leading-edge mini-series format, though long-form 'soap' is not exempt from this tendency). Now drama is categorized not as tragedy or comedy, but according to what it *looks* like: action, landscape or costume drama. Acting becomes a succession of poses, not lines, as grunting sociopaths (action), prissy middle-class couples (landscape), or brain-dead walking clothes-hangers (costume) stumble their way through plots whose main purpose is to get the special effects aligned with the best camera angle, and to propel their bodies into, or out of, a succession of expensive explosions, exotic locations or extravagant frocks.

To know, know, know you

The Politics of Pictures is designed to appeal to a wide variety of readers; it is interdisciplinary in approach and application, drawing, as occasion demands, on anthropology, philosophy, politics and history, as well as from media and cultural studies. Its method of 'forensic' examination of primary texts is an extension of literary studies, while its arguments about the relations between media and politics are important to political and social scientists. It has new insights into the history of journalism, which is approached through the concepts of truth, community and readership, rather than by following the usual alarms and excursions of the insider industry. Cultural and media studies are taken in a new direction with the attempt not only to understand popular media but also to popularize that understanding. The issues raised in this book are not only central to contemporary public life but also important for every reader, who is, in the end, that point of unity around which all the disparate strands of knowledge cohere: the public.

The book is divided into two parts: the first half deals with the pervasiveness of popular pictorial politics, and the textual, discursive and representational mechanisms media use to create and address their publics; the second half deals more specifically with the symbiotic relationship between readership and citizenship in the history of journalism. Both parts are concerned with political struggles over the status of knowledge and truth, as well as that of the public and of its mediated visualization. The book as a whole is interested in what I've called the 'three Ds' – drama, didactics, and democracy – three public virtues which according to classical political myth are coterminous; democratic participation is at the same time both performative and pedagogic, dramatizing and

7

explaining, showing and teaching, at the very moment of responsible self-representation and decision-making. Now, however, the three Ds have been institutionalized; they're no longer what people do, they are the gigantic social institutions of media, education and government. Each of these institutions strives to create the public in its own image, and it is part of the argument of this book that of the three, the one which creates a public closest to that of the classical model – that is a public which is simultaneously performative, participatory and pedagogic – is the one with least social prestige and fewest political credentials; the media.

Chapter 1, 'Popular Reality', discusses cultural studies, a theoretical perspective which this book explicitly adopts but also implicitly criticizes. For a generation cultural studies has been interested in the connections between culture and politics, meaning and class, media and society, aesthetics and power. It is now going through a period of rapid disciplinary consolidation, gaining ground in tertiary institutions around the world as a subject in its own right. Chapter 1 traces the twin tendencies of 'institutionalization' and 'ancestralization' in cultural studies, showing how some of its founding concerns have still to reach a wider public, and how its interest in the popular has not enhanced its own popularity beyond the campus wall. Here then are some problems to which the book as a whole is a response; there are real differences between popular and intellectual culture, between action and understanding, between the teaching that is done in universities and that which occurs in the media. While cultural studies, as a formal mode of intellectual inquiry with its own history, personnel and fields of study, cannot avoid its fate, which is to take root in universities as an academic subject, equally it cannot afford to abandon its interest in popular culture, political action and public pedagogy. It must avoid mere scholasticism, but equally it must outgrow some of its earlier tendencies, among which was a willingness to subordinate the quest for knowledge to the quest for power. As the inscription on Marx's tomb doesn't quite put it, the point was not to understand the world but to reinvent it in the image of a political philosophy based on Marxism, which in cultural studies, as in so many other spheres of knowledge, has proved itself an absolutely indispensable guide to *reading* the world but an ultimately disastrous guide to *ruling* it. 'Wanting to know' remains a prime motivation for cultural studies, and this politics of knowledge is also cultural politics, but the old slogan 'Knowledge is Power' shouldn't be taken too literally – cultural studies is not a political programme. However, it is very well placed, because of its own interdisciplinary history, to analyse knowledge and power in both theoretical and popular contexts, and this book is designed as a contribution to that enterprise.

Chapter 2, 'Agoraphilia', takes some of the methodological concerns hinted at in the first chapter a stage further, by criticizing the tendency towards binarism in western cultural and political thought, even while recognizing the power of binarism as it is deployed in both popular and theoretical domains. Instead of accepting binary categories (like reality: illusion), and analysing the world according to them, I propose 'forensic analysis' as an alternative, where forensic means not only the search for objective traces of people's actions and intentions, but also the science of argumentation in public in search of the truth. Chapter 2 begins the forensic analysis of the public domain by tracing it to its classical roots, the Greek agora or Roman forum: the physical public space at the centre of the city state, wherein the public actually congregated in order to conduct political, legal, religious and market affairs. Now it's gone; there is no public space. It hasn't disappeared but gone private (a process the Greeks would have described literally as idiotic), and turned into pictures.

Chapter 3, 'No Picnic', is a forensic search for the public in the history of photography. Part of its purpose is to show how just one signifier, in this case a *picnic*, can occur throughout various photographic media, which means that analysis based on just one of them, even TV or the press, necessarily misses the way that images suffuse and pervade the realm of popular reality. I have chosen the picnic because it is at first sight ideologically inert; what could be more natural? But of course it soon turns out that the humble picnic can bear all sorts of potent meanings, and pictures of picnics are circulated not as natural and neutral but as cultural and political, representing the most important elements of social and civic life: family, empire, race, nation, science, heroes, fashion, gender, age group, art, sexuality. Picnics are part social institution, part medium in their own right, part activity and part symbol, constituting the public even while appearing to let it out for a relaxing walk. Nature, the countryside and private leisure turn out to be products of (not binary oppositions to) urban, public, scientific culture; and picnics, pictured in any medium, turn out to be politically and historically charged. As we cut a swath through the tangled undergrowth of visual meaning, they let us glimpse new branches of knowledge in the thickets of popular reality – a sociology of discourse, a history of semiosis, a geodemographics of meaning, a politics of picnics.

Chapter 4, 'Power Viewing', actually finds the public that the previous chapter sought. As you might have guessed, they're at home watching the telly. But guessing is not reckoned a scientific approach to knowledge, so *how* you know that what is sitting at home watching the telly is in fact the public, or *how* you know what they're actually doing as they watch, become serious problems. These can be addressed by taking seriously the conclusion reached so far: that the public is a fictionalization of citizenship, and the audience for popular media is a discursive production too; an 'invisible fiction' produced and deployed by the institutions which have most to gain from its existence. If the public and the audience are indeed discursive productions, there's not much point in barging into people's living rooms to watch them watching telly. Better to look at the discursive production of audienceship, and to reconceptualize the activity people undertake in their homes as something neither autonomous nor authentic, but the end product of a discursive strategy in which viewers are participants but not original sources. Better also to look for the meaning of viewership not in what viewers confess to on survey forms, whether administered by the industry or the academy. For what such confession reveals is not the true or real audience but the efficacy of the media's construction of their ideal readers, to whom actual viewers either approximate or not. There is no 'empirical' audience, in fact, that is not already fully textualized, suffused with discourses that organize actual practices. Such practices include what I have called power viewing, which is both the obsessive engagement of the telly addict and media academic (power viewing in depth), and a pervasive, anthropological 'will to watch' (power viewing in width), which, it seems to me, characterizes our entire species, and which underlies not only prime-time TV and fashion, but philosophy too; the politics of Aristotle and the philosophy of Socrates were both founded on the will to look.

Part of Chapter 4 is taken up with a critique of current trends in audience ethnography; it concludes with an example of what can be achieved from evidence that is both empirical and fully textualized. The audience is investigated in its photographic and epistolary form, not in its living room, resulting in some semiotic history that is based on audience self-representation, not on turning it into a powerless, ethnographized, 'other'.

Chapter 5, 'The Smiling Professions', pursues the philosophical underpinnings of the will to watch by tracing their history. From Aristotle to Gramsci, via Hobbes, Veblen and Kropotkin, philosophers have worried about the education of the public. They have also worried about the ability of institutions of higher learning to do the job. Conversely, popular media have been very successful in gaining readers, and, when looked at from the perspective of public-creation, they have a better teaching record than they're usually credited with. There is in fact a politics of knowledge, a struggle between intellectual culture and popular media, for the creation and education of citizen readers. Because media publics are created in the name of pleasure and voluntary entertainment during leisure time (i.e., not in the name of politics or pedagogy directly), I have dubbed the media as being among the 'smiling professions', whose relationship with the public is based on mutuality and participation, not on duty or coercion. The contemporary emblem for the smiling professions is, it transpires, the Olympian sport of smiling, namely synchronized swimming. Synchronized swimming, at least on television, is the ultimate aestheticization of politics.

Chapters 6, 7 and 8, 'Heliography', 'Common Sense', and 'Journalism in a Post-Truth Society', comprise a history of journalism since 1644 as the visualization of order, the discourse of truth, the creator of publics, and the mediator between common readers, common sense and common-wealths. It is in this context that the traditional distinction between picture and print, image and word, most needs to be superseded, for the print media are media of visualization whether they use words or photographs to achieve their ends. One way of getting beyond the often silly comparisons that are made between television and the press, or picture papers and posh ones, is to think not in terms of the form in which visualizations of social order and disorder are published, but the profession that has arisen to do this work – journalism. Journalism is a social force, a pervasive and central component of contemporary global culture. But it has a comparatively short history; it achieved formal, professional status soon after John Milton proclaimed the freedom of the press in the mid-seventeenth century. Since then the theory and practice of journalism have been developed by writers including Addison, Dr Johnson, Tom Paine, John Fairfax and Winston Churchill, and contributed to in papers as diverse as *Fog's Weekly Journal*, the *Daily Sketch* and the Melbourne *Truth*. In these unlikely hands the themes of journalistic truth, political order and public participation were developed and internationalized, at the same time as readerships, both actual and intended. Somewhere along the line, between John Milton's 'Virgin Truth' and the *Truth*'s topless 'Gulf Girl', stands the figure this book set out to find: a contradictory figure that is both universal and adversarial, popular and produced, participatory and performed, powerful and pervasive: the public.

And that's about it, really.

Part I
PUBLIC PICTURES

1

POPULAR REALITY
A (hair)brush with cultural studies

For many years, my father was a hairbrush. He, that is the hairbrush, was improbably made of perspex. The real thing died before I got to know him, so I carried this hairbrush around, and for me it became the real thing. Ever since then I have been interested in ancestries, in authenticity, and in reality. I've also had a longstanding sympathy for perspex, which I like as a word, as well as a plastic. What all this has to do with cultural studies is, as you read what follows, for you to decide.

Pissed off and pouting?

In the wake of political developments in Europe and the Soviet Union in the late 1980s, 'the left', as a unified western political culture, ceased to exist. Although it was true, and not only of the USA, that 'the country is turning browner, yellower, blacker, more female, more unemployed and more pissed off',[1] it was not the case that these and other disaffections and oppositions saw in each other the mirror and hope of their own struggles; radicalism, like so many other aspects of postmodern culture, was fragmenting, localizing, becoming suspicious of totalizing metaphors of unity which would allow all-inclusive statements and actions to be made, by general intellectuals or activists, on behalf of specific interests. In consequence, it was no longer possible for radicals to presume the coexistence of an international community within which their own work could not only be understood by others but also justified to themselves; to others it might not appear radical at all. So, an unexpected *casualty* of the *cessation* of Cold War hostilities was the sense of shared opposition, that is solidarity, so naturalized that it could appear self-evident, and therefore often remain unspoken.

Cultural political intellectual work was radically destabilized with the demolition of the Berlin Wall and its equivalent metaphorical binary oppositions, resulting in such a pervasive doubt about the existence of 'the left' – broad, ultra, sectarian or whatever – to which we all belong,

15

that there was no longer any ready referent for the pronoun 'we' in cultural politics, including in cultural studies, which had until then been unquestioned as a radical academic enterprise, despite the mixed ambitions and allegiances of its practitioners.

Cultural studies is politically a child of the 1960s, when political radicalism was not only liberating but hip, when public affairs expanded to encompass the mind (and vice versa), when the boundaries between politics, music, sex and drugs became blurred, and when alternative, counter and sub cultures sprang up to claim attention like so many doggies in the window. But institutionally it came of age in the 1980s, a decade whose fashion statement was, according to *Vogue*, the pout, and the pout was 'symptomatic of spoilt, arrogant, eighties behaviour'. But now, says *Vogue*, 'we'll have none of it'.[2] The pout is out, at least at work (it's still permissible in the bedroom, especially on men). Meanwhile the 1960s are back in, to inaugurate the last decade of the millenium. This is not total recall, however, but mannerist copy, clothes shorn of politics, bringing back to the future just enough of the 1960s to hang on a fashion model's newly slimline, thin-lipped and tousle-haired body.

Cultural studies has also changed over the last thirty years, following not so much the cycles and recyclings of fashion, but rather the slower biorhythms of an ageing intellectual generation, which is rarely brown, yellow, black, female and unemployed, even if it retains its politically pissed-off credentials. In fact the question for cultural studies is whether it has changed enough in response to, or even in anticipation of, wider social and cultural developments, or whether it has survived into middle-aged respectability with many of its youthful prejudices intact. If so, any apparent innovations that are associated with cultural studies as it gains a firmer foothold in academic institutions (a process most notable in North America), may not be so bold and radical and new after all, but merely the beginning of a spoilt, arrogant, *pouting* phase for a discipline which has abandoned its 1960s idealism and commitment to social change in favour of a belated discovery of its own 'me generation' selfishness.

Institutional ancestors

So who are 'we'; what is cultural studies? Silly questions in this existential form, perhaps, but nevertheless a response is already discernible to these unasked, post-Wall questions, in new publications, at conferences, among colleagues, in journals. The response takes two forms: first, institutionalization; cultural studies is no longer an intellectual enterprise of the left, but an academic subject increasingly of the centre, that is to say, taught at universities. Second, meanwhile, ancestralization; 'we' become not so much a synchronic pattern of like-minded intellectual political workers around the world, but a diachronic succession of names.

Prodigal parents (mostly fathers) are invented as ancestors, blessed by reiterated invocation in opening chapters and exigetical articles; the return of the reposed in cultural studies, if you like, precipitated into identity by genealogy; and Hoggart begat Williams begat Hall begat . . .

Ancestralization is a tribal, or at least national, narrative. In British cultural studies the First Book of the Chronicles would name Williams, Hoggart, Hall and others (notably E.P. Thompson, whose devotion to history and dislike of (French) theory ensured that later on his face would be quietly airbrushed from the official photo). In North America the names would be different: Harold Innes and Marshall McLuhan would figure in any Canadian genealogy, while in the USA there are numerous autochthonic godfathers, many of whom were gathered together in the 1983 'Marxism and the Interpretation of Culture' conference, and the 1990 'Cultural Studies' conference, both held at the University of Illinois. In Australia the 1990 'Inaugural' Cultural Studies Conference at the University of Western Sydney, designed to launch Australian Cultural Studies as a professional association, empanelled Tony Bennett, John Frow, John Hartley, Lesley Johnson, Meaghan Morris, Stephen Muecke, Graeme Turner and John Tulloch as living proof of its prehistory. What matters, in each country, are not the names themselves, but the inter-continental drift towards 'naming the father' in cultural studies around the turn of the decade. The global circulation of these national genealogies is ensured, however, by publication; a good example being a book on British cultural studies, written by Australian Graeme Turner for an American publisher.[3]

What was begotten by these prodigal parents is not easy to name. Cultural studies is notable for its participants' squeamishness about orthodoxy, manifested positively in a commitment to interdisciplinarity, and negatively in the avoidance of authority; it has no unified theory, textual canon, disciplinary truths, agreed methodology, common syllabus, examinable content or professional body, no bodily integrity at all. It is, in fact, getting to resemble its centenarian grandparent English, from which it recruited many of its personnel, not only among teachers and writers but, more significantly, among students, where it is beginning, perhaps, to usurp English's hegemonic mantle as 'Queen of the Human-ities', if by that might be meant a subject which attracts large numbers of disciplinarily uncommitted undergraduates, most of whom are women, interested in a general arts or humanities education which combines textual analysis with moral high ground, public affairs with artistic creativity, social change with personal skill.

Questions arise. As cultural studies is becoming institutionally instated, is it going back to the 1960s to clad its post-political pout in the clothes of canonized ancestors? What has been gained in the thirty-odd years since Williams and Hoggart and *Universities & Left Review* (*ULR*), edited by

Stuart Hall, came down from the high ground of literary criticism with the tablets of democratic popular culture? Have 'we' come very far since then, towards the promised land? What are the social successes of an intellectual enterprise whose only unity was the commitment of its adherents to progressive social change? What are its political achievements, given its democratic rhetoric? What is the popular resonance of one of the few academic disciplines which is truly interested in the popular (though not in popularity), theorizing ordinary people as part of political struggle, and everyday life as creative in ways that had previously been looked for only in fine arts and high society?

It is far too early to answer these questions, though it may be timely to ask them; the work of cultural studies thus far has been intellectual ground-clearing, conceptual tillage and theoretical seed-sowing; its political harvest, social fruit and popular propagation are still to come. At least I hope so – cultural studies had better have a future, or it may be condemned to endless reruns of its past. It is, in some respects, exactly where it was thirty years ago, at least in the wider world of popular politics and political consciousness.

An absolute beginner

The perspex hairbrush of cultural studies is Stuart Hall. In 1959 in his last issue of *ULR*, before it was transformed into the *New Left Review*, he wrote an article called 'Absolute beginnings', (reviewing Colin MacInnes's teenager-novel *Absolute Beginners*) in which he posed some questions: 'We have very little understanding of the roots of cultural deprivation, and of its relation to the pattern of class culture and education in this country. Where does it begin?'[4]

Since this is, as it were, the absolute beginning of Cultural Studies, it is also appropriate that he should pose his questions around the adolescent figures of what was then called 'youth', the hope of the future, the generation of the 1960s, the teenager. Hall begins to answer his own questions, and the path he takes is decisive – at least for cultural studies:

> What we have to do is to begin to disentangle what is real and what is phony in the responses of young people today. What is real are the feelings and attitudes involved, the interests aroused: what is phony are the *ways* the feelings are engaged, the trivial and inconsequential directions in which the aroused interests are channelled. The revolt and iconoclasm of youth today arises because of the contradictions between the true and the false elements in their culture: because the wave of post-war prosperity has raised them to cultural thresholds which offer rewards unequal to the expectations aroused. Instead, therefore, most young people compensate for their frustrations by an escape into the womb-world of mass entertainments.[5]

18

If that isn't the Genesis of cultural studies, it is certainly the Exodus: fleeing the tyranny of high culture towards a promised land where culture may be analysed in terms of class, where consciousness may be true or false, where feelings and attitudes may be political not psychological, where economics (prosperity) connects with meaning, and where, crucially, it is *important* to understand 'the womb-world of mass entertainments'. It's worth adding that the article as a whole already displays some characteristic moves of subsequent cultural studies; it combines political with literary analysis (Hall says '*Absolute Beginners* is still the closest we have come to a "British" (Mr. MacInnes is Australian!) *Catcher in the Rye*');[6] it is happy to use for its own purposes the statistics and discourses of the advertising industry (in the shape of a trade pamphlet called *The Teenage Consumer*); and – amazingly for a left publication – it is published with photographs and a design which are *part* of its consideration of its subject matter.

Here is the generation which entered the 1960s as teenagers – somewhat younger than Stuart, slightly older than me. He calls them the 'L-P, Hi-Fi generation', describing them bodily, in terms of their hair, clothes and make-up. 'The girls are short-skirted, sleekly groomed, pin-pointed on stiletto heels, with set hair and Paris-boutique dead-pan make-up', while the boys are Italian suited, hair brushed into a 'brisk, flat-topped French version' of the crew cut, their shirts are continental and 'jeans are *de rigueur*':

> A fast-talking, smooth-running, hustling generation with an ad-lib gift of the gab. . . . They despise 'the masses' (the evening paper lot on the tubes in the evening), 'traditionals', 'cops' (cowboys), 'peasants' and 'bohemians'. But they know how to talk to journalists and TV 'merchants', debs and holiday businessmen. Their experiences are, primarily, personal, urban and sensational: sensational in the sense that the test of beatitude is being able to get so close you feel you are 'part of the act, the scene'.[7]

However, in the very same issue of *ULR*, Hall is already in trouble for his preoccupation with style, sensation and culture. He writes a response to a number of his critics (including representatives of sectarian socialist factions for whom 'Aunty Dogma still rules the roost'), where he defends himself thus:

> I do not anywhere suppose that we can read straight from advertising copy to the attitudes of working class people. True, the ad-men can only 'suggest'. But the result *could* be, not a break-up of the class system (a thing I never suggest), but a sense of confusion about what class *is* and how much it matters, and where 'class' allegiances lie. I described this as a 'sense of classlessness and a sense of class

confusion', and I think if he [E.P. Thompson] got out on the knocker instead of on to the shop floor and said to the first head that came round the corner 'Vote Labour', he would see what I mean. . . . In other words (this was my ideological point), the superstructure of ideas (in this case, false ideas, false consciousness) *is* going to affect directly the course of events. And if the admission of this fact makes us reconsider some of the more primitive notions – still current – of *how* to interpret Marx's dictum that 'It is not the consciousness of men that determines their being, but, on the contrary, their social being that determines their consciousness', I, for one, can only say, 'Long Live the Revisionists'.[8]

And he adds, for good measure, 'I do not see how the "feel" of the Age can be described without reference to the qualitative changes which have taken place in the media of attitude-formation and opinion manipulation.'[9]

Between them, these preoccupations, with 'feel', style, consciousness, beatitudes as much as attitudes, the interpretation of Marx in the light of media, the relations between class and popular culture, and the consequent centrality of culture to political theory and action, are a founding manifesto for cultural studies. And it is remarkable, rereading this thirty-year-old document, to see how stable they have remained as its 'subject', how similar some of the intellectual controversies are, and how 'we' in the 1990s are still those 'Revisionists' (who have indeed Lived Long). 'We' have yet to convince activists and adversaries alike that *discourses organize practices*, that the real is constructed (partly through media), and that, therefore, reality is materially affected by media discourses, that there are direct political consequences of apparently immaterial and supposedly ahistorical phenomena like feeling, style, suggestion, not to mention confusion, contradiction and allegiance.

(Girl) you know it's true

In fact, it can be argued, 'we' haven't come very far since 1959. Here's how far we haven't come: exactly thirty years later there was still no public recognition of perhaps the most fundamental tenet of cultural studies – that of the constructed nature of the real. Reality's status as a product simply hasn't got through, and the material effect of public allegiance to authenticity is measurable, at least if you happen to be the lead singers of pop band Milli Vanilli. Their 1989 US Grammy award for 'best new artist' for 'Girl You Know It's True' was taken away from them when it was subsequently revealed that the voices heard by 10 million purchasers of the record were not their voices.[10] Now of course the record-buying public has become used to a certain amount of reality-production, finding, it seems, little to sue for when singers mime on TV and even at 'live' concerts, when the good bits on popular singles are in fact played by anonymous session musicians, or when the entire industry of music video is dedicated to breaking the nineteenth-century nexus between reality and representation by dissociating sound and sight, sense and sensibility, singer and song. No matter: the buck, or in this case a few million bucks, stops here; the Board of Trustees of the National Academy of Recording Arts and Sciences has decreed that singers' voices are evidence of the self-presence of person and creativity, individuality and emotion, and neither cultural studies nor Milli Vanilli has succeeded in busting apart this ideology of authenticity by saying that 'Girl You Know It's True' actually *is* true; truly produced reality, at least authentic enough to sell 10 million copies.

However, there's no such thing as bad publicity; at the last count Rob Pilatus and Fab Morvan, the offending Milli Vanilli, were: 'considering a number of offers to record for real, three offers to star in TV movies, two offers to sell their story in book form, and one offer to serve as spokespersons for a new board game, Read My Lips'.[11] Of course, no one will mind if the words they utter in the TV movie are written by someone else, no one will sue if their book is ghost-written, and no one has so far ousted President Bush after having 'read his lips' and then found themselves paying new taxes. Perhaps, in fact, Milli Vanilli are doing more right now than cultural studies ever has done to expose the apparatus of reality construction, to convince the public once and for all that feeling, sensibility, style and culture are neither false nor authentic consciousness, but, on the contrary, they're *popular reality*.

Some things have changed since 1959. One of the great strengths of cultural studies has been the importance attached to the connection between textual and social matters; too late to save Milli Vanilli perhaps, but useful in the institutional politics which itself has determined how and in which 'Academy of Arts and Sciences' cultural studies sets up shop. Traditional textual disciplines like literary studies and linguistics were at that time notoriously insensitive to the economics of production or the ideology of the texts under scrutiny. *Literature*, for instance, could be studied without any reference to *publishing*, so that a novel might be made sense of as an abstract form, conveying the author's imaginative genius, but not as a physical book, with crafts, trades and markets to account for its material form, and factories, distributors, bookshops and publicity to account for its social reach and success, and government policy, regulation and censorship to account for internal features and external impact. I remember, as an undergraduate in the later 1960s, having a furious argument with another student about whether an unpublished novel is in fact a novel, or whether publication – and readership – is an *a priori* requirement for literary status. What I remember about that argument is the fury, not the outcome. Both of us were vehement; I that getting the

21

message across is the *sine qua non* of the whole literary enterprise, she that imagining the fiction was enough, on the grounds that a thing of beauty is just that, whether or not anyone sees, knows or understands it. Well, in our beginnings are our ends: I went off to specialize in communication(s), she became a form designer for the Department of Health and Social Security.

Meanwhile, and conversely, the political and social sciences of the time thought themselves able to analyse the structure, ownership and power of popular media, and even to pronounce on their individual and social influence, without paying any attention whatever to the peculiarities of the textual systems through which such influence was conveyed to the supposedly unsuspecting public. Television, for instance, was divided into two distinct phenomena. Factual output became the province of sociology (an ascendant discipline of the 1960s), which pronounced on the politico-social impact of news by looking at the ownership of news media, not at the news itself; while fictional output was left to the psychs (who also enjoyed a vogue in that peculiar decade of disembodied mind expansion), and they managed to tell us what TV did to other people's behaviour by looking at the people, not the TV.

Popular reality

Well, thank God (or Raymond Williams), that's all over now. Cultural studies combines social and textual matters, focusing on power through its textual deployment, and on the social distribution of the resources and products of sense-making, whether they be the technical and corporate 'hardwares' of the global media industries, or the codes and conventions of various semiotic 'softwares' (from language to continuity editing), by means of which people might make sense of themselves, each other, and the world at large. With such interests as these, it follows that the texts and media chosen for analysis in cultural studies differ from those traditionally associated on the one hand with literary analysis, where disproportionate attention is paid to elaborate works of fiction belonging to an authorized canon of art, and on the other hand with sociopolitical analysis, which accepts the status if not the accuracy of the established 'truth media' like news, overstating the political power of editorials and opinions which circulate between elements of the governing apparatus through the columns of what their owners and letter-writers would like to think are 'influential' newspapers. The social diffusion of the resources of sense-making cannot be seen from such vantage points, preoccupied as they are with high art and high politics, with the decisions of management and judgements of posterity.

However, there's another vantage point from which the doings and sayings of the high and mighty can be looked at, but not taken as the be all and end all of human meaning. From the perspective of cultural studies, there are anthropological and historical dimensions to meaning: how sense is made in ordinary circumstances, how the 'power of speech' is socially distributed and historically developed, what meanings have become established in the widest popular context. The aim here is to discover what is *special*, not about the chosen few, but about our entire *species*, and thus also to determine how the cutting edges of textual productivity in the domains of politics and literature, truth and fiction, news and art, history and imagination, actually *work* socially. Cultural studies has made a start on such investigations.

However, cultural studies has its own history, which has shaped its intellectual agenda. Its most enduring concern has been with the media. Strictly speaking, literature and cinema are media too, and elaborate, artistically shaped fiction is a central part of media fare. But in cultural studies, 'the media' as a term has come to signify television above all, along with the daily press (radio rarely gets a hearing, although the recorded music industry does).

What distinguishes post-Frankfurt School cultural studies, in fact, is not a comprehensive theory of 'the media'. Perhaps the last such attempt was Hans Magnus Enzensberger's Frankfurter essay, 'Constituents of a theory of the media', first published in English in *New Left Review* (the successor journal to Hall's *ULR*) in 1970.[12] It is also among the most challenging, prescient and as yet unanswered attempts, because since then critical-analytical attention has fragmented; for the last twenty years, during the period of its most intensive self-invention, cultural studies has been preoccupied not with 'the media' but with *popular* media, and not with how such media work internally (both textually and socially), but with how they measure up against an externally applied yardstick, namely *reality*. Here's why:

> Any socialist strategy for the media must . . . strive to end the isolation of the individual participants from the social learning and production process. This is impossible unless those concerned organize themselves. This is the political core of the question of the media.[13]

So, it seems, the politics of the media is not what 'the masses' are doing with the means of media production that are already in their hands, but 'why these means of production do not turn up at factories, in schools, in the offices of the bureaucracy, in short, everywhere where there is social conflict'?[14] The masses *ought*, it seems, to leave off snapping their children, archiving their weddings and holidays, and tape-recording bird songs, and get on with 'aggressive forms of publicity which were their own', and so 'secure evidence of their daily experiences and draw effective lessons from them'.[15]

23

From the perspective of the cultural politics of the late 1960s, the fact that 'the masses' already had in their hands the means of media sense-making was simply ruled out of the discussion, because they didn't use these media for organized, self-consciously socialist politics. Popular *reality* was deemed to be what left intellectuals had decided in advance, while what the populace actually did was regarded as phoney or false. Enzensberger's argument suffers from a blind spot which is emblematic of the period: while arguing for the appropriation of the means of discursive production as an essential element of socialist strategy, it disallows the evidence of what 'the masses' might actually want to do with the media for themselves.

In fact, Enzensberger's notion of 'masses' is contradictory, wanting them to be active and self-determining, but only if such action is organized along existing political lines, to support existing (socialist) strategies, and only if it is *mass*. Evidence that populations are not masses, and that the new media technologies may suffuse popular culture in ways that challenge socialist orthodoxies, is dismissed as the result of corporate manipulation, leaving a view of the masses as, by default, passive, depoliticized and in need of organization. But, Enzensberger admits, transforming media into an emancipatory 'social learning and production' is only possible if those concerned organize *themselves*.

What if they don't? Do 'we' sit and wait for them to cotton on? The alternatives are either that someone organizes them whether they like it or not, which is 'democratic centralism', otherwise known as Stalinism, or else that whatever they do, even self-determined political action, is not deemed to be political because it doesn't conform to the preferred model of collective organization. The contradiction inherent in Enzensberger's argument ultimately defeats it, for any media politics becomes dependent on something else (the self-organization of the masses) which may or may not occur, while the existing use of media by individuals is ruled out as a-political, no matter what's going on, and the disabling distinction between 'we' vanguardist intellectuals and 'they' masses is reproduced, to the frustration of the former if not the latter.

The sorrows of success

This problem has trickled into cultural studies in the form of its curriculum. Media production itself is still downplayed as it always has been, on the wrong side of the Veblenesque binary divide between 'academic' and 'practical' subjects, suited to vocational students and unpublished tutors. On the high ground of theory too, in contemporary cultural studies, there is a tendency to take reality genres like news, actuality, documentary and journalism much more seriously than the same genre industries are taken in film and literary studies, which have neglected them in favour of narrative fiction (this is despite the fact that actuality genres are found on the big screen and the printed page as well as on TV, and, conversely, elaborate artistic fictions are just as common in popular TV and print media as they are in art cinema and literature). However, cultural studies has dwelt on popular reality as part of a more general intellectual endeavour, namely to demonstrate the way in which reality is not only constructed textually and socially, but also popularized in line with political and ideological dispositions of power.

The agenda of cultural studies, then, predetermines its object of study. Its interest in how political and cultural hegemony is established and maintained among the popular classes of contemporary nations has resulted in a kind of critical common sense which has created a demarcation line between cultural studies and the aesthetic disciplines (film and literary studies), and further demarcation lines between popular and other media, between reality and art, truth and fiction. All such demarcations do violence to the facts of the situation. Cultural studies has taken an interest in 'the media' (i.e. popular reality) in order to establish and maintain another kind of hegemony: its own claims to moral authority and intellectual leadership in the field of cultural criticism.

In fact it might be argued that the oppositional intellectuals whose early efforts established the theoretical and analytical agenda for cultural studies as an academic subject were interested in television's potential to manipulate the masses because some time in the future they hoped they'd be able to have a go at doing that too. What's the point of Gramsci if not to show how the hegemonic can be countered, and, once the strategy is determined, who's going to direct it if not the strategists? Theory in this arena is far from otherworldly or impractical, it's an apprenticeship for power. So theory is also far from disinterested, nor is its interest primarily in being correct. Its interest is in success. But as Stuart Hall put it in 1959, 'The gravest danger in the coming years could be that we fail to *make socialists*, and yet have "success" in building another socialist sect.'[16] (Point taken, but I think Hall was wrong here; socialists, either successful or sectarian, are not for 'us' to make, socialists make themselves.)

Perhaps an interest in being correct (not necessarily ideologically correct), might have been a good idea all along, for theories of media manipulation are wrong, and one consequence of this is that the strategies for the takeover of popular reality based upon them did not work out. Certainly the utopia of self-organized masses appropriating the means of representation as part of a socialist strategy for counter-hegemonic revolution did not occur. So the potential leaders, cadres and 'democratic centralists' of popular utopia, who flocked to the Communist University of London in the late 1970s to watch Stuart Hall and other beatified culturalists strut their stuff, learnt the language of the corporate-media adversaries without getting to push the buttons and pronounce the sentences for themselves.

Long live the revisionists

However, some of them, in fact, ended up under contract to the corporate-media adversaries, working as TV producers. And some of those, true to their own false consciousnesses, ended up making TV drama about their dreams and nightmares. Recently repeated on Australian TV, for instance, has been *A Very British Coup*, which happens to be a good TV play, and which pissed off the British Tory party by showing a Prime Minister (albeit a left-Labour one) pissing in a toilet, which at least led to pompous questions in the House of Commons, if not a popular appropriation of parliament. Along the way, however, *A Very British Coup*, written by a left-Labour MP and co-produced by someone who might (until the 1990 scrapping of the 'are you now or have you ever been . . . ?' question) have had trouble getting a US visa, is the true image of the kind of theorizing that has cost socialism its foothold in popular reality. It's a combination of utopia and conspiracy – *our* utopia and *their* conspiracy. Harry Perkins, from the People's Republic of South Sheffield, is the true representative of the people, and the people see this, elect him, and would support his programme, if only *they*, namely Philip Madoc done up to look like Rupert Murdoch, wouldn't conspire to use his media influence to confuse the people's consciousness and precipitate a very British coup, which is of course an anti-democratic conspiracy done up to look genteel.

This, then, is the tide-mark left round the empty bath of cultural studies: dammit, we *ought* to have won – not least because Stuart Hall is a more congenial, inspiring and convincing political theorist than the 'Countess of Finchley' – but we didn't, so *they* must've manipulated the masses.[17] Girl, you *know* it's true.

The masses are no more; the politics of mass organization is redundant. But cultural studies needn't throw the baby out with the bathwater. The aim of understanding media retains its utility, in seeking to analyse the media in the here and now, in their current dispositions of power, their social reach, diffusion and uses, and not only in their utopian potentiality. What is implicit in the politics of popular reality, these days, is a new understanding of politics, as well as of popular reality, and running through post-Wall critical analysis is a new, fragmented, politics of knowledge too, a sensitivity to the relations between popular reality and intellectual culture (where the uncertainty resides with the latter, not the former), and a sense of distinction between different lefts. Whether this turns out to be nothing more historic than the post-political pout of the Old New Left, or the rejuvenating revisionism of a newly constituted field of study, remains to be seen. In the meantime, as Stuart Hall put it in 1959, the success of cultural studies won't be primarily to '"arm us for the struggle against capitalism"' (risking, when you get the theory wrong, 'scientifically constructed bent pitch-forks'); success will be measured against a different yardstick: 'I wrote my article,' says Hall, 'because I wanted to know.'[18]

Me too. Whether you'll find knowledge or bent pitchforks in what follows, is not for me to say. All I know is that I seem to have lost my hairbrush.

2

AGORAPHILIA
The politics of pictures

No picture is pure image; all of them, still and moving, graphic and photographic, are 'talking pictures', either literally, or in association with contextual speech, writing or discourse. Pictures are social, visual, spatial and sometimes communicative. As visual text and social communication they construct literal social space within and between the frames and fields of which they're made. Pictures of all kinds are aesthetic, textual works, capable of personal appreciation and individual interpretation, but at the same time they are institutionally produced, circulated within an economy, and used both socially and culturally. Not only is their own internal space organized or framed, but also relations are developed between them and spectators, users, audiences or publics, real or imagined, outside the frame.

Pictures are political *as such*; it is not merely that some pictures, because of their subject matter, are more obviously public and political than others. Consequently, because they circulate in the domains that are traditionally deemed private, both 'commercial' and 'domestic', pictures take public politics into the private and personal realm, where contemporary politics is in fact conducted.

It so happens that the conceptual lexicon of contemporary politics is derived to a large extent from classical Greek and Roman terminology, although political organization today is very far from such antecedents. In fact, classical terminology may get in the way of a clear view of the current situation. The same applies to pictures; they're surrounded by a conceptual penumbra which is at least as old as politics. Pictures have traditionally been associated with art, individual emotion and pleasure, and with the symbolic domain of representation; they are not normally considered within the public domain of politics. The strategy of this chapter is to look at both politics and pictures in the light of the concepts by which they have become known. Part of the argument is that politics and pictures are in fact much closer to each other than the conventional (classical) wisdom would have us believe, while conversely contemporary politics and its classical 'origin' are much further apart than the similarity of wording might imply.

28

To refer to classical antecedents is not to search for an ultimate authorizing origin for contemporary meanings and activities, nor is it to endorse the classical meanings, but to use them as points of comparison, opening up conceptual history to see how things have changed. This is a somewhat risky undertaking, for merely to mention Greece and Rome is to place oneself in the shadow of 'glory' and 'grandeur'; whereas for most of their inhabitants the classical societies were neither glorious nor grand. Thus, although Greece and Rome bequeathed to later ages the *concept* of democracy, they never *practised* it. Classical politics was not the rational and desirable model for democracy that it is often taken to be, because the theory applied only to adult, free men. For women and slaves, on whom the survival, productivity and security of the classical city state depended, things were quite different; they were not subjects of political theory at all, having neither freedom nor rights. So classical democracy is only utopian if it is taken out of context. One of the differences between contemporary democracy and its ancient model is that, despite its many flaws, democracy nowadays is much more worthy of the name – the 'demos' includes, in principle, all members of our species.

This chapter is concerned with conceptual ground-clearing, which will, perforce, take the form of the ambiguation of some classic and classical opposites. Ambiguity in this context is not confusion; on the contrary it is the clearest picture possible. The first part ('Framing the subject') considers some of the analytic procedures that might help to establish the politics of pictures by reference both to inherited modes of thought (especially binarism) and to the strategies of analysis (forensics) which characterize the present study. The second part ('Wide open spaces') traces the classical (binary) distinction between public and private space in the most solidly real and public of the visual media, namely architecture, taking both public space and the public itself to be 'talking pictures'.

FRAMING THE SUBJECT

Forensics

Pictures are objective traces of socio-semiotic struggles (conflict), allegiances (consensus), and ideologies (sense-making practices), right across the spectrum from big-deal public politics to intimate personal culture. The material reality of pictures allows for the recovery and critical interrogation of discursive politics in an 'empirical' form; pictures are neither scientific data nor historical documents, but they are, literally, *forensic* evidence.

The word 'forensic' (Latin: *forensis*) strictly speaking means 'of the forum' or agora. The classical Roman forum (Greek agora) was the place of citizenship, an open space where public affairs and legal disputes were conducted, and it was also a marketplace, a place of pleasurable jostling, where citizens' bodies, words, actions and produce were all literally on mutual display, and where judgements, decisions and bargains were made. 'Forensic' is derived from this notion of cheek-by-jowl public politics, whence it has been applied to courtroom practice (adversarial argumentation in search of the truth), and thence to forensic *science* (rather than argument).

In forensic science, the search for truth is based on clues. The crumpled sweater, the blunt instrument, the damp cushion; such objects are turned into subjects, because they are transformed, by forensic investigation, from the realm of physics and chemistry into the language of discourse and argument; they're caused to 'talk' as mute witnesses, *things* that are coaxed into *telling a story*. The *medium* which carries or transmits that story from the past to the present, in forensic science, is typically one that the untrained eye can't even see; it might be a tiny piece of hair, minute chemical traces, bodily fluids or fibres of fabric. Forensic scientists *interrogate* these media, transforming a crumpled sweater into a text, making that damp patch on the cushion into an interlocutor or narrator which is able to tell them who was there, what happened, and – hopefully – whodunnit.

But forensics need not be confined to blood samples and the identification of telltale messages discovered under fingernails; 'forensics' as 'material evidence' can be combined with the older notion of 'adversarial argument', and applied to the analysis of pictures. For, as evidence, pictures are more real than the people and events they seem to be images and reflections of. People and events pass on, but often enough pictures remain as clues to assist the search for who those people were and what they did. In other words, the 'politics of pictures' begins not with the textual content and social use of images, but with their *status*; what their status is determines how their textual and social politics will be understood and conducted, but their status is not self-evident. On the contrary, it is a product of the way they are looked at.

Binarism

Status is a comparative concept; things don't 'have' status as a body has mass, but only by comparison with other things. One classic method of comparative analysis (inherited from classical times) is *binary* thought; sorting things out into polar opposites, black and white. Binaries include, in the analysis of social phenomena, the opposition between public and private domains, and in the analysis of texts, between reality and illusion. The latter, an abiding figure of thought going back to Platonic philosophy, survives where reality is construed, on the model of physical science, as comprising only empirically observable material objects and actions, a move which simultaneously consigns sense-making, pictures, writing, discourse, and so on to the equal and opposite pole; i.e. to the status of illusion.

Such binarism 'forgets', however, that while physical objects are real enough, their reality is a product of knowledge. The world goes round whether we know it or not, but the idea that the world goes round (historically a relatively recent one) is still an idea. Indeed, it is the knowledge of the earth's rotation that has had material effects on human society, not the rotation itself, which went on unnoticed for aeons without troubling anyone. But still there's a widespread belief that knowledge and ideas are *merely* representations or reflections of a reality located somewhere else; discourses, media, and the meanings they carry belong to the domain of non-material, untrustworthy illusion. Against this, it might be better to say that ideas *make* the world go round. Discursive knowledge is precisely what is real for our species, and reality is what we imagine (make into an image).

The real takes the form of texts, discourses and media, within which visual images coexist with speech and writing, although here again a binary distinction is common between writing and pictures. Script (especially print) is taken to be capable of rational truth, while pictures are suspected of seductive duplicity. For example, 'glossy' (i.e. seductively cosmetic) photographs are prohibited in company prospectuses, though print, especially in its extreme 'rational' form of lists, tables and numbers, is encouraged (naturally the Stock Exchange rules apply only to publicity aimed at shareholders: for information aimed at consumers, the converse philosophy holds sway – seduction by visuality is much preferred to statistics). Against this kind of binary thinking, it might be useful to assert that pictures and other modes of writing like print are all equally capable of rationality and desire, and their opposites. Print can mislead and pictures tell the truth, and while pictures are clearly full of artifice and appeal, the same applies to every other mode of communication, even statistics.

However, binarism should not be understood as 'wrong' (illusory) thinking, for the textual tendency towards binary classification is a powerful material, social and therefore political force. For instance in the media, binarism structures the macro-social organization of entire industries (into public/private sectors), and the micro-semiotic organization of whole classes of texts (into art/entertainment), and these structures determine not only who makes what kinds of cultural product, but also how individual productions will be read and evaluated by both critics and audiences. Hence, cultural analysis must not only be aware of binarism in its own analytical practices, but also be alert to the material socio-textual *force* of binarism in the structuring of sense-making.

Cold War rhetoric was militant binarism, assigning polar values to the distinction between the two superpowers. It was only after the thaw that media and journalistic representations of Russian people and the USSR began to construct them into what might be called 'like-usness', where for the first time in forty years western populations were able to see Soviet people at home, in the shops, talking, and expressing hopes, fears and ideas that were strangely familiar. Of course it's hard to feel comfortable about obliterating 200 million people if they are obviously people, and not mere opposites or adversaries (for which the Hebrew word is *satan*); conversely, western popular support (or toleration) for the Cold War had been promoted and managed during all those years by means of foe creation; turning people into binary opposites so that 'we' can, if it should come to that, nuke the binary, not the people. In short, the Soviet people's status as an 'evil empire' was the product of binary thinking, not of their reality, but the product of binary thinking was the reality of the Cold War.

Creative cross-dressing

It is therefore important to recognize binarism when it is most forcefully at work, not when it has become a mere historical relic. An aid to recognition is to look deliberately at the 'black' side of any equation to find traces of 'white'. It is often the *distinction* between the opposites that blinds innocent bystanders, for although it stands to reason that black is black and no amount of analysis will make it white, it is nevertheless rare, in both physical and cultural domains, for things to be in fact as black and white as binary thought makes them appear.

The binary between science and art, reality and illusion, has, despite its persistence, always been of doubtful or ambiguous status in the most important area of innovation and creativity. On the 'science/reality' side of the divide, for example, the science of rocketry, on which intercontinental ballistic missiles and the exploration of space both depend, is a product not of 'reality' but of fiction:

> The greatest pioneers of modern rocketry – Tsiolkovsky, Goddard, Oberth, and their successors Korolev, von Braun, and others – were not inspired primarily by academic or professional interest, financial ambitions, or even patriotic duty, but by the dream of spaceflight. *To a man they read the fantasies of Jules Verne, H.G. Wells, and their imitators.*[1]

Konstantin Tsiolkovsky, widely credited as the founder of space flight, himself recorded how his 'hard' science was precipitated by its discursive opposite, i.e. the illusion of fantasy:

> I thought of the rocket as everybody else did – just as a means of diversion and of petty everyday uses. I do not remember exactly what

prompted me to make calculations of its motions. Probably the first seeds of the idea were sown by that great fantastic author Jules Verne – he directed my thought along certain channels, then came a desire, and after that, the work of the mind.[2]

So science may result from art, intellectual work from desire; and although binary classification remains forceful (Tsiolkovsky's rockets worked in the sky, Verne's in the mind), the dynamics that produce *change*, both physical and cultural, occur precisely at the moment of the ambiguation of binaries.

Turning to the art/illusion end of this binary, it is hardly necessary to mention how many fictions are founded on science, including the science of forensics. For instance, at the extreme outer limit of fictionality is pastiche. This form refers not to pre-discursive 'scientific' reality but to another reality, that of textuality, genre and the conventions of narrative drama, which become the self-reflexive subject of the fiction. A well-known example is David Lynch's TV soap-pastiche *Twin Peaks*, which despite its artistic textual mannerism is narratively driven by science; FBI Agent Cooper's classic position in the story is as the 'agent' of discovery, knowledge-broker from the diegetic world to the viewer. His forensic detection makes inanimate objects like Laura Palmer's corpse or a gold necklet into talking witnesses. This being pastiche, Lynch jokes with the investigative 'scientism' of the genre by making Agent Cooper's discovery of empirical truth result from dreams and Tibetan mysticism; like Tsiolkovsky, Agent Cooper succeeds where others fail at the exact moment when opposites (forensic detection and Tibetan mysticism) are ambiguated.

More generally, the status of pictures *as such* is more ambiguous, and therefore more productive, than is commonly supposed. That is, pictures are both real and primary, *and* illusory and vicarious. Thus, a picture is not a 'simulacrum' or a simulation of a reality which is (apparently) located somewhere else, and pictures are not 'hyper-real', signifying whatever anyone likes. 'Talking' pictures are, at the same time, imperative, a governing *regime*, for the communities into which the public is organized, and the public uses them to constitute and contemplate itself. In an inversion of what common sense declares to be the case, it is the public that turns out to be a fabrication, while talking pictures are, in this respect, the only reality there is. Such apparently obvious, empirical phenomena as the public domain and the public have become of doubtful status in point of physical fact, while pictures, despite their reputation for illusion, seductiveness, manipulation, and for duplicity of meaning, are hard evidence.

Forensic ambiguation

The politics of pictures occurs in the least public, least political places. 'Talking pictures' constitute the public domain – the most private pictures are implicated in political processes. Instead of looking at mug shots of presidents and potentates for evidence of these processes, it is more decisive (and more interesting) to sift through the detritus of everyday life, to find the politics of pictures in nooks and crannies that present themselves as apolitical.

The politics of pictures occurs across different media, so it is important not to confine any forensic analysis to the most obviously public media like television and news. All pictures 'talk', and the public domain is the space inside picture frames, so visual media need to be connected and compared with each other to see how regularities, or regimes, can be traced across them. How-to-do-it manuals, record covers, postcards, museums, advertisements, academic texts, popular literature and magazines are unlikely neighbours in this context, but to see how meanings circulate from one to another is to interrogate the very concept of 'media'.

At the same time, the media of social sense-making share many representations and even individual pictures among themselves; just one referent may turn up in a variety of media. However, the meaning of such a referent will differ depending on when, where and how it is deployed, so an analysis that traces a single photographic subject across different media will find that it covers a great many other subjects, ending up with meanings about, for instance, personality, family, gender, nation, youth, art, censorship, class, history, imperialism, heroes and fashion. The same pictures also raise questions about the institutional site of their production. Society is maintained in formal and informal institutions, from government to 'the family', as well as in persons and their mutual activity. Such institutions are sites of prolific discursive productivity – symbols, meanings, knowledge and representation are their products and by-products, so to study society is also to study meanings in themselves and in their institutionalized production, circulation and history. There's a sociology and history of discourse, in which the existence, scope and purposes of communities and individual persons can be traced. Different institutional sites, different media and different times produce not only different but also competing images, and so the study of social sense-making is also the study of semiotic struggle – the politics of pictures.

Just as it's very hard for photographers to get their subjects to remain still for long enough to be photographed, so pictures themselves are never still, either in signification or in social circulation. It is just as important for the analyst to trace the flux and circulation of sense-making as it is to fix an image into a more or less permanent and therefore legible form. It is also important to realize that the institutional sites of discursive productivity are both social and semiotic, both actions of people and representations in media, and that social institutions over which semiotic struggle occurs are much more widely diffused than the obvious kinds, with walls round them. As a result, one photographic subject, of one social

34

institution, is rare; part of the politics of pictures is that various institutional sites are invested and invaded by other institutional purposes and meanings, appropriated or colonized by institutionalized media, and so on.

WIDE OPEN SPACES

The politikos of pictures

Pictures are political when they enter the public domain. But the public domain is not what it used to be: a physical location you can walk into, as in the classical era from which modern political terminology is derived. The English word 'public' is derived from the Greek word for adult male; in classical Greece and Rome, assuming you were a free man – rather than a woman, slave, or foreigner – you could walk into the agora or forum and participate in public life directly, as a voter, a jurist, a consumer, or as an audience of oratory in the service of public affairs. In Greek parlance, the city was the *polis*, the citizen was the *polites*, and that which pertained to citizens as a whole was therefore *politikos*, meaning 'popular' (of the populace), hence 'politics'.

But nowadays there is no physical public domain, and politics is not 'of the populace'. Contemporary politics is *representative* in both senses of the term; citizens are represented by a chosen few, and politics is represented to the public via the various media of communication. Representative political space is literally made of pictures – they *constitute* the public domain.

Members of the public, who are both audiences and citizens, may enter into more decisive relations with photography than with each other. When judging the merits of candidates for public office, for instance, the public must use photographs and talking pictures to decide the issue; acting as citizen means engaging in the politics of pictures. But the *place* of citizenship has shifted out of the classical agora, from participation in judgement and decision by the assembled public (the enfranchised few), to the family home and the private consumption and contemplation of pictures by whole populations. However, the actual activity of looking at persons to decide politics is not new; it is integral even to classical political organization. Aristotle himself grounded politics upon the faculty of looking, limiting the ideal size of a state to the largest number of citizens who could assemble together and still 'be taken in at a single view'; the idea being that looking – citizens seeing each other, and seeing candidates for public office – was a prerequisite for good government and accountability.[3] The 'single view', the mutual gaze of all the citizens assembled together, was a participatory, live, talking picture, as it were.

In modern times Aristotle's prescription as to the size of a state has been exceeded, in some cases by a millionfold and more; states are now

35

normally nations rather than cities, against his advice. Also, a physical separation has occurred between the places where public issues are decided (government) and the places where citizens congregate. Public affairs and public space are now quite distinct. Citizens do not congregate in one public space, in single view of one another, to perform acts of government. Typically, they go (or are encouraged by publicity to go) into public places for leisure, culture and recreation, or for shopping; the agora is still open for business, but not for government.

Although the political importance of collective looking was recognized by Aristotle as the foundation of political action, the mode of looking in modern societies is quite different. Modern politics is still described in terms borrowed from classical Greece, but what is described has changed so much that the nomenclature makes the contemporary picture hard to read. The public domain is in modern times an abstraction, its realm is that of representation and discourse, it is graphic and photographic but not geographic. As a concept, 'public' no longer refers to adults, but to a complex of institutional and largely professionalized collective practices; government (public affairs), administrative bureaucracy (public sector, public service), utilities (public lavatories, public works), and the representation – not the practice – of citizenship (public opinion). As a concept, 'the public' also has its meaning in opposition to 'the private', a vast realm which encompasses both 'private enterprise' and 'private life'. So although references to 'the public domain' are quite commonplace, it's not always clear whether they signify a system of government or a lavatory.[4]

Complex uncertainty and abstraction into the discursive realm is what representative democracy has come to mean. Democracy is conducted through representations circulated in public, even though no public (no *demos*) assembles in one place to constitute and govern itself. The process of abstracting and representing politics has gone so far that the public itself is now circulated as a representation, in the form of public opinion, which is an industrially produced fictionalization of citizenship.

The public domain

One of the binaries that contemporary politics has inherited from the ancients is the distinction between public and private. In classical politics, the public domain was a wide open space, an architectural site. This is no longer true, and in contemporary nations the public and private domains have become thoroughly ambiguated. But taking the classical distinction at face value allows questions to be raised about what shape and size the public domain should be, and how its space might be organized to enable or constrain the activities it encloses. In fact, to design a wide open space is to propose a theory of citizenship. Charles Jencks, perhaps best known in critical circles for having dated the moment postmodernism began,[5] enjoyed an earlier incarnation as a radical critic of modernist architecture, which he denounced on the grounds of its anti-participatory concretization of the public realm. In *Modern Movements in Architecture*, Jencks says:

> For brief moments in . . . history there have emerged forms of political organization that reveal an enormous ability for realizing certain human potential. . . . The Greek agora, the Roman forum, the medieval communes and American townships were all variants of an institution which allowed particular human qualities to emerge and furthermore protected their continuing ability to do so.[6]

Jencks looks at architecture not as an art but as a realization (making real) of political organization. He praises these four historical 'variants of an institution' (agora, forum, commune, township), because each of them organizes size and space in such a way as to enable citizenship to flow directly, at a single view, from social congregation and active participation in the conduct of affairs. The institution of which they are all variants is *local participatory democracy*, and its first historical concrete example is the agora, which can thus serve as a point of comparison for the way that public space is organized nowadays.

The desirable human qualities associated with the agora include such obvious political benefits as self-government, free and open discussion, and control over decisions affecting oneself. But they extend to two essential but less celebrated aspects of democratic participation: *performance* and *pedagogy. Participation* is a practical impossibility without these, but they are not often included as components of democratic theory. Performance (drama) is now binarily excluded from the 'real' world of politics, while pedagogy (Greek: 'boy's guide') is commonly understood to be what is done to people by authoritative others, rather than what people 'draw out' (Latin: 'educate') of themselves, so teaching now frequently appears to be the very opposite of self-determination. Even more strangely, along with *drama* and *didactics, democracy* itself is not now seen as a practical, participatory component of public self-realization; all three of these classical political skills have been subjected to a division of labour, to professionalization by semi-exclusive elites, and disintegration from one another. Drama is now a province of the media (not just in fiction but also in journalism), didactics belongs to teachers and democracy to politicians; the one group to which none of the three 'belongs' is the public.

Jencks sees the satisfactions to be had from making public performance as an intrinsic part of democratic decision-making. Such 'attributes of acting' are:

> areas of enjoyment which sound almost quaint to our ears: 'public happiness,' the delight of appearing in public to disclose one's personal identity, the enjoyment of debate, sharing one's opinions

with others even including an opposition, the pleasure taken in public speaking, rhetoric, the art of persuasion where artifice becomes a satisfying substitute for physical coercion.[7]

Whereas the *drama* of democracy was fully integrated in the classical models (where performative arts were intrinsic to political processes and politics was intrinsic to drama), it is only apparent today at rare moments of political and social crisis, when mass, collective, performative and mutually educative action occurs, taking a remarkably similar form across the world, as in Paris and Grosvenor Square 1968, the pro-democracy movements in Eastern Europe and Tiananmen Square of the late 1980s, American and South African civil rights movements, Moscow in August 1991, and so on. The same kind of 'feel' may arise in certain cultural events (like sporting or pop music festivals), where, as Jencks puts it, the 'nature of a spontaneous talented gesture is immediately shared in a collective, but credible, way'.

As for didactics, Jencks cites Rousseau to claim that local participatory democratic organization is educational because it 'forces' individuals to be responsible citizens by the discipline of sharing control, which in this context brings with it 'the development of accountability, foresight, tolerance and intelligence',[8] and these qualities are civic, not personal. This is not to deny that the same discipline of shared control can at times 'draw forth' vengeance, intolerance, and so on, as numerous classical examples, including the trial of Socrates, attest.[9] But the point is that such actions become in themselves a kind of autodidactic 'case law' for participatory democracy, which develops through the 'media' of education and drama, both of which are produced in and by the public in the course of their democratic practice rather than being supplied to them by any centralized elite bureaucracy. The people involved 'keep an eye' on themselves, for good or ill.

Public architecture

However, democracy, government and citizenship are, between them, only one specialist department of politics, including the politics of pictures. Pictures are political *as such*, which means they're all politicized in more or less formal ways, caught up in myriad power struggles, large and small, by means of which people sort themselves into different communities with allegiances to different ideologies. In the binary classical tradition, the private realm is apolitical and therefore unworthy of architecture. Greek, Roman and medieval architecture was exclusively dedicated to the public realm, the spatialization of politics and religion. But in the post-medieval word the private realm is not unworthy. On the contrary, America was founded on it.

The free private individual and free private enterprise are among the foundations of the American economy, and hence of its constitution, so much so that it can be argued that societies like America (i.e. western market economies with liberal democratic governments) have no public realm, at least in the physical fabric of their cities and their architecture, and thence in the collective activities of their citizens. The consequence of this for architecture has been to produce confusion. According to Jencks:

> The public domain is exactly what didn't exist in American architecture. . . . Lacking a believable or even credible political base, it was not surprising that the public domain continued to look like the Lincoln Center or all the other pseudo-classical cultural centres across America. . . . And even when such attempts as the Lincoln Center were declared a 'disaster' by everyone involved . . . it was still copied with equanimity because of its monumental classical look.[10]

Classical monumentalism is the result of a paradox: public architecture for private enterprise, classicism for purposes directly at odds with the virtues that classical architecture concretized. In consequence: 'There is . . . one aspect of [American architecture] which is all too clearly comprehensible and that is the official architecture of American corporations and the government. Its resemblance to Fascist architecture of the thirties is, alas, all too great.'[11]

The private domain

As individual is to state in the public realm, so family is to private enterprise in the private realm. If the macro end of the scale (private enterprise and the state) is hopelessly compromised by seeking to fill public space with private meanings (or, more accurately, to clad private space with public façades), a structural flaw that makes the whole edifice lean towards totalitarian monumentality, then what of the micro end of the scale – the private individual and the family?

In the classical tradition, the private realm is not very much to write home about.[12] On the contrary, it's an object of derision, and the Greeks, once again, had a word for it. A private citizen who was concerned only with himself (women were private, but not citizens), and who was therefore ignorant of public affairs, was known as an *idiot* ('private, own, peculiar': *OED*). The classical idiot is one who lacks knowledge and reason, because these qualities are produced exclusively by engagement in the *public* realm; they're a product of the agora, not of the individual.

Here again an application of the classical to the contemporary world produces paradox, and again Jencks is instructive. He analyses Le Corbusier's influential modernist Unité d'Habitation in Marseilles, a multi-storey building to house 1,600 people, erected soon after the Second World War, complete with communal services like an athletics track and childcare centre on the roof, and a market on the seventh floor. According to Jencks, Le Corbusier's

> major, social intention was something of a paradox – although a paradox which was shared by most modern architects. This is that family life, the domestic everyday life of the home, is elevated to the level of a public monument. Here is the closest modern equivalent to the Greek Temple.[13]

Le Corbusier's solution to the problem of how to organize public space is to design a block of flats within quotation marks, so to speak; the building's rhetoric ('I'm a public monument, a Greek temple') is emancipated from its use ('I'm mass private housing').

Architecture cannot escape rhetoric; as Jencks says, it 'must by its nature explain and dramatize certain social meanings'. But its communicative role is compromised today: 'when the whole public realm and politics are in doubt, architecture also must lack credibility.'[14] Architecture's credibility gap is structural, if it is held to its classical job of concretizing the public domain in the absence of the public. Its job of *education* is impossible if it tries to explain the *social* meaning of, for instance, banks and insurance companies (classically the 'meaning' of private lending was 'avarice' or usury). Its job of dramatizing the *social* meaning of a private citizen at home is impossible by classical means, since classically the meaning was 'idiot'. Banks and apartment blocks are not the same as the Forum or the Parthenon, so when these are quoted the result is bathos behind a fascist façade.

Contemporary buildings don't mean what they say. Behind their rhetorical façade there is use, and that use is private. Classicism can't explain or dramatize this domain except by paradox, bathos and monumentalism, because contemporary society is not organized along classical lines. The classical primacy of public politics and public religion, conducted in the agora–forum and the temple, has been turned upside down; contemporary primacy goes to private enterprise and private life, conducted in the (abstract) market and in the home. Says Jencks:

> It is this general loss of credibility in politics and religion which, in a strange way, has even been the cause of 'modern architecture'. . . .
> Like Le Corbusier, [architects] tried to elevate the house to the palace, the private to the public and the utilitarian to the cultural.[15]

It may be said that the same applies to pictures: attempts to see contemporary photographic and 'talking' pictures in the light of traditional notions of public and private, reality and illusion (truth and seduction), are doomed to failure. Pictures no longer mean what such binarism says.

It seems that this investigation of the problem of the public domain through its concretization in architecture has raised a more serious problem: if there is no public space that constitutes the people as political actors, then there is, strictly speaking, no public. The 'place' of citizenship is abstracted from the physical forum of collective action and relocated into the individual bodies of private persons. The 'place' of democracy, conversely, is abstracted from those same bodies and delegated to representative government and bureaucracy located elsewhere.

Meanwhile, the bodies in question, privatized, agoraphobic, with leisure begotten of delegating their sovereignty to the abstract body politic, and with nowhere to go in the privatized public spaces of the built-up *polis* but shopping malls, have other binaries to play with: not the city but the country, not culture but nature, not politics but picnics.

3

NO PICNIC

For all flesh *is* as grass

'For all flesh *is* as grass, and all the glory of man as the flower of the grass. The grass withereth, and the flower thereof falleth away.' St Peter is quoting the prophet Isaiah: 'All flesh *is* grass, and all the goodliness thereof *is* as the flower of the field: The grass withereth, the flower fadeth.' And Brahms quotes St Peter: 'Denn alles Fleisch es ist wie Gras und alle Herrlichkeit des Menschen wie des Grases Blumen. Das Gras ist verdorret und die Blume abgefallen.' And I quote Brahms, thereby keeping contemporary a transcendental theory of the relations between humanity and nature that is already several thousand years old.[1]

The grass withereth, and the flower thereof falleth away

In an essay called 'The critic as clown', Terry Eagleton raises what he takes to be a thorny problem of critical, especially Marxist, theory – the problem of nature: 'Few words have rung more ominously in Marxist ears than "natural," and we have all long since learned to rehearse the proper objections to it with Pavlovian precision.'[2] Having donned his intellectual welly boots, Eagleton trudges off to cross some perennial binaries. He discusses the *pastoral* form of writing, which he sees as an ironic allegory on such (apparent) polarities as:

$$
\begin{array}{rcl}
\text{critic} & : & \text{text} \\
\text{critic} & : & \text{society} \\
\text{intellectual work} & : & \text{manual work} \\
\text{self} & : & \text{other} \\
\text{nature} & : & \text{society}
\end{array}
$$

Some see a lamentably uncrossable gulf between these binaries, but Eagleton argues that it is time to get beyond such an impasse and see what 'fertile pacts and allegiances' might be made with nature, on the model not of cloistered high theory, but of the ecology movement. Thus, the debate Eagleton conducts around the pastoral is not just about cultural form, but is also an intervention into the politics of intellectual work. He describes the politics of the pastoral in terms that I find suggestive for understanding popular media:

> All propaganda or popularization involves a putting of the complex into the simple, but such a move is instantly deconstructive, for if the complex *can* be put into the simple, then it is not as complex as it seemed in the first place; and if the simple can be an adequate medium of such complexity, then it cannot, after all, be as simple as all that. . . . If one has a cultural form in which simple characters are made to voice highly wrought rhetorical discourse, or sophisticated figures to articulate simple feelings, then the political effects of the form are likely to be ambiguous.[3]

Such an ambiguous form – where the sublime *is* the cor blimey – is one way of 'coming to terms with the fraught relations between critic and text, intellectual and society'.[4] Eagleton argues that despite the gap between intellectuals and the common people, and despite the gap between consciousness and nature, it is not the case that the intellectual is the eternal 'other' of the masses, nor that the mind is the eternal other of nature. On the contrary, intellectuals and others are part of a 'common humanity' (and what's more 'the intellectual must be taught by the masses'); while 'the mind is, after all, a *part* of nature and not just its other'.[5] For a Global High Theorist like Eagleton, this is living dangerously, for such a position is both transcendentalist and evaluative, flying in the face of a certain critical orthodoxy which is even more suspicious of judgements than of totalizing fictions like 'nature' and 'humanity'. But the risk is worth taking (i.e. that nature be valorized over mind, humanity over intellectuals), precisely to transcend the theoretical impasse that can recognize 'nature' and 'human nature' as ideological fictions, but is then unable to rework these concepts, or connect one with the other.

Such theoretical difficulties stem not from the nature of nature but from the opposition of intellectuals to society; Eagleton suggests that: 'There seems something strangely self-thwarting about a culturalist or historical Marxism that sternly forbids itself to describe as "unnatural" a wholly reclusive life or a society that finds sunshine disgusting.'[6] He says, 'some people feel repulsed and alienated by staring at the roots of trees, while others just sit down and have a picnic'. Contemplation of the otherness of nature need not be tragic at all, but an occasion for acting socially. From Isaiah to Marxism, High Theory has found little to enjoy in the country beyond cutting down tall poppies and/or watching them wither. Perhaps it's time for something simpler and more active.

Let's just sit down and have a picnic. To do so is to pursue the pastoral, to interrogate action in its dramatic, performative form, to think about the

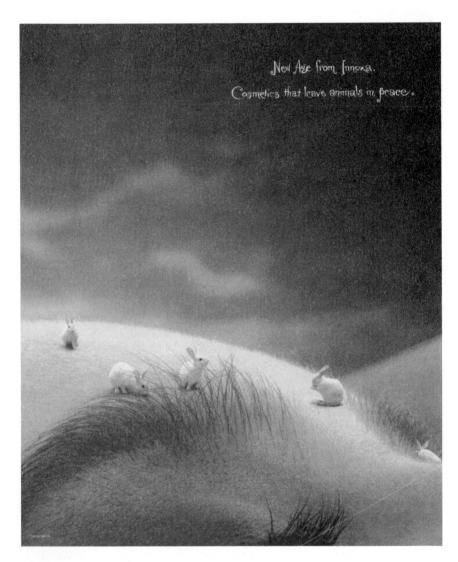

New Age from Innoxa.
Cosmetics that leave animals in peace.

Figure 3.1 'New Age Nature': 'For all flesh *is* as grass . . .' (Innoxa Cosmetics)

gap between intellectuals and society, the relations between critics and texts, and to look for the mediated representation of the picnic in popular culture. Along the way, the picnic, as a playful, politically neutral concept or activity (the word has no 'ominous ring', no ring at all, in contemporary theory and criticism), may serve to show how media, discourses and

44

ideological meanings are attached and fixed in different contexts, media, times and places. To go on a picnic, in short, is to go looking for the politics of, among other things, pictures.

'The picnic' is a social activity, a form of social organization, fully participatory for all involved. In sociological terms it's a social institution, though not one that displays the centralized control functions which are designed to ensure survival and reproduction for other social institutions (from medicine to media). The survival, cultural form, reproduction and internal organization of picnics are ensured not by codification in centrally enforced regulations (picnics are not a *regime*), but in the unrehearsed participation of myriad dispersed and mutually unacquainted picnic parties. Picnics are highly codified, by time (leisure), place (countryside), activity (eating and looking), and in their signs (hampers, gingham cloths, plastic cutlery, disposable crockery). Thus there is a 'right' way to have a picnic (it has 'looks' which can be recognized), but no one polices it, and while all picnics are the same, each is different. Everyone is free to draw from the discursive knowledge bank as much picnic 'currency' as they like, as often as they like, in whatever denominations they want, to dispose of as they see fit. It's an 'economy' that escapes all current definitions of that term, especially as picnics have no utility, except as ritual or ceremony.

The picnic as a social institution is not a 'mass medium' as commonly understood, even though it is socially pervasive, indifferent to cultural, historical and demographic difference, and it is a ritual of leisure consumption undertaken by the very same units of people (families, friends) as constitute the unit of self-present audience for popular media. The picnic is thus an ambiguous category – it is both 'A' (media) and 'Not-A' (not media) simultaneously, which means that the following analysis of picnics is both 'media analysis' and something else as well, namely a forensic attempt to locate not the media but the public. To go in search of the lost assembly of the agora is to relocate performance, pedagogy and participation in a contemporary 'public space', but in order to arrive at such a destination, it is necessary first to digress, to travel through unfamiliar country.

Our family picnic: agoraphobia tames the country

While the scientist is concerned with the analysis of natural phenomena in objective terms, the artist seeks to interpret both the natural and metaphysical world in terms of emotions, feelings and aesthetic perceptions portrayed through a particular medium. The philosophy behind a work of art, the ideas, the intellectual message and the meaning are conditioned by the thoughts and aspirations of the artist. The technical possibilities for conveying these perceptions and aspirations have been influenced dramatically by scientific

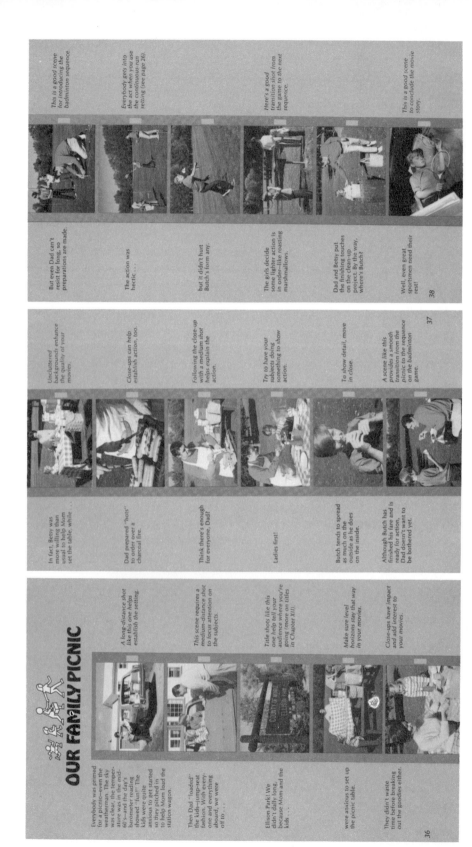

Figure 3.2 Our family picnic (Kodak: Home Movies Made Easy)

discoveries. This is particularly illustrated in the discovery of the photographic process.[7]

The discovery of the photographic process continues, for each and every practitioner of the art. All media are pedagogic, containing within their message systems guidance on how to use them. Kodak's *Home Movies Made Easy*[8] is one such guide, whose advice is summarized in 'OUR FAMILY PICNIC', starring Mom, Dad, Betsy and Butch, in a banal tale of travel, food preparation and consumption, playing games and clearing up. The family is cast in traditional roles: mother and daughter set the table and roast marshmallows, while Dad oversees the barbecue and sets up the badminton in response to Butch's demand for 'action'. It's not hard to see these sequences as a politicization of family life; Kodak's fictional family teaches discursive organization as well as technical tips. Advice on how to film sexual divisions of labour is also endorsement and propagation of them, while the integration of movie-making into family activities is 'naturalized' by associating the family with the consumption of technology. So a family picnic is the site for gender and consumer politics, made into a meaningful story, which is what is being taught.

The status of the pictures is complex, for they purport to show a home movie, but they are printed stills 'authored' by Kodak, and the whole point of the story is that the family is not at home. They depend on the impression of reality created by both the profilmic picnic and the diegetic narrative, but while it is common to make films of events that never occurred (fiction), in this case the film never occurred either – 'OUR FAMILY PICNIC' is the name of a movie, which is itself part of the diegetics of Kodak's instructional technique. Kodak's picnic sits on the ambiguous boundaries between different media, connecting movie-making with publishing, still pictures with moving ones, home movies with Kodak's corporate image of the family, and pedagogy with entertainment.

The meaning of 'picnic' is not so complex. The country is essential, but as site not sight, as setting not action: 'We didn't dally long, because Mom and the kids were anxious to set up the picnic table.' No concessions are made at all, in fact, to nature, with food, cooking, table settings and games reproducing exactly the urban indoors from which a picnic is designed to deviate. The American family goes to the country with as much of its own life-support system on board as the space shuttle. It's as if the only reason for going outside is to get enough light for the camera, loaded as it no doubt is with the very slow-speed Kodachrome II filmstock (25 ASA in daylight). This is not mentioned, although unsigned traces of Kodakery may be visible in the choice of a red car and yellow and red sweaters for the adults. These colours contrast with the country greens, following a familiar device in landscape postcards, where the little red sweater highlights the scenery so well that many an unwitting hiker has ended up wearing, in postcards, a red sweater that they never owned in fact. As it happens, these are also colours to which Kodachrome is technically especially suited.

'OUR FAMILY PICNIC' is ideological and manipulative in its vision of 'the family', but the politics of its pictures includes an unstated struggle between Kodak and the purchaser, whose filmmaking plans may not include a family, to say nothing of a picnic. There is in fact a forensic trace of such possibilities in the text, for there are scenes which destabilize the gendered ideology by making cinematography itself indifferent to it; e.g. 'Ladies first!' shows Dad, Betsy and Butch – so Mom must have shot it. And although the imagined family and the cute euphoria of their picnic is not everyone's cup of tea, Kodak's pedagogical advice is still useful both technically and in terms of composition and continuity editing. The cuteness and euphoria are a teaching device, easily legible as such (readable in quotation marks). In the end, what consumers make of that advice is not determined by Kodak, as is demonstrated both by the number of home movies (and videos) which cheerfully ignore it in favour of an untutored camera technique (best described as hosing), and conversely by the considerable use of the so-called 'amateur' 8-mm format in art, independent and music filmmaking.

When you compare your amateur 8-mm picnic with *Picnic at Hanging Rock*, the home movie version might appear to be rather paltry, and far from political. But it is clear that politics is embedded in the heart of home movies (and video), and in the relations between Kodak and the purchaser of Kodak's equipment. Furthermore, this politics is pervasive and 'anthropological', extending into the myriad and unspectacular rhythms of everyday life a technology of visualization. By such means consumers can do what Enzensberger requires of 'emancipatory' media: use them to 'secure evidence of their daily experiences and draw effective lessons from them'.[9] It's just that the lessons, once learnt from Kodak, are both simple and self-taught; this is the politics of pastoral popularization, not *necessarily* of 'aggressive forms of publicity' conforming to the political programme of the organized masses.[10]

Heroes of Britain: to see is to Speke

Despite their mobilization in the service of all branches of human knowledge and endeavour, books are among the easiest media to avoid. Purchasers of cameras don't need to buy the manual, and even the owners of books don't necessarily read them. It's not entirely a matter of chance whether an ideological text gets through to its target or not, but it's by no means a foregone conclusion. This observation leads to the next picnic, and takes the discussion from politics of families to national, imperial dimensions. However, the family is not forgotten. In this case the family is my own, and the question of avoidability arises because of a book belonging to my grandfather, presented to him at the Crystal Palace in 1894 by HRH the Duchess of Fife on behalf of the RSPCA, for which he had, it seems, written an essay on 'Man's duty towards animals'. The volume he received for this effort is called *Heroes of Britain in Peace and War* by Edwin Hodder, and the first question is whether anyone had ever opened it before I did nearly a century later. It shows no sign of use. So although my family was donated imperialist and nationalist propaganda by a worthy ideological state apparatus, it is possible that I'm the first member of it to see the picture of a royal picnic shown in Figure 3.3.

On a journey in search of the source of the Nile in Central Africa in about 1860, Captain John Hanning Speke entered the territory of Uganda, where he stayed several months at the court of King M'tesa.

" M'tesa was about to strike her down with a thick stick, when Speke, whose British blood was roused by this appeal to him by name, rushed at the tyrant, caught his upraised hand, and demanded the poor victim's life " (*p.* 265).

Figure 3.3 Speke saves the king's wife (*Heroes of Britain in Peace & War*)

He found M'tesa to be the incarnation of despotism and tyranny, and his reign a reign of terror. . . . His wives were legion, and scarcely a day passed that Speke did not see one or more of these unhappy creatures dragged off to execution, no one daring to raise his voice on her behalf. On one occasion, at a pic-nic, when the king was accompanied by a selection of wives from his harem, one ventured to pluck a fruit, and offer it to her lord. It was intended to please him, but he took it as an offence, and ordered her to death. Immediately she was surrounded by the page boys – hundreds of whom are kept to look after the women and to run errands – boys who are always on the run, and are killed if they dare to walk. As soon as these little black imps threw their cord turbans around her, she attempted to beat them off, but failing, cried out in anguish to Speke to help and protect her. M'tesa was about to strike her down with a thick stick, when Speke, whose British blood was roused by this appeal to him by name, rushed at the tyrant, caught his upraised hand, and demanded the poor victim's life. It is a wonder he did not lose his own, but the whole affair seemed to afford only amusement to the capricious chief, who failed to see what difference a life more or less could make, and he therefore ordered the woman to be released. It was obvious, however, that Speke could not interfere in domestic matters with impunity, and this appears to have been the only instance in which he was instrumental in saving a condemned life.[11]

Here then is another family picnic, but the relations between Mom and Dad are represented in somewhat different terms in this one, to say nothing of the fate of all the little Butches who don't do as they're told. If the story is read to isolate what actually happened, very little remains; a defused domestic dispute in which no blow was struck but which stirred up the usual passions and terrors among those concerned. Perhaps, shorn of its tribal exoticism and imperial blood-upmanship, this is just as familiar a picnic scene as was the golly-gosh harmony of Kodak's happy family.

This fantasy of Britishness in the face of sexuality and violence is accompanied by what can only be called a *proto-photo*: an engraving which gives in photographic realism the details of the picnic, complete with abandoned fruit in one corner, M'tesa's condemned wife kneeling in the other, with M'tesa in the middle, grasped by the towering figure of Speke, eyes staring in righteousness. The status of this picture is to illustrate a story, part of which is given as its caption. There's nothing remarkable about it, except that it never occurred. No artist ever beheld that scene, and so the verisimilitude with which the event is depicted is a lie. Like photographers from that day to this, the artist has sought to illustrate the 'decisive moment' of the story, but unlike photographers has succeeded in

50

this from a distance of thousands of miles and several decades. Such engravings, well-established components of popular (and unpopular) literature and magazines in the nineteenth century, paved the way for photography in mass publishing, by illustrating not only events but also such fictional qualities as roused British blood, capricious tyranny, profligate African sexuality and carelessness of life. This mythical African picnic serves to teach the readers of *Heroes of Britain*, if there were any, that binary opposition does indeed organize the world, along familiar racist and imperial lines.

Before photography became a mass medium, the publishing medium had solved the problems of making pictures not only meaningful but pedagogic, not only specific records of what-the-camera-saw but also transcendent dramatizations of moral and political values, teaching readers how to see in nature the cultural values promoted by the text. So M'tesa's picnic, which in terms of food content seems rather paltry, is nature filled with culture with a vengeance, overflowing with the proto-photo's naturalized imperatives. The picture relies on (requires and promotes) an 'eyewitness ideology' that still structures news, a philosophy of knowledge borrowed from empirical science: it celebrates the hero explorer/journalist who can bring back new knowledge by having been there and seen that.

It may be of interest that the ideology of looking was at this time more significant than the ideology of truth. Speke's stated aim was to find the source of the Nile; his mission was accomplished at the moment when he was able to *look with his own eyes* upon some water which, though not in fact that source, would do. Speke's act of looking was sufficiently powerful not only to represent the presence at the event of his entire race ('Europeans'), but also to claim what he saw as an imperial colony, and because of its ethno-political import the actual moment of seeing is given high narrative status:

> When Speke reached Tanganyika, he was unable to gaze upon the lovely view in consequence of severe inflammation of the eyes. . . .
> While camping out one day, Speke was attacked by a host of small black beetles, and one of them, finding its way into his ear, bit its way farther in, causing fearful pain; at the same time it acted as a counter-irritant, and drew away the inflammation from his eyes. After many difficulties and dangers in ceaseless journeyings, Speke . . . discerned at a distance of a few miles a sheet of water. . . . On the 4th of August, standing on a high hill . . . he was rewarded for all his toil, for there burst suddenly upon his gaze the whole vast expanse of the Nyanza![12]

The decisive moment: to see, which is to know, which is to imperialize. Speke was 'the first European who saw the Victoria Nyanza, and it was he who opened up a rich and extensive region hitherto unknown, but with which the English people have since become painfully familiar'.[13] Truth, progress and national power are attendant upon the individual eyewitness hero, unbowed by tradition, custom or fear of reprisal, who ventures into the unknown.

Unfortunately, worms, or perhaps hosts of black beetles, have withered the flower of this pretty grass even before *Heroes of Britain* has finished arranging it. Speke did not, despite his belief and his three-year quest, find the source of the Nile;[14] the proto-photo of his bravery at a picnic is a realistic portrayal of a scene that never took place; and the moral of a story that teaches heroism in the face of tyranny while poring over details of brutality, sexual humiliation and death is ambiguous – not at all a pure record of the power of scientific exploration and of rationality over supposedly baser humans, of truth over mumbo-jumbo. No, the heroic picnic is something much more familiar – another wife-bashing with the intervention of a well-meaning but ultimately ineffective neighbour. In the end the picture is not a representation of darkest Africa, but darkest suburbia, in fancy dress, and Speke didn't have to make a three-year trip to be its eyewitness, nor is seeing it normally accounted very heroic.

Pique-nique, pique Nièpce

National pride and science are among the originating discourses not only of British heroism in the exploitation of Central Africa but also in the history of photography, and the history of the picnic too, come to that. The word picnic came into the English language from the French *pique-nique*, becoming an 'English institution' around 1800, according to the *Oxford English Dictionary* (*OED*), when it was 'a fashionable social entertainment in which each person present contributed a share of the provisions'. At about this time, in 1802, Thomas Wedgwood, a member of the pottery family, another English institution (one which plays but a cameo role in this narrative, however), discovered how to record light on materials sensitized with silver nitrate.

Later the essential feature of a picnic changed from the individual contribution to 'a pleasure party including an excursion to some spot in the country where all partake of a repast out of doors: the participants may bring with them individually the viands and means of entertainment, or the whole may be provided by someone who "gives the picnic"' (*OED*). Later still the picnic was popularized beyond the fashionable social classes into the widest reaches of global-American family ideology and consumer culture, as we've seen.

Figure 3.4 shows a postcard from Paris. I've had it for years, and I don't know now whether I bought it, was given it or found it. On the obverse, a *pique-nique* (but no picnickers), laid out to illustrate a verse by Emilie Bernard that is printed on the reverse.

Figure 3.4 Pique-nique (postcard)

There is of course very little science here, although there's plenty of Frenchness, but the absence of science is not insignificant, for picnics are intelligible as a social institution only after a binary opposition between town and country, work and pleasure, knowledge and entertainment, culture and nature, has been naturalized, not only in formal discourses but also in the practical activities of social life. A picnic excursion is not heroic exploration of unknown territory in the manner of Speke, it is pleasurable congregation and a ritual of crossing, and thereby confirming, the binary boundaries mentioned above. That is why it is essential to travel to the country, and why eating is transformed into an autochthonous reclamation of the relationship between food and the ground. The knowledge gene-rated by picnics is magical (the binary opposite of science), enacting a scientific society's belief in an inside and an outside, the performance of an irrational ceremony in praise of rationalism's reductions of the world to opposition. You cannot go on a picnic unless you believe in science.

Meanwhile, national pride and science are the dominant discourses of the history of photography too. Historical accounts always raise the question of origins, of causality, and of the trustworthiness of original documents, and the history of photography challenges all such questions. Photography was not originally invented by any one person, nor is it clear

Figure 3.5 Set table (J.N. Nièpce)

what inventions led in causal sequence to new developments, and there is no original photograph – no 'first picture'.

So Figure 3.5 is not the world's first photograph. It is a picture of a repast out of doors, and like the *pique-nique* postcard from Paris, there are no human figures, and no landscape. Perhaps it is not even a picnic, and certainly it is not a photograph in the usual sense, but a concoction of light reacting with a type of asphalt called bitumen of Judea, and lavender oil. It was taken in 1822, by J.N. Nièpce, an amateur inventor of Chalon-sur-Saône in France, whose earliest experiments in light-fixing had been sparked off when he heard of Thomas Wedgwood's work in England.

> If any one individual has a particular claim as the discoverer of photography it belongs to the Frenchman Joseph Nicéphore Nièpce; the subsequent development of the process was due to a collaboration between Nièpce and a compatriot, Louis Jacques Mandé Daguerre.[15]

So says a volume published by the Australian Academy of Science to coincide with a 1986 'art–science' exhibition on photography called

Images: Illusion and Reality, co-sponsored by the Société française de Photographie and the Académie des Sciences. The first image of this exhibition was Nièpce's proto-photo of a *pique-nique manqué*. The exhibition's avowed purpose was to bring art and science together, not least to counteract the current funding of science by administrators and entrepreneurs rather than on the basis of vision:

> Artistic creation and scientific creation depend on precisely the same mechanisms even though the end results of the two processes are quite different. An artistic creation is of its nature evanescent whereas a scientific fact or a natural law is characterised by persistence, reproducibility and universality.[16]

It does seem as though photography too is characterized by persistence, reproducibility and universality, but as Bede Morris says in the preface to the book, 'Nièpce could never have been funded through a peer review system – all he had was a dream, an inspiration, a passion and a conviction.' It also has to be noted that he wasn't a scientist but an amateur, and his discovery wasn't exploited by a scientific funding body but ripped off by Daguerre, a commercial scene-painter and showman. Because of its photochemical, optical and physical complexities, photography is often claimed as a product of science, but the claim is unfounded. It was a product of amateur inspiration, artistic flair and commercial showmanship, and science came limping along behind, trying to work out what was going on. Nor is the origin of photography unequivocally French – the inventor of the positive/negative process in use today was the Englishman William Henry Fox Talbot, whose prototype 'Calotype' dates from 1839, and the inventor of photography as a mass medium was the American George Eastman, who launched the first Kodak camera in 1888. In short, neither science nor nationalism can claim photography for its own.

In this context it is interesting to observe how photography was first understood as a social as opposed to artistic or scientific medium. It became socially significant in the Victorian era, and the earliest social historian of that period in Britain took it to be not only a popular but also a pedagogic medium. George Macaulay Trevelyan (a national institution by himself), in *English Social History*, a book of history-as-propaganda written to boost popular national sentiment during the Second World War, saw photography as a teacher of family values; like TV and home movies later on, popular photography was understood as a domesticating medium, teaching not civic or public values but private discipline. Trevelyan cites contemporary opinion in support of his view:

> In the Twentieth Century, drink has found fresh enemies in the cinema at the street corner, and the wireless at home; and the

increase of skilled and mechanical employments, particularly the driving of motor-cars, has put a premium on sobriety. . . . In the Victorian era photography made its effective impact on the world. Already in 1871 it was acclaimed by an observer as 'the greatest boon that has been conferred on the poorer classes in later years.'

'Any one who knows what the worth of family affection is among the lower classes, and who has seen the array of little portraits stuck over a labourer's fireplace, still gathering into one the "Home" that life is always parting – the boy that has "gone to Canada," the "girl out at service," the little one with the golden hair that sleeps under the daisies, the old grandfather in the country – will perhaps feel with me that in counteracting the tendencies, social and industrial, which every day are sapping the healthier family affections, the six-penny photograph is doing more for the poor than all the philanthropists in the world.'

(*Macmillan's Magazine*, Sept. 1871)

By the cheapest and most accurate form of portraiture possible, photography had indeed brought to all classes a prolongation of poignant and delightful memories of the dead, of the absent, of past years, incidents and associations.

Its effect on art was of more doubtful benefit. . . . By reducing the importance of picture-painting as a trade, and surpassing it in realistic representation of detail, it drove the painter to take refuge more and more in theory, and in a series of intellectual experiments in Art for Art's sake.[17]

So entered the new poignant and delightful communications media of cinema, radio, automobiles and photography into social history: as laudable antidotes to alcohol, as props to family life, and, in the case of photography, as the culpable cause of theory.

Trevelyan counts the social influence of cinema, radio and photography to be benign, though his 1871 source shows that long before the exponents of mass society theory popularized the idea of social atomization there was a perceived connection between the new media of mechanical reproduction and the loss of traditional ties. In this case, however, the villains of the piece are those unspecified 'social and industrial tendencies' which 'sap family affections' and which photography can 'counteract'. In other words the new visual-mechanical medium is seen not as the cause of those tendencies (as in later theories of media effects), but quite the reverse. Similarly, Trevelyan makes no adverse comment about the social effect of cinema and radio, the then mass media of broadcasting, claiming them as allies (against drink) for his own brand of conservative social evolution. Cinema civilizes the street corner, wireless the home; motoring induces sobriety and skill, photography protects the family.

56

The only blot on Trevelyan's landscape, as far as the social effects of the media are concerned in 1942–4, is the unfortunate tendency of art to retreat from representation of the real (a task it had in fact only taken on in Ramist post-Reformation Europe[18]), routed by photography, to 'take refuge' in theory. Now theory has become so popular it can be used to sell gravy in the most popular women's magazine of an entire continent (see Figure 3.6).[19]

There is no word in Trevelyan of audiences or consumers, or even of the public; merely of classes, the poor, the Twentieth Century and the Victorian era. But there is quite clearly an attempt to account for the mechanical mass media of communication as social phenomena, explaining them in terms of the uses to which they were put by the public at large. This move is not innocent; Trevelyan is engaged in an intellectual colonization of audience practices, making the relationship between media and their audiences a matter not for them to decide between themselves, but for his historical narrative to explain on their behalf, naturally enough in terms of worthy social and political goals.

These goals are missionary; the civilizing mission of progressive, rational modernization, in which the wild and disruptive population spawned by industrialization and empire, living in London and Glasgow but children of M'tesa, is at last domesticated, tamed by education into home, family and sobriety. Jacques Donzelot[20] has analysed historically how in nineteenth-century France a private, social, domestic domain was produced – engineered – as a branch of national policy; Trevelyan's civilizing rhetoric belongs to the same politics, and his recruitment of popular communications as an ally is itself an important reminder of how the media were integrated into social policy at an early stage, with no misgivings as yet about their individual behavioural effects. The cinema is a vanguard medium, combating the enemy on the street corner (perhaps partaking of the pleasures of the street corner too, though this is not allowed by Trevelyan). Meanwhile, radio, photographs and, paradoxically, the driving of motor cars, are all seen as constructing on the site of the urban industrial labourer an ideology of immobility – of staying at home (out of harm's way).

Hero(in)es: fashioning the bush, taking tea with beloved Billy

The driving of motor cars is by now an inescapable attribute of picnics. The urban industrial labourer is not what he used to be, either; as often as not, nowadays, he's a woman. Out in the country, the picnic is feminized and updated. Photography has come far enough since the days of amateur inventors like Nièpce to be able to sell back to the consumer an image of her own amateur practice. Figure 3.7 shows a fashion spread from *Hero*, a shortlived, big-format, highly produced Australian bi-monthly magazine

CUBISM

When a certain group of continental painters created
their masterpieces, they restricted themselves to cubes.
  And in recent times, so too have Continental cooks.
But now you can break away from these restrictions.
  Our experience at Continental suggests certain cooks
prefer a little 'light and shade' in flavouring their meals.

Figure 3.6 Cubism/postmodernism (Continental gravy)

*P*ost ODERNISM

So we offer the flexibility of Continental Powdered Stock.

Which means, whether you choose the beef or the chicken, Continental can help let your animal urges run wild.

Release your creative juices with Continental.

Figure 3.7 Album (*Hero*)

Everyone. All smiling.

A nice one of me.

Jonathon and me.

Miss Jones Marguerite photograph in black collar, $50, with cream blouse in sky blue and white striped cotton, $95, from Dynasty. Jonathon wears a cotton shirt with peppermint, black and white jumpsuit outfit $45, from City Boys. Felt Hat wears cotton trousers, $50. Jim Jones Mark Robinson pullover in palm-collar shirt, $180, with City Boys grey drill trousers, $120. Jim tie wears Miss Jones for Women black and white checker-pressed set, tucked into lovely Osaka Bracelet black denim jeans with white stitching, $45. Michael wears Pips white drill jacket, $75.

cotton blue and white stripe drill undershirt, $45, grey grey drill trousers, $45. Tie wears a white shirt with denim collar, $50, by Marquette with blue and white striped drill pleated skirt, $50, from Dynasty. A cream linen print with a line hanging around her head, by Lee wears a navy blue cotton jersey dress, with a floppy brim and full skirt, $90. In Miss Cundy Jonathon wears to his little dungarees shirt, $90, with City Boys cotton stripe jacket and Mark Oxford cotton tie, $50.

Candid shot of Jim and Kat –
who would have thought it!

" Our last shot.

Kat and Michael ready to go home "

Kat in the bedroom.

" Jim snaps Mike, Kat and Jonathon.

dicks not out

Jonathon looking cool.

for the older teen market.[21] It shows a trip to the country (in Australia 'country' means farming, so the trip is in fact to the bush, a wilder, more dangerous country, where picnics may have to cohabit with snakes, or so the copy says), by three young men and two young women, to have a picnic. The spread takes the form of a photo album of the event, complete with wavy-edged prints captioned in a youthful scrawl, supposedly compiled by one of the female participant models.

Like most of the other picnics featured so far, this one never happened. The snaps are carefully numbered, itemized and priced, and while the handwritten captions celebrate personal relations, emotions and pleasure, naming the models and using personal pronouns (especially 'me'), the pictures perform the realistic function of illustrating the languid self-awareness of those who know they are being made to look as good as the landscape, simultaneously hinting at teenage moods, and parading city fashions to potential customers.[22]

These potential customers, the teen and early twenties market, are not domesticated; on the contrary, they are in that phase of life where they are detached from both family of origin and family of destination, and they're not immobile at home but in transit, from school or unemployment to job, from officially asexual children to gendered adult sexuality, from the mendicant poverty of childhood to independent spending power. The *Hero* picnic makes a virtue out of ambiguity: what looks like a picture of heterosexual love proves, on reading the caption, to be sibling affection (allowing that 'my brother' is a figure of the picnic-fiction, and may not describe the models' propinquity), so the image of girl + boy and the practice of rehearsing poses on one's brother or sister can coexist wittily in the same photograph. *Hero* takes the lifestyle of people with little money not as its subject but as its form, using the picnic viands (which are unsophisticated cheap fresh fruit), the photo-album format, and the young people lolling about with books and magazines, to naturalize circumstances in which the clothes on offer might look and feel appropriate to someone on a bus who might never have left the city, but who knows about clothes, boys, girls and mementoes.

The Australian bush is not often feminized in the languid *Heroic* style,[23] nor seen as an appropriate venue for a picnic (a city-folks import). On the contrary, after *Picnic at Hanging Rock*, we all know what happens to girls who venture out into that ancient and mysterious landscape for a picnic (Figure 3.8). In the mythological landscapes of art, film, literature and nationalism, the bush is more commonly regarded as home to the male, and what you eat there is *tucker*. What tucker is was most recently demonstrated by the hit Australian ABC TV series *Bush Tucker Man* (1990–1), starring Les Hiddins, whose job in the Australian Defence Forces was to collect information on how soldiers can live off the land in the far north of Australia, but who became a popular celebrity through

HISTORIC AUSTRALIAN MOMENTS: PICNIC AT AYERS ROCK

Figure 3.8 Picnic at Ayers Rock (David Arthur-Simons)

this series by wearing an unlikely hat and chewing enthusiastically on all manner of unlikely objects as he introduced traditional Aboriginal foods, landscapes and methods of collection to the wider Australian public.

One thing the Bush Tucker Man never did was to drink billy tea, but no matter, this isn't the bush, it's the outback. What you drink here is not some traditional Aboriginal concoction, for you have your own traditions to invent and uphold. To explain, Figure 3.9 shows a 1957 advertisement for Brooke Bond tea, called 'Waltzing Matilda', part of a 'taking tea with the world' series for the British tea-drinker. The ad shows a picture which is invested with the authenticity of both art and nation, being captioned with an artist's name and titles, and acknowledging the Australian High Commission in London. The picture shows a group of eight men, one on horseback, round a fire, boiling their billies. The copy tells us that 'in their homes', the Aussies make tea 'as we do. But not the man who works in the "out back"!'

In his swag (or Matilda), the roll or bag which holds his personal possessions, he carries his beloved billy. He fills this with water to

Waltzing Matilda

ILLUSTRATED BY
ROBERT JOHNSTON, R.I., S.M.A.

Tea is almost as popular in Australia as it is here, but the Aussies like it stronger. In their homes, they make it as we do. But not the man who works in the 'out back'!

In his swag (or Matilda), the roll or bag which holds his personal possessions, he carries his beloved billy. He fills this with water to boil, throws in a good measure of tea, for strength, and allows it to boil again. Then—an old custom—he swings the billy round and round over his shoulder.

Bushmen usually have a 'sweet tooth', and add plenty of sugar—with often a gum tree leaf for its subtle flavouring. Like you, they find tea a wonderful thirst quencher, cooling in the heat, warming in the cold, a good morning freshener and a soothing night-cap.

(With grateful acknowledgement of the help given by Mr. Finley, of the Staff of the High Commissioner for Australia)

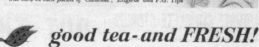
Figure 3.9 Waltzing Matilda (Brooke Bond tea)

boil, throws in a good measure of tea, for strength, and allows it to boil again. Then – an old custom – he swings the billy round and round over his shoulder. Bushmen usually have a 'sweet tooth', and add plenty of sugar – with often a gum tree leaf for its subtle flavouring.[24]

So this is not a picnic. No picnic in English English perhaps, but in Australian English the word picnic has a special association with rural horse races, which are called picnic meetings or picnic races. A 1923 citation in the (Oxford) *Australian National Dictionary* offers this explanation of how such picnics reproduce for white settlers some ancient, traditional customs: 'The joy or excitement [of a kangaroo hunt] to the blacks was on a par with that of the picnic races to the white people at the present time in the same district.' So Brooke Bond's horsy bushmen are authentic enough picnickers after all, and closer to Aboriginality than appears at first sight, even to themselves.

But the image of a repast out of doors is one of simultaneous enjoyment of the same joys and excitements around the world – while you sippa cuppa in Surbiton, these manly but not Aboriginal lads are gazing into the warm glow of Brooke Bond tea out there in Woop Woop, New South Wales, going native with gum leaves, perhaps, but endearingly instituting ancestral customs of their own with the famous billy-swinging ceremony and the indispensable language of the Aussie 'out back' where tea is billy and a bag is a swag (or Matilda). For all that, they're like us, and the bush is not alien nature but masculine workplace, unpeopled by Aboriginals or women simply because our heroes have a job to do, which is to represent the myth of Australian mateship for the benefit of the largest tea company in the world.

Go wild in the country

See Jungle! See Jungle! Go Join Your Gang Yeah, City All Over! Go Ape Crazy! is the name of an LP released in 1981 on the RCA label by Bow Wow Wow, a British band made up of the former Ants of Adam (Dave Barbarossa, Matthew Ashman and Leroy Gorman), and fronted by fifteen-year-old lead singer Annabella Lwin, a discovery of Malcolm McLaren, who managed Bow Wow Wow.

The album cover (Figure 3.10) became instantly notorious, not because it is a careful and witty pastiche by photographer Andy Earl of Manet's *Le Déjeuner sur L'herbe*, a celebrated Impressionist picnic, but because Annabella Lu Win appeared in the photograph, and thus on the album cover, wearing no clothes. It seems that because she had not been accompanied by her legal chaperone (supplied by the Greater London Council) on the day of the shoot, her mother, Amie Dunn-Lewin, was within her rights to claim that 'her daughter was being portrayed as a sex object without her prior knowledge'.[25] Hence most of the transparencies were destroyed, but the photograph nevertheless appeared in the *Los Angeles Times*, the New York *Soho News*, the London *Sun* and *The Face*, not to mention on at least some album covers, one of which I bought at the time. The cassette version, meanwhile, was presented as a photo-package called 'Your Cassette Pet' (Figure 3.11), and sported fold-out photographs of the band (also by Andy Earl), with Annabella draped but two of the male members wearing no clothes, though there was no furore about this.

Here's another politics of pictures; not exactly censorship, not exactly sexual exploitation, but perhaps more than a little jostling over the economics of a fifteen-year-old female body. The politics of this picture is not so much ambiguous as laminated; a thick pile of mutually reinforcing binaries:

art	:	entertainment
freedom	:	regulation
painting	:	photography
high culture	:	pop music
artist	:	manager
Manet	:	McLaren
erotica	:	pornography
public	:	private
adult	:	'child' [minor]
male body	:	female body

You only have to look down each side of this list of oppositions to see that something odd is going on. Manet, an accredited master painter of high cultural art, is ambiguated into McLaren, whose reputation was then and has remained as the great 'rock n'roll swindler', scourge and beneficiary of monopolistic record companies. As manager of the Sex Pistols, McLaren used punk to criticize the music business from the very belly of the beast, raising violence to an art form. After violence, which is a bodily politics, sex, which is another. He launched Bow Wow Wow with a 'Cassette Pet' whose lead song, 'Sexy Eiffel Tower', sung by the then fourteen-year-old Annabella Lwin, ambiguates the experiences of fucking and falling just enough to escape litigation. Bow Wow Wow's début full-length album was to be called *Go Wild in the Country*, an anthem to the eroticization of picnics, if you like, but the title was changed to *See Jungle! See Jungle! Go Join Your Gang Yeah, City All Over! Go Ape Crazy!* (which means much the same) when the cover got into trouble (a change no doubt calculated to get right up the noses of the bland talk-over DJs of pop radio).

Bow Wow Wow's picnic *déjeuner sur l'herbe* was, then, not an innocent pastoral idyll but an intervention into the politics of pictures, a public

Figure 3.10 See Jungle! (BowWowWow album cover)

SEE JUNGLE! SEE JUNGLE! GO JOIN YOUR GANG YEAH, CITY ALL OVER! GO APE CRAZY!

Side One

JUNGLE BOY
CHIHUAHUA
SINNER, SINNER, SINNER
MICKEY PUT IT DOWN
(I'M A) T.V. SAVAGE
ELIMINATION DANCING

Side Two

GOLLY! GOLLY! GO BUDDY!
KING KONG
GO WILD IN THE COUNTRY
I'M NOT A KNOW IT ALL
WHY ARE BABIES SO WISE?
ORANG-OUTANG
HELLO, HELLO DADDY
(I'LL SACRIFICE YOU)

IKE RONNIE REAGAN, SUE ELLEN, CASANOVA, BOTTICELLI, IN A TIME NEVER NEVER, QUEEN DIANA, ROCKEFELLER... MATTHEW ASHMAN, ANNABELLA LWIN, LEROY GORMAN, DAVE BARBAROSSA

esign Nick Egan photography Andy Earl

69

Figure 3.11 See Jungle! (BowWowWow cassette cover)

provocation, legible as part of McLaren's public image as an entrepreneur of ambiguation in the music, style and cultural politics business. The McLaren/Manet scene quotes art while treating it with derision; any challenge to the decency of the cover would at least be compromised by the artistic allusion. Reporting on the furore, and taking the opportunity to print the 'banned' photo in full colour, *The Face* wittily headlined its story 'ART' (Figure 3.12).[26]

McLaren's politics of ambiguation is not confined to cocking snooks at high art. Annabella's picnic enters the public domain to promote not only Bow Wow Wow but also adolescent sexuality; both picture and music are dedicated to its pleasures for teenage participants and general audiences alike, neither arguing for nor against that sexuality, just flaunting it. If the cover is offensive, it is partly because of McLaren's 'Svengali' image as the band's all-too-knowing manager. Commercial entertainment by manipulative media and suspect methods is traditionally no place for children. But, as Bow Wow Wow's manager well knows, people of Annabella Lwin's age are nevertheless the prime market for the music on offer. Popular music is founded on sex, even though a sizeable proportion of its fans are legally under age. Moreover, sex is both culturally and legally confined to the private sphere, hemmed into the marital bedroom by law, custom and suburban architecture, and so popular music's public status is always on the ambiguous boundary between safety and scandalousness, merely for being public.

Annabella's picnic finds a weak spot of contemporary culture; using public media (music and album covers) to promote a formally illegal pleasure (underage sexuality), which at any age is the most privatized of all private-sphere activities, but simultaneously one of the most heavily policed. As Larry Gross has argued, the *right to privacy* in matters sexual is a longstanding political issue, but it can be a two-edged sword, since that right, whose legal recognition eventually enabled the decriminalization of homosexual activity to be secured, can also be used by the forces of reaction to *insist* on privacy, that is to force any sexuality other than the approved monogomous marital heterosexual variety back into the closet.[27] Back into the closet was just where Annabella Lwin's body had to go, and it remains an open question whether the politics surrounding her *déjeuner sur l'herbe* was a victory for women's (in this case a mother's) right to the privacy of their own (and their daughters') bodies against commercial exploitation by manipulative managers, or whether it was a victory for the forces of reaction against real but regulated participation in sex, music, art and public cultural politics by people under sixteen.

Entertaining the picnic girls

'Jimmy Edwards entertaining the picnic girls' is the cover picture of the British weekly *Illustrated* for 31 August 1957 (Figure 3.13).[28] It adds to

Figure 3.12 Exclusive Art (*The Face*)

TAKE THE MANET & RUN

EXCLUSIVE

You're looking at a rare surviving copy of the photograph that *would* have made the cover of Bow Wow Wow's debut album, had singer Annabella Lu Win's mother Mrs. Amie Dunn-Lewin not intervened and arranged for almost all of the transparencies to be destroyed. Mrs. Dunn-Lewin objected to the shot as, according to an aide of Malcolm McLaren, Bow Wow Wow's manager, "Annabella was without legal chaperoning from the GLC on the day of the session and her daughter was being portrayed as a sex object without her prior knowledge." Presumably they're assuming it would have been OK if only she'd been asked first. The photograph, a careful pastiche of Manet's celebrated "Le dejeuner sur L'herbe" has already appeared in the Los Angeles Times and New York's Soho News but, apart from a bit being reproduced in black and white in the Sun, this is its first exposure here. With the fifteen-year-old Annabella still legally required to have a chaperone when working with the band, McLaren continues to tread a thin line between "fun" and exploitation. He's stepped off it once—with his Bow Wow Wow-associated magazine *Chicken*, which failed to find a sufficiently courageous publisher. This time, he's been legally forced to find a new cover; the most unfortunate consequence is that the album title has been altered from "Go Wild In The Country" to "See Jungle, See Jungle, Go Join Your Gang Yeah, City All Over! Go Ape Crazy". Let's hear you get your laughing gear round that, Peter Powell!

Words STEVE TAYLOR
Photo ANDY EARL

this series of picnics at least one element not seen so far: television. Here is portable TV, sitting *as* a picnicker on one of the portable chairs, upstaging the thermos and sharing the occasion with the picnic girls right down to the mutual iteration of facial expressions; TV is one of the family, going wild in the country, as it reaches the then legal age of majority, twenty-one years old.

Can TV go wild in the country? Is this the birth of postmodernism, the moment when a social institution turns into its simulacrum? Has simulation usurped authentic experience once and for all, reducing the picnic to a bad, outdated copy of a Jimmy Edwards grimace? Of course, the telltale signs of a Baudrillardian shock of the neo are all there. The picture is self-referential, cheerfully faked, with no truth claim but high recognition value (so long as you share the codes of women's magazine covers and are active in the economy of 'telebrity' faces). It is a reduction of the picnic to one attenuated but plastic-coloured signal: portability (portable TV, thermos flask, portable seating), which in turn signifies not nature nor even country but mere mobility (with no destination, and no sense of the country traversed, which is militantly excluded from the picture), so this is not mobility as action but as consumption. It all adds up; but only if you 'read' the cover of *Illustrated* as an illustration of a real picnic. If you do do this, however, Jimmy Edwards the TV comic will have the last laugh on the 'critic as clown', for this is not a representative picture, not a picture of a picnic at all, but a mock-up belonging to no other world than that of magazine cover; it celebrates an 'event' that never occurs (TV's anniversary) but which can be 'covered', and it illustrates not action but discourse. It says, briefly: 'open me'; and its logic is this: to see (recognize), is to act (buy), is to forget (turn the page).

Putting TV into the picture does nothing more than to conflate some pleasures of popular culture – reading magazines, picnicking, watching TV – which are alike not because they're all emancipated from the real as soon as mass communication happens along, but because they are all versions of yet another activity, long neglected in cultural theory: the activity of 'people-watching' or social looking. People-watching is a pervasive, anthropological and inexpensive component of popular culture, upon which much of TV's own fascination rests for viewers. It is also one way of conducting forensic research: the Mills and Boon writer Helen Bianchin (author of twenty-three books) uses this familiar form of visual doodling in a professional way, as the inspiration for her fictional romances: 'I love people watching,' she says:

'I might be sitting in a cafe and I'll see an attractive girl who has something that makes her stand out – the way she walks or wears her clothes – and your imagination wanders. You think: "I wonder what she does for a living. I wonder if she has a boyfriend." Then I might

74

Figure 3.13 The picnic girls (*Illustrated*)

see an attractive man and my creative juices flow. I might put them together and build a life for them, a reason for meeting and some sort of conflict.'[29]

This describes more than just a familiar everyday practice indulged during indolent moments by café society. Doodling with the eyes has been professionalized, even industrialized. For the likes of Helen Bianchin it becomes a *textual method* of visual research; social looking for the purpose of publication. This *textualized* people-watching is not confined to romance or even fictional writers; it is prevalent in the popular factual media too, where it is taken to an almost metaphysical sophistication. People are scrutinized, pictorially and verbally, in obsessive detail, in a practice that is nothing short of 'popular literary criticism'; that is, textual analysis and interpretation for the general public, and furthermore the purpose of such semiotic and interpretative analysis is straightforwardly didactic; it's intended to teach 'the people' about people, the public about its personality.

Happy families and sizzling sexiness

One 'attractive girl who has something that makes her stand out' is the Princess of Wales. And 'wondering', in the manner of Helen Bianchin, what she does for a living, whether she has a boyfriend, what kind of life she has built with her attractive man, with what sort of conflict – this is the stock in trade of the popular papers. In their eyes the Princess of Wales is precisely a 'fairytale' princess; she's far from being emancipated from the real, but she marks the boundary between textual and social power – between fiction and fact, private and public life, between emotional, personal conduct and cultural, national identity. Her relationships and conflicts are used in commentators' columns as a 'calculating machine' to measure and adjust the current boundaries of socially acceptable and transferable behaviour, thereby generalizing, in the manner of algebra, the myriad particular dilemmas experienced by a myriad of readers. And the evidence used to make these calculations is almost entirely textual – published stories and pictures. The Prince and Princess of Wales are icons of the *social* body, bearers of mythologizing speculations about family life, love, sex, children . . . and picnics.

It will be remembered from the outset of this chapter that Kodak's 'Our Family Picnic', promotes 'the family' as well as the skills of movie photography. But the identity of the actual family in question is not relevant; Mom, Dad, Betsy and Butch are, like the parts of a Ford automobile, fully interchangeable with every other American domestic consumer unit. This interchangeability is evident in fictional media too: the Mom, Dad, Betsy, Butch functions are endlessly recycled, as for

Figure 3.14 Royal Family picnic (Photo: Lord Snowdon)

instance in the self-referentially ironic form of Peg (Mom), Al (Dad), Kelly and Bud Bundy in *Married . . . With Children*. The family is interchangeable in its individual parts, in art as in life. Similarly the identity of the photographer is necessarily anonymous (interchangeable), given the enunciative status of a Kodak instruction manual ('anyone can do this'). But at the same time the Kodak family is unique, as is each photo of every picnic, and it is this very uniqueness which its members are encouraged to record on amateur movie film; uniqueness being the 'commodity' that is sold to the mass consumer. Simultaneous sameness and difference is logically impossible, but it is very common, being the essence of 'Fordism', that is, the founding principle of the capitalist consumer market.

While Kodak's family, picnic, and movie, are all presumably of interest only to the family whose picnic it is, the picnic of Charlie and Di, Wills and Harry, pictured by Uncle Tony, is quite the reverse. As a *picnic* it is of no significance to its participants, being hardly more appetizing in food content than was King M'tesa's. Even as a picture it is not especially memorable, but nonetheless it was published all over the world and subjected to intense critical attention at the time. Clearly, even though they are married . . . with children, the Wales family cannot be substituted for the Bundys (except satirically); but this unique (different) royal family is in fact made interchangeable (same) with other families, and the way it is done shows how the representative popular media teach their readers what it means to be members of the (textualized) public family.

Lord Snowdon's portrait was released on 17 October 1991 as part of a set to coincide with a tour of Canada by the Prince and Princess of Wales, a tour dubbed 'happy families' in Buckingham Palace publicity, because the two children, Prince William and Prince Harry, were to accompany their parents. Like so many other picnics, this one didn't occur. And although nothing had 'happened', almost every British morning newspaper ran the picture that day, though the stories they made up to accompany it varied considerably. It appeared on news pages, fashion pages, as a colour spread in the middle pages, and as a pin-up – the *Sun* printed it on page three, in place of the topless model, with:

TALLY HO, TOFF THEY GO
Canada Di dresses up to meet the Mounties
In her 'Canada Di' look the 30-year old Princess is pictured wearing a £110 Foxley checked hacking jacket with leather-covered buttons over a £120 pure silk designer shirt.[30]

The *Daily Mail* used the photo in its *Femail* pages as a fashion feature: 'It looks like a glossy advert for American fashion designer Ralph Lauren. . . . Indeed, it is an advertisement of sorts – but for a very royal kind of firm.' Commenting that 'it would be difficult to find anything less like a relaxed happy family snap than this one' (a comment that is repeated as the picture's caption), the *Daily Mail* settles for the commercial fashion angle, laced with sex:

> The star of the shot is Princess Diana who is well aware that riding clothes allow one to combine eminent respectability with sizzling sexiness.
>
> Her tight, grey corduroy Eurostar jodhpurs show off her fabulous legs better than any swimsuit, while the button down man's shirt, tweed fashion hacking jacket and tight black leather riding boots, hand-made at Lobb's, add just the right hint of glamorous authority.
>
> There is no doubt that the whip hand in this picture is Diana's. Not for nothing has she graced the cover of Vogue; this is a highly styled fashion shot.[31]

So much so, in fact, that the *Daily Mail* reckons that 'It is difficult to decide which looks the more uncomfortable – Charles, Wills, or the garden seat.

On balance, it is probably Charles, . . . whose traumatised gaze gives a whole new meaning to the term fashion victim.' The feature continues with a detailed reading of the expressions and clothes of the people – and the pony. It analyses the picnic hamper, the crockery, the food, and the photography; Snowdon's portrait ('suitably regal') is contrasted with others by Jayne Fincher ('easy informality') and Patrick Demarchelier ('smouldering sensuality'). It decides that Snowdon's picture is, after all, 'unwittingly . . . commercial'.

Today claims that this is 'the most extraordinary royal portrait ever seen', and gives its readers a lesson in the history of art. It prints the picture alongside a colour reproduction of a 1748 portrait by Gainsborough (of Mr. and Mrs. Andrews in the park of their house), using 'Christie's fine art expert Mark McDonnell' to validate its reading of the 'princely picnic' as 'Gainsboroughesque' (both groups are 'in the shade of sturdy English oaks,' both are 'in the grounds of their own homes', and both are 'centred on green iron benches' with 'the wife sitting on a bench and the husband standing behind her'). While the Gainsborough portrait was 'one of the first paintings to show land as a possession', this is one of the first royal portraits where all the clothes, props and stylistic influences can be labelled and priced, for possession not by the sitters but by the readers. *Today* makes the connection between art and designer-labels a matter of artistic expertise: 'In addition to the Gainsborough connection, Christie's experts also see similarities with the style of the American fashion house Ralph Lauren or the British fashion house Mulberry.'

Today agrees with the *Daily Mail* that the Princess's jodhpurs are 'skin-tight', but it identifies them as the 'Harry Hall "Montana" collection' (not Eurostar), and it reads them not in terms of Diana's 'sizzling sexiness' but of their wearer's known tastes: 'Diana was even prepared to don riding gear – a sport she reportedly loathes'; while for Prince William, conversely, it was 'a welcome change for him to dress in riding gear once again', after having been 'barred from riding – his favourite pastime – since he was hit on the head with a golf club last June'. Unlike the *Mail*, *Today* emphasizes not the ('traumatised') facial expressions of the sitters but the fact that 'the relaxed family shown in Snowdon's photograph are all touching'; Charles' hands rest on a shoulder apiece, and Harry holds the horse: 'As the last link in the chain, the youngest prince holds the reins in a clever compositional device which links all the figures in the picture together.'[32] Actually the last link in the chain is Diana's jodhpurs; a 'clever compositional device' indeed, which draws attention to those 'fabulous legs' even as they unite the 'happy family' by touching Prince William.

For the *Daily Star*, what links everything in the picture together is price; it prints an outline diagram of the items shown, each with a price tag, under a headline that is superimposed over the picture itself:

NICE PICNIC
(Shame about the Price . . .)

In this respect the *Star* is at one with the *Sun*, which also gives some prices, although the prices themselves do not agree. Depending which paper you read, Diana's jacket is £110 or £430, her shirt is £120 or £50, the wicker hamper £1,600 or £165, Charles's jacket is £345 or £750, and so on. But the *Star* goes one better in the end; it even tallies up the cost of Snowdon's services – he can 'charge up to £10,000 a day' – and, although 'Buckingham Palace says Lord Snowdon is donating his cut to charities', the 'going rate for publication' of the royal picnic pictures is given as '£250 for colour prints and £175 for black and white'.[33]

The *Daily Mirror* is less concerned about cost than class, and it can tell fun from a fake too. It uses class difference to distinguish the *false* royal picnic from *authentic* ones, comparing the 'worst children's treat any mum and dad ever dreamed up', with what 'the rest of us' might take on a family picnic, including 'soggy Marmite sandwiches', 'cold sausages, salt 'n' vinegar crisps and Hula-Hoops', 'sticky sweets, chocolate biscuits or melting ice-cream', washed down with an 'exploding can of Coca-Cola'. The *Mirror* comments: 'You wouldn't believe what fun they're having. In fact you've never seen a picnic like it. . . . But then, as anyone could tell, this wasn't a real picnic.'[34]

Perhaps it isn't a real family either – the popular media are quite prepared to use pictorial evidence to think this problem through too. Later that same day, the *Evening Standard* ran another picture from the set showing the two princes alone, and concentrated on the official 'happy families' theme promoted by the Palace, quoting 'Royal expert Mr Harold Brooks-Baker, publisher of Burke's Peerage' as saying: 'Being surrounded by a cosy, loving family atmosphere is clearly having a healthy influence. The way they are being brought up is clearly turning them into well-adjusted young men.'[35] This is just as well, for the Royal Family isn't *necessarily* a Happy Family. On the very next page, following its reproduction of the princely picnic, *Today* reported that Margaret Thatcher's daughter Carol, employed as the London correspondent of a US TV show called *Now It Can Be Told* (hosted by 'confrontainment' legend Geraldo Rivera), had 'accused the Queen of shunning Katherine Bowes Lyon', her mentally ill cousin:

> Millions of US viewers yesterday saw the 64-year-old, who has a mental age of six, staring blankly at the camera with her tongue hanging out at the NHS [National Health Service] Royal Earlswood Hospital, Surrey.
>
> Presenter Geraldo Rivera said the secretly-filmed footage showed that the Royal Family had done nothing to ease her plight since it was first revealed in 1987.

Against a backdrop of the Houses of Parliament, the former Premier's daughter replied: 'You are absolutely right Geraldo.'[36]

Today is published by the same international media corporation that puts out the *Sunday Times* in Perth, not to mention *Married . . . With Children* in the US.[37] Its concern for the Happiness of the Royal Family is global, but not in the least convinced by the Wales's 'happy families' visit to Canada. On the occasion of the Queen's later visit to Australia, (23 February 1992), the *Sunday Times* in Western Australia ran an article on how Diana is out with the kids more often than Charles is, and that therefore she 'has slowly turned . . . into almost a royal one-parent family, where dad hardly plays a part'. Armed with this, 'Psychiatrist Dr Robert Howard of the London Institute of Psychiatry' is then able to deliver himself of the opinion that 'Wills and Harry' may 'develop feminine traits – like crying over the slightest thing for attention', or they may become 'very naughty or aggressive in a bid for stronger discipline'; they 'run the risk of becoming "mummy's boys"', or of having 'difficulties in their relationships with women when they grow up'.[38] And all this unspeakable drivel is based on the premise that 'the royals are no different from the rest of us when it comes to the effects of life without dad'.

But 'dad' is in fact never far away, even from 'the rest of us'. *The Independent on Sunday* (20 October 1991)[39] ran an editorial under the picnic photograph, in which Diana hardly figured (and the only jodhpurs mentioned were those of Prince William). The *Independent* was more interested in the Prince of Wales. Here is a man given to making speeches about how 'the way forward for humankind lies in spiritual resources rather than "lifestyle" and possessions' (and other 'mystic mumbo jumbo' based on the ideas of his 'hero' Carl Jung). The *Independent* comments: 'What . . . the rest of us must wonder is: can the figure in the picture . . . be the same man? And, if so, can . . . we believe what he says?':

> For here is not a portrait of a soulful prince, or a prince with a conscience, or a 'loony' prince, or even a princely prince. A slight knowledge of social or art history suggests that this is HRH the Prince of Wales as Victorian coal-owner. . . . A slight knowledge of *Country Life*, or *Vogue*, or *Tatler*, suggests something else: that the prince and princess may have taken out shares in a wicker-work factory; or that they are assisting the profits of Aquascutum, Harrods or Fortnum and Mason; that, above all, they are taken up – forget Jung, forget the saintly van der Post – with the lifestyle of the newly-enriched Britons of the Eighties; that their happiness depends upon possessions.

And so the 'happy families' portrait is hoist with its own petard, used as evidence for an analysis of what in fact constitutes happiness. *The*

Independent on Sunday proposes that the picture might be entitled *A Portrait of National Humbug*, and suggests the possibility that:

> Lord Snowdon has caught some aspect of the truth. That although the prince wrings his hands about a divided Britain, he continues to own 128,000 acres of it. That although he has said 'I am not in favour of an élite if it is solely based on birth and wealth', he shows no sign of relinquishing his own membership.

Is this the face of the last of the yuppies, more interested in being identified with (and *as*) the display of designer-labelled possessions, than in the credibility of putting one's money where one's mouth is? Is it the face of a regal Al Bundy, head full of unfulfilled dreams, house full of feuding family, dominated by an acquisitive and overbearing wife? Is it a portrait of well-adjusted children, or of a functionally one-parent family, of happiness or humbug? Is it art or commerce, fashion or pin-up? Are the royals unique, or interchangeable with 'the rest of us'?

Let the last word go to those who know. The November issue of (English) *Vogue*, published a few days later, included the whole Snowdon set as a feature called A PRINCESS AND HER PRINCES. As is only proper for a magazine devoted to fashion, *Vogue* 'reads' the pictures as photography not news, giving them maximum space and minimum commentary. It merely announces, with the pomposity of a family retainer, that: 'To celebrate their tenth wedding anniversary, The Prince and Princess of Wales were photographed by Snowdon at Highgrove with their sons Prince William and Prince Harry'.[40] This caption is printed over the picnic photograph, quietly organizing the reader's gaze in the direction of the Princess (and 'her' Princes), and even more quietly forgetting the Canadian visit and the 'happy family' theme altogether (in favour of a wedding anniversary mentioned nowhere else). The following month's *Vogue* had even got rid of the Princes; its cover shows the Princess of Wales as patron of various dance organizations, photographed by Patrick Demarchelier (of 'smouldering sensuality' fame) to promote a 20-page feature called 'Come Dancing'.[41] This is no more than another win for the sexualization of the body politic – sizzling sexiness *as* happy families, both domestic and national – a tendency of the modern popular media which will be taken up further later on (Chapter 8).

Clearly, each publication finds in the royal picnic exactly those meanings which are proper to that publication, from couture of the very *hautest* for *Vogue*, to critique of the cor blimiest from the *Star*. Equally clearly, the 'creative juices' of the press have indeed flowed freely, though by no means implausibly, in this one instance of textualized people-watching, which amounts to an informal *sociology of discourse*, meditating in public upon the same categories of civic life which have recurred throughout this chapter: race, empire, nation, family, heroes, gender, age-group, sexuality, science, art, fashion. The *form* in which this intellectual work is undertaken is *pastoral*, both literally, in the case of the picnic, and also in Eagleton's sense (see the beginning of this chapter), where 'the pastoral' is the cultural form which involves putting 'the complex into the simple'; and where simple characters are made to voice 'highly-wrought rhetorical discourse' (as in Trevelyan's account of the family snapshot), or sophisticated figures to 'articulate simple feelings' (as in the picnic of the Prince and Princess of Wales).

This chapter has not been a history of photography, if by that is meant a chronology of inventions and technologies, or of a cultural form. It is, however, concerned with the *history of semiosis* (changes in meaning over time, which can be investigated via a single sign like 'the picnic'), as well as with the *geo-demographics of meaning* (where and by what segments of a population meanings are deployed and changed). Looked at in this way, a history of a cultural technology like photography can turn out to be a forensic analysis of white discourses on race and the family, via the 'simple' form of the picnic. But in order to recognize the sociological, semiotic, and geo-demographic importance of those discourses, and therefore the ambiguous politics of picnics, it is necessary to cross from formal intellectual classifications of knowledge into the realm of popular reality, where they've been thinking these matters through for a couple of hundred years, and where the public is invented, visualized, and taught about itself in front of its very own eyes. There's a name for this activity too, and it is the subject of the next chapter: I call it power viewing.

4

POWER VIEWING

A glance at pervasion in the postmodern perplex

What follows is an attempt to take TV audiences seriously as fictional constructs, their fictionality not being taken as a disqualification from but as a demonstration of the social power (even truth) of fictions. The energy with which audiences are pursued in academic and industry research bespeaks something much larger and more powerful than the quest for mere data. The TV audience is pervasive but perplexingly elusive: the quest for knowledge about it is the search for something *special*; literally, knowledge of the *species*. The chapter is in two parts: a theorization of power viewing, and an appropriately 'empirical' study of the socio-semiotics of looking: 'Show Piece'.

Textual and social power

The question of the power of the visual media is traditionally posed as their power over the populace and the power of economic or political elites over them. The question of media power is thus a social question. But the media are encountered by those over whom they are supposed to hold sway, the audience, only in textual form. So to study television is to study the relationship, if any, between social and textual power. If the media exert power and influence over their audiences, i.e. socially, how is it done textually? And if media texts exert power, what is the place of meaning in the analysis of power?

If politics, the economy and society are systematically meaningful, how can meaning be investigated? Television at the moment represents one of the most fully developed and globally pervasive phenomena for the production and distribution of meaning. To investigate it culturally is to ask how *humanity* makes sense, not as primitive or prehistoric species, but here, now. As I have argued elsewhere, TV is the 'power of speech' as transformed and developed in relation to material forces and social power.[1]

From this cultural perspective, which is close to the anthropology of meaning of Marshall Sahlins,[2] the TV audience can be theorized quite simply, not by reducing it to a false unity, but precisely because it is *not* a specific group. It represents a way of conceptualizing not a group in society but what *constitutes* society as a whole in its specifically sense-making mode.

Social totality

Watching TV is not merely useful (economic), it is meaningful (cultural); those for whom TV has meaning are the audience. But from a cultural perspective audiences are not 'individual viewers'. Individual people are not merely individuals, opposed to or distinct from society, they are the totality of society; as Marx put it, the 'ideal totality – the subjective existence of thought and experienced society present for itself'.[3] What this helpful insight means in practice, however, is that the notion of the 'individual' is far too complex to deal with as an analytical unity ('writing' individuals as social totality has long been the province of fiction and drama, not least on television, but is not common in academic analysis). Hence I am reluctant to equate 'audiences' with 'individuals', for individuals are not always audiences, while the point of Marx's statement is that though individuals are particular they are totally social at the same time. Instead of trying to decide between them, cultural analysis might do better to show how the individual and the social are in fact connected. My argument is that the connection between the individual and the social is textual, and one way of investigating it is to look at a specific instance; television can be studied as a meaningful system (rather than in terms of its power effects alone), whereby social meaning is circulated among particular individuals by textual means.

The textual and discursive forms of television are by no means unique to it, and they're not confined to the screen, so by text I mean more than a programme or even 'supertext'.[4] Television's textuality includes the industrial, regulatory and critical discourses that literally channel what's on the screen, without ever appearing on it, and of course it includes the dialogic participation of its viewers, both during and beyond viewing time. However, I do think such texts and discourses, representations and meanings, are real; they can even be observed in their 'exosomatic' or empirical form, where they display the properties of what Karl Popper calls 'objective knowledge'.[5] I take audiences to be textual too (rather than somatic – though of course bodies are both textualized and legible). It is not just a matter of finding fictive representations of audiences in other texts (addressed to them or about them), but also I think the practice of 'being' an audience cannot be understood except textually. Certainly the act of making meaning cannot be observed directly. Our 'behaviour' as audience is an act in the performative sense, the role we play is rehearsed and our lines have been scripted, and the scene we're in is a dialogue with the social totality. As a matter of fact I have always been impressed by how difficult it is to think, experience or know anything, as an individual, without discovering it has already been done. Buckminster Fuller once wrote a quirky little book called *I Seem to be a Verb*; well, my auto-biography should be entitled *I Seem to be a Quote*. But then '(since, as Emerson wrote – "By necessity, by proclivity – and by delight, we all quote"),' so should everyone's.[6]

Pervasive power

The fundamental attribute of TV viewing is pervasion. It is global, insistent, and quite indifferent to any demographic boundary you can name. Give people a chance and they'll buy TV sets, give them time and they'll watch TV. Not even totalitarian governments can stop the will to watch; it belongs to the species. At the same time, no one *just* watches television, as far as I know. Just as television is pervasive, so it is pervaded. Its meanings circulate in a context of talk, other media, and the myriad semiotic systems from clothing and housing to industrialized production itself. To understand television's textuality some notice needs to be taken of such concomitant goings-on; it's very hard to see how 'family television' makes sense (to itself or to an observer) without an account of the meaning and history of housing, the domestic ideology that turns houses into homes, and a productive industry that depends on the consumption of symbols in the form of commodities. Television makes sense in such a context, and I think, given time, that the 'totality' of the society which is 'present for itself' in a family watching television could be described. But it would be a big project, and who'd do it justice except a playwright or novelist?

Textual and social power, connected in the form of meaning, can be justified as a proper object for television studies, novelists notwith-standing. Power is not merely sovereignty or the power to command; after Foucault, it has been rethought as occurring in all the myriad transactions and networks of everyday life.[7] Although television is radically different from the classic Foucauldian disciplinary institutions in that watching it is strictly voluntary, it's certainly not exempt from its own internal power relations, which are much better understood through a Foucauldian notion of power than by means of earlier versions – no one has the 'right' to watch, produce or appear on television, so a notion of power as sovereignty (which generates rights), for example, doesn't apply. Never-theless, television's institutional power relations are constantly worked out among its participants on both sides of the screen.

Within the repertoire of viewing practices, the power of the viewer escapes that of the institution, its controllers, regulators and textual regimes; the disciplinary apparatus not only circulates to the viewer from the screen but also in the reverse direction. Watching television is exercising the power to turn one's own disciplinary gaze or glance on and through the screen, using the act of looking to keep an eye on the social and discursive organization of the world at large, and to make judgements and take actions which are themselves exercises of power, often enough of a directly political kind, over which the forces of disciplinary domestication have much less control than they or their critics would like to think. Television does exercise social power, but half of the equation has historically been ignored; the social power of surveillance exercised by audiences in the meaningful use of television as a cultural resource of their own.

Postmodern power

Although it would be a simplification to argue this too strongly, it is nonetheless tempting to suggest that while Foucauldian notions are being applied to the terrain previously occupied by questions of television's social power, questions of textual power have been abandoned to the postmodernists. Taking their cue from such writers as Derrida, Baudrillard and Lyotard, the postmodernists rode into town looking not for power but for difference. They found it in the act of reading. It seems that TV texts are at their viewers' command and mean whatever they decide. However, those who read television texts in the name of postmodernist techniques tend to be less interested in the social and textual power of television than in performing feats of postmodern criticism – a form of textual display that celebrates fragmentation, difference, the dissociation of sign from reference, text from readership. Far from producing exemplary readings on behalf of less astute audiences (the traditional literary method which has its roots in biblical exegesis), postmodernist readings begin from the position that texts are not in the first place acts of communication; they don't have addresses written on them, or even if they do they may never reach their destination.[8] However, television and other media texts are still readable, even if they don't have an interlocutor, for what they reveal to postmodernism is something like this, and I quote:

> Once upon a time our world was enslaved by teleological meta-narratives like History which told our story for us in terms of an ending which never occurs but is endlessly deferred, while in the meantime we spend our intellectual energies trying to prove that the story is true and the world is real, authentic, beyond discourse and in a state of existence that is not only separate from our knowledge of it but capable of being known directly. But now, instead of using such totalizing fictions to prove how authentic our picture of reality is, we have taken the path of the computer animation artist, whose

claim to fame is that the object revolving in front of our eyes is *completely simulated*, despite the fact that

(a) it looks more real than the object it simulates . . . and
(b) it is now doing things that cannot really be done . . . and
(c) the things that cannot be done are in fact being done in front of our very eyes, so they're real . . .

Which means that the simulation is the real, that there's nothing outside the text, and that the authentic icon of postmodern art is the fake. Where this leaves television is uncertain, for television promotes itself on its realism while cashing in on computer animation; it rhetoricizes the world even while telling the truth, and its audiences are drawn to, held by and glory in its trashiest fakery while simultaneously asserting an earnest commitment to realistic portrayals of real life, including those performed by glove puppets purporting to be alien life forms posing as cute emotive child-pets.

Unquote. This quotation is of course a fake. The postmodernist perplex is not fazed by any of this.

People power?

Recent intellectual currents have proved exciting but somewhat frustrating for television studies. In spite of Foucauldian, postmodernist, feminist and other interventions, or perhaps because of them, it seems as hard as ever to explain the link between textual and social power. There are contending and incommensurable theoretical approaches, and there are real difficulties in isolating a coherent object of study; the act of watching television is itself a widely dispersed and variable cultural practice, undertaken by a community (the audience) which is never encountered as such, while on screen television is what I've called a 'blivit'; i.e. a 'dirty' textual form in which fact, fiction, faking and fabrication are all mixed up like 'two pounds of shit in a one-pound bag', in Kurt Vonnegut's phrase.[9]

Is it possible to supersede the variety, difference, 'blivitousness' and elusive complexity of both TV texts and viewers, not to mention theories, encompassing the whole lot into a general framework which can say *how it works* without having to bother too much about *what it is*? Or is it proper to abandon general frameworks as fictional and imperializing totalizations, and to content ourselves with local analysis, done in the flux of the 'ceaseless reformulation of symbolic relations within the national social life',[10] which not only form our object of study, but our subjectivity too, and also constitute the raw materials for the creative personnel who make symbols saleable in the industries we analyse? I think cultural studies, at least my own, retains a commitment to both of these positions, the global and the local, illogical though that may be. For one thing, a recognition of the textual productivity of contemporary culture requires both engagement and analysis, while scepticism about general frameworks does not mean they are not ceaselessly produced and deployed, comprising a major component of textual and social power, and a major component of academic research too.

Meanwhile, the focus of critical attention in cultural studies has switched from ideology and its effects towards audiences or readerships, since it is at this point that meanings generated in and by media discourses actually spark into life socially, where textual and social power intersect, and where the distinction between them is meaningless. Ethnographies of reading ask 'what (in fact) *do* audiences do with the media?' Meanwhile critical readings, mindful that the polysemic qualities of texts open them up to any reading that may plausibly be brought to bear upon them, ask 'what (in principle) *can* readerships do with the media? The proof is looked for in the eating, not in the pudding.

But the conceptual gap between social and textual power is if anything widening in these moves, because instead of seeking to analyse its intersections these approaches reproduce the gap. Ethnographies of reading must presuppose that they'll reveal something in the 'other' that can be observed – the act of reading, the real or 'natural' audience. So ethnographic research runs counter to textual theory, which holds that nothing outside meaning exists for humans, that discourses organize practices, and that when you ask people what they think of texts, or how they read, even when you go into their very living rooms to do it, you don't end up with the real, but with more text, requiring just the same sort of critical reading as is given to television texts themselves. The direct reflections of participants in a process are *reflections*, already mediated, theorized, fictionalized, and selecting them for analysis is a further act of textual creativity, as any television documentarist will tell you. The return to audience studies might look like a welcome return to common sense after some rather bizarre theoretical excursions, but if it is then it has already forgotten that common sense is an effect of texts, not a cause.

Decolonizing ethnography

The *Oxford English Dictionary* derives 'ethnic' from the Greek *ethnos*, 'nation', making clear that its arrival in English was associated with biblical translations of the Hebrew *goyim*, 'the nations', i.e. Gentiles. In fact early lexicographers thought 'ethnic' to be the same as 'hethnic' – heathen. In other words, 'ethnic' referred to non-Christian or non-Judaic nations; it meant heathen, pagan, *goyim* (first citation 1470). What then is 'ethnography'? 'The scientific description of nations or races of men, with their customs, habits, and points of difference' (1834).

In the 150 years since then, ethnography in its home discipline of anthropology has changed, of course, not least in its sensitivity to the politics of the 'other', of the relationship between researcher and subject, researcher and knowledge, researcher and his or her own self – including *its* other; the 'heathen or infidel' *within the self*. How ethnography came to be applied to TV audiences is of course a matter of institutional history not etymology. But what worries me about the current upsurge in the use of 'ethnography' to describe how viewers may be brought into the purview of cultural studies is that history may be repeating itself as farce; a careless reinstatement of the old distinction between believer and heathen, between the imperial colonizer and other nations, but now in the ludicrous form of a distinction between TV researchers and TV viewers, as if they are not one and the same.[11]

Ethnography must be founded on *distance from self*; the object of study must be 'other' in order to be written. But ethnographies of audiences ought not to be *orientalisms*, in Edward Said's sense,[12] 'Heathen-ography' if you like, descriptions of the other, imagined by the research project which nevertheless pretends exemption from its own otherness. The otherness of the television audience has historically taken many forms, not only of ratings but also of deviant, dissident, disadvantaged and politically disabled groups (children, women, working-class men, adolescents, racial minorities). Social and psychological scientists tend to look for 'others' who are in need of correction or protection – watching TV causes violence and passive behaviour (all at once!) – while oppositional intellectuals look for political resistance in 'others' who will vindicate the intellectual stance of opposition.

Such tendencies indicate to me that there's a need to 'decolonize the audience'. But this means decolonizing *our* 'other', it does not mean looking for new ways to capture a purer, less partial conception of the audience, for example by doing more sophisticated research into what the 'natural' audience really does. For the 'natural' audience of academic researchers comprises academic readers. Research is conducted along lines, and in pursuit of questions, that are agreeable to colleagues, editors, conference organizers, students. It is not disciplined by television audiences; what they think about it is normally neither here nor there.

The glance: there's the rub

Given that we are what we study, I'd like to find a different metaphor for power, one that is appropriate to television, while recognizing the public's capacity and willingness to don the garb of an audience and our ability to wear it for our own purposes in our own style. If acting as audience means playing a role, then the fashion industry can supply a description of the costumes people are wearing for the part. Marshall Sahlins, in his analysis of American clothing, 'La Pensée bourgeoise: western society as culture', concludes with an insight into the function of the clothing system which is suggestive to my own project; the power of looking:

'Mere appearance' must be one of the most important forms of symbolic statement in Western civilization. For it is by appearances that civilization turns the basic contradiction of its construction into a miracle of existence: a cohesive society of perfect strangers. But in the event, its cohesion depends on a *coherence* of specific kind; on the possibility of apprehending others, their social condition, and thereby their relation to oneself 'on first glance.'[13]

Sahlins claims that this kind of looking has logical precedence over rationality, and indeed forms the base on which reason's superstructure is constructed:

This dependence on the glance suggests the presence in the economic and social life of a logic completely foreign to the conventional 'rationality.' For rationality is time elapsed, a comparison: at least another glance beyond, and a weighing of the alternatives.[14]

At this point I'll direct only the most fleeting glance towards my own suggestion that the pleasure of television is akin to *frottage*: 'a glimpse, a frisson of excitement provoked by taking private pleasure from public contact',[15] the pleasure of watching television to keep 'in touch' by means of 'the brush, not with skin . . . but with clothing, surfaces, textures, furtive appropriations of the *look of otherness*'. . . . 'Prime time presents Americans with the clothed body of America.'[16]

Textual and social dressing

Be that as it may, I am interested in pursuing the idea that 'mere appearance' and 'the glance' may be neglected or undervalued concepts in cultural studies and also in the idea that fashion can help to identify some larger issues. In fact, I'm searching for a metaphor which will unite two kinds of power – textual power and social power – in the name of a 'comprehensive theory of the audience'.[17] But rather than searching through time-elapsed, weighty textual and social theory for my rationale, I turn to something immediately to hand as I write: a fashion feature in the weekend magazine of *The Australian* newspaper:

Each decade within reasonable memory has had a distinguishing fashion feature: 1920s, the Little Black Dress; 1930s, the Bias Cut; 1940s, the New Look; 1950s, the A-Line; 1960s, the Mini; 1970s, the Big Look; 1980s, Power Dressing.[18]

It is tempting to match these changes in the history of looks with a history of looking. The 1930s of the 'bias cut' was certainly also an era of biased looking, what with totalitarian propaganda, the Frankfurt school and the Leavises' journal *Scrutiny*, and I suppose the New Look/New Deal, A-line/A-bomb decades show some connection between high fashion and high politics. The New Look 1940s also marked the cultural (if not technical) début of new-look TV, and the A-line 1950s was the period when TV viewing was cut most simply; half the nation plugged into one show, ideology and domesticity harmoniously balanced while the eye was drawn uninterruptedly from hemline to head, or from suburbia to centrality, from *I Love Lucy* to 'I like Ike'. The 1960s, decade of the mini, was also the decade of the little screen's displacement of the big screen, when television, like miniskirts, used less but showed more, abandoned the high-definition artistic pretensions of cinema and flaunted the greater social (but not sexual) equality of its apparent freedom. The 1970s and 1980s coincide with questions of social and textual power very neatly. The era of the 'big look' and 'power dressing' in fashion; here's a useful metaphor for the politics of looking in the popular media. The big look and Althusserian Grand Theory of the 1970s gave way in the 1980s to a new phase in the history of looking and a new type of audience participation in the forum of media citizenship. The couch potato was wearing shoulder-pads and going in for the ocular equivalent of power dressing; suddenly, around the world, the new look was *power viewing*.

The *Weekend Australian*'s laudable acknowledgement of historical change leads it to predict that the 1990s will be 'an era of fashion driven by consumers, not designers'. If so, the prediction for 1990s television is that the fashion in looking will be for audiences to 'drive' programming. But the lines have softened and the look is fragmented; power viewing continues, but the shoulder-pads are giving way to their bodily simulacrum – power bodies decked in sportive fashion, fashion decked in the prowess of sport.

Sovereign power

Power dressing is in principle available to everyone, but as in fashion, so in looking; not everyone is dressed to kill. So who is wearing the new garb of power viewing; who is willing to be seen in public flaunting a style of looking that to other eyes appears ludicrous, even dangerous? Fashion-conscious people will often reserve their most powerful statements for clubs, which in turn are apt to restrict entrance to those who dress appropriately. Such places are public but private, open but restricted, village communities flickering to life here and there, part of but distinguished from the social terrain they both camp within and illuminate. Similarly, power viewers will not be distributed evenly throughout a given population; they often gather into clubs too, where they can flaunt their excessive obsessions in public but in safety. These clubs have a name. They're called universities.

Robert Park, writing in 1916, compares modern politics to primitive society; 'we' groups of insiders known to one another, scattered across an urban landscape, for whom the rest of the city, the outsiders, are not quite human, not quite alive. The relations between insiders is personal and feudal, based on fealty; the relations between outsiders is mediated and modern, based on publicity. In the latter groups and in the city 'fashion tends to take the place of custom, and public opinion . . . becomes the dominant force in social control'. Hence, for Park, 'the medium of the press, the pulpit, and other sources of popular enlightenment' are the disseminators of public opinion, which itself is a creation of agencies of publicity, not of the public *per se*, since 'members of the public are not as a rule personally acquainted'.[19]

So power viewing coexists with other kinds of looking, as insiders coexist with others, while all are connected via the communicative apparatus of fashion and the media. There are no doubt citizens who watch television in more traditional ways, uncritically and sympathetically, in cardigans and carpet slippers, and there are those who watch critically but unsympathetically – dressed like Margaret Thatcher and keeping a beady eye on television in order to find fault, finger poised for wagging. There are cross-cultural differences between cultures of ethnicity, nation, class, gender, age group and so on, and doubtless the way people look is differentiated along such lines too – though looking also transgresses those cultural divides. No doubt looking is not only characterized by historical change, but is also synchronically very complicated, displaying many modes at once. One piece of evidence for this is that in Mandarin the very word for television is – almost – 'power viewing': that is, *dianshi* or 'electric looking'. And there is evidence that power viewing is not confined to academics, but is already being reworked into a new generation's cultural politics:

> Some young people even self-consciously consider themselves as beyond postmodernism. Thus, one young local media activist from Amsterdam who calls himself an 'illegal intellectual' says, shrugging his shoulders, 'Postmodernism is for older people, for people who are still struggling with their pasts. We don't have that problem. We are sovereign.'[20]

A glance at the gaze

However, before age or utopianism overtake me, I want to backtrack and show how the connections between Park's personal and mediated, feudal and modern communities might be thought, not only in terms of fashion and publicity, but in terms of power viewing. For insiders like legal and illegal intellectuals, sovereignty is achieved within their own communities, and their textual productivity may be mediated more widely by the 'sources of public enlightenment'. These sources, television most of all, are taken to be forces of social control, especially by those who claim sovereign exemption from their sway. But what is the situation for the general audience, the public which is 'not personally acquainted'? How is Sahlins's 'miracle' of a 'cohesive society of perfect strangers' achieved?

I think one answer to that is hinted at in Sahlins's own observation of the power of 'mere appearance', the power of the look, of the glance, of the 'first glance', which is *constitutive* of social cohesion, of social totality in a particular individual. Such looking, glancing at appearances, is commonly taken to be an attribute of television viewing; the unengaged glance, the distracted look, the uncritical apprehension of an unordered surface. John Ellis, for instance, makes much of a distinction between television and cinema which he locates in the difference between glancing and gazing (where gazing is intense looking).[21] I don't think such a distinction is valid to separate TV from cinema. Indeed I think Ellis's position is just one more example of the pervasive binarism of western intellectual thought which constantly reinvents a Veblenesque[22] distinction between the *honorific* and the *serviceable* – between prestigious cinema and humble television. But I do think glancing and gazing are different modes of looking – both of which can be applied to television.

Where gazing may be favoured as honorific by critics schooled in rationality (the second glance), glancing – the apprehension of social totality through appearance – seems to me to be the serviceable version of power viewing. But, like Veblen and Sahlins, I'm impressed by social productivity as well as individual skill, and the power of the glance is not that of individual skill but of anthropological pervasion. Its analogy in natural attributes is the 'power of speech'; its analogy in the historical world of material production is fashion. Furthermore, even in western political mythology, glancing is the very foundation stone of politics.

'Loytering and prating'

Aristotle is definite about the fundamental importance of the agora to politics and to the state. As noted in Chaper 2, he concludes that the optimum size of a state is limited by technologies of looking: 'Clearly, then, the best limit of the population of a state is the largest number which suffices for the purposes of life, and *can be taken in at a single view*.'[23] The Aristotelian 'single view', where citizens can judge each others' merits 'at a [Sahlinsesque] glance', is an apt description of contemporary politics on television. However, given that television is literally a technology for *distant* looking (it's what the word means), it is clear that such mediated appearances are not the same as a jostling crowd in the agora. But before we dismiss the idea that a marketplace like television cannot be used for politics, and philosophy too, it is worth noting where our (i.e. western) philosophy, as well as our political terminology, came from.

According to the political philosopher Thomas Hobbes, writing in 1651, the original occasion for philosophy was leisure: '*Leasure* is the mother of *Philosophy*.'[24] Philosophy flourished as a form of conspicuous consumption, a leisure entertainment for the underemployed youth of a city that had become wealthy by conquest and dominion. 'They that had no employment, neither at home, nor abroad, had little else to employ themselves in, but either . . . *in telling and hearing news*, or in discoursing of *Philosophy* publiquely to the youth of the City.'[25] Says Hobbes: 'From this it was, that the place where any of them taught, and disputed, was called *Schola*, which in their Tongue signifieth *Leasure*; and their Disputations, *Diatribæ*, that is to say, *Passing of the time*.'[26]

It is worth noting in passing that the *OED* gives as its first historical instance of the word 'agora' in English this highly pejorative view from the year 1800: '*The agora or forum was the resort of all the idle and profligate in Athens.*' It seems the agora–forum was not Anglicized as a respectable concept (it's remembered as Aristophanian not Aristotelian). Small wonder, since the root causes of western philosophy turn out to be leisure, underemployment, and what Hobbes calls *loytering and prating*,[27] not to mention attending to the news. Furthermore, philosophy was from the beginning pedagogic, dedicated to 'passing of the time' in the pursuit of teaching through discourse.

I mention all this not only because I think television deserves a better reputation, and what better than a classical pedigree, but also because I'm aware that my emphasis on power *viewing* has ignored television's propensity for *talk*; the model supplied by Hobbes and Aristotle suggests that power viewing is not just personal display but also dialogic, and that talking, teaching and watching are the attributes of today's 'idle and profligate' medium of television. If we give it a second glance, may we see in television the beginnings of some new philosophy, some new politics; the miracle of social cohesion in the era of an urban public whose members are 'not personally acquainted' but span the world?

Under my thumb

Meanwhile, back in TV land, a ceremony is taking place even now. While of course the godlike audience cannot be known in its entirety, there is one metonymic attribute of its power which can be named. I refer of course to the *thumb*; the latest disembodied image of the power viewer, as shown in a cartoon from the New York *Village Voice* (Figure 4.1).[28]

While you contemplate the terror of network executives as they ponder the fate that awaits them under the thumb of the 'deadly "click" of cancellation, termination', let me bring this analysis back down to earth

Figure 4.1 Washingtoon (Village Voice)

with some closing remarks. Power viewing: the audience as tribal other, or as god. Perhaps not. But if you think these are far-fetched metaphors, I should point out that they are not of my own invention. Social scientists and television providers (producers, executives, presenters) are not known for their flights of fancy; on the contrary, they pride themselves on prosaic, no-nonsense understandings of the world, and often espouse some pretty uncomplimentary theories about viewers. But within the industry and among its observers there circulates a view of the TV audience that amounts to a secularization of *medieval* conceptions of God. That is, for those whose livelihoods depend on its power, the TV audience is ubiquitous, unknowable, omnipotent, mysterious, capricious, benign and cruel. It needs constant propitiation, endless offerings which it may or may not deign to accept.

Furthermore, monastic sects have arisen which are dedicated to the contemplation of this mighty but elusive being, erecting a fantastic edifice of writings, knowledges, methodologies and metaphors to encompass its myriad manifestations. These learned but unworldly clerics are withdrawn from the contagion of everyday life behind the walls of secluded university campuses. They're divided into various orders, like their medieval counter-parts the Dominicans, Franciscans or black Benedictines, and like them there's intense rivalry between and within the sects of psychologists, social scientists, political economists and culturalists, not to mention ratings agencies, public opinion pollsters, market researchers and media analysts. Charges of heresy are common. Each sect claims privileged knowledge of and access to the only thing that unites them: their belief in the existence of something that can never be observed directly, their faith in a being which is never present but ever-present, pervasive but perverse.

Fashioning meanings

I suggest that the television audience ought not to be imagined in terms of individuals with identities, experiences, motivations or personalities, for in that direction lies the trap of deification, turning the audience into the ultimate 'other'. Instead, I have characterized TV viewing in terms of 'power viewing', invoking fashion and the power of the glance – the capacity of our species to apprehend social totality through mere appearance at a single look. Power in this context is not conceived as moral or political power – the power to select authoritatively or correctly what has been judged good or right. Power is not dominion over others. Power is not even sovereignty within a system of differentiated domains. In a cultural theory of television, power is pervasion: the power of the species to do, on an individual basis, what the species is capable of doing, the power of Veblen's 'matter-of-fact knowledge of mankind and of everyday life'.[29]

My analogy with the fashion industry and my emphasis on the anthropology of looking does lead to a cautionary note for those who would undertake audience research. In the case of fashion, attention is focused on the clothes, not exclusively on the model. The human body is essential to fashion, as it is to television, but fashion is strictly speaking exosomatic – outside the body. Here it differs radically from most audience research, which is dedicated to looking *inside* the body, interpreting inner states from outward signs, whether it uses electrodes and galvanometers or ethnography and participant observation to do it. What would you make of a study of the fashion industry which took off everyone's clothes and tried to work out the meanings of fashion by gazing intently at the models' naked bodies? It is my feeling that audience research is somewhat too interested in what's going on beneath the surface. My own modest proposal is that the television audience ought not to be treated like some naked, tribal, fetishized body, but rather that it should be imagined as the bearer of fashioned meanings which, like clothes, are at once public and private, personal and economic, real and rhetorical.

Finally, like fashion, 'power viewing' can also be judged on its merits. Those who understand clothes will know at a glance whether a particular ensemble is good or bad, taking into account who's wearing it, on what occasion, for what purpose. TV audiences are likewise more or less successful in their appropriation of the textual and social power of television, and once they are understood as wearers of meaning rather than as natives, 'others' or gods, the proper business of television studies can begin – teaching the public (our other self) how to get the most out of the available resources; where to find, how to fit and when to wear the most appropriate outfit.

While TV audiences are understood as persons, they will paradoxically be imagined as both sub- and superhuman (tribal others and god), under- and overvalued at once in the classic Lévi-Straussian manner. The alternative is to develop a theory of TV audiences which is based on the anthropological pervasion of the human species' power to make sense 'at first glance', and to 'read' TV audiences within a history of looking based on fashion: power viewing.

Tactile power

One way of looking at television's social impact, bearing in mind these points, is to regard it as a physical, tactile object; a thing. Instead of fretting fruitlessly about the effect of TV on people's behaviour, morals or politico-aesthetic sensibilities, it is possible (with a good deal more certainty) to study the effect of television sets on people's living rooms. Furthermore, there is a body of objective, exosomatic, 'forensic' evidence which exists, or which can be called into existence, to assist in such studies.

The private war of Allo Allo's Rene

'The scar is very noticeable ...I'm trying to forget it'

Marky Mark pin-up

EXCLUSIVE PICS

NICOLE STUNS HOLLYWOOD!

SNEAK PREVIEW

'IT HURTS...'

SOPHIE REVEALS THE CRITICS HAVE LEFT THEIR SCARS

Keep playing Dial For Dollars

Graham at home with his horses

FIRST COLOR

RAUNCHY KYLIE: 'I'm not trying to do a Madonna!'

GREAT CONTESTS
● Match the stars —2 cars to be won!
● Tour Europe
● Visit Hollywood

WANDIN VALLEY STARS LET THEIR HAIR DOWN!

Figure 4.2 Sophie Lee; 'eye-catching looks are the essence of TV . . .' (*TV Week*, Melbourne)

When television was very new, people not infrequently took photographs of the set and its spatial environment. Those same people can be called on to record their recollections of early television, and their comments then become a further textual resource for the analysis of the history of looking.

Thanks to the Museum of Contemporary Art (MCA) in Sydney, which devoted its inaugural exhibition in 1991 to 'TV Times', a history of thirty-five years of television in Australia, I have been fortunate enough to get hold of some of this type of forensic material. The MCA advertised in local newspapers around Australia for people to send in photos and letters, and I managed to solicit some more via my weekly 'popular culture' slot on ABC Radio 5AN in Adelaide, South Australia. The results are as follows:[30] an empirical but textual reading of the personalization of television sets, and of the viewing environment, in the early days of Australian TV (1956–63); a literal form of *power dressing*. This is a forensic foray into the real textual–social world of the audience, the 'invisible fictions' of power viewing, whose unselfconscious actions constitute the history of looking, and who do occasionally represent themselves.

SHOW PIECE

After Margaret Thatcher retired from government, she was still not ready to embrace the joys of domesticity. She told an interviewer in the USA: 'Home is where you come to when you have nothing better to do.' Coming from her this sentiment isn't surprising, but it is out of step with the times, saying that only public life is worthwhile, that home is a lack, a mere pause from 'better' activities. An odd thing about Mrs Thatcher's sharp line between public and private life, which places no value on the private side, is that her opinion was actually offered for domestic consumption; broadcast via the media into those very homes around the world whose status she deni-grates, but whose occupants she had for a decade sought to reach and teach, guide and govern, in her relentless, inimitable style. One of the keys to her perennial political success, in fact, had been her ability to use TV to appeal to domestic audiences directly – over the heads of party and parliament.

Domest-Oz

Mrs Thatcher's philosophy may not be homespun, but it owes more to the domestic, homely sphere of life than she's willing to admit, and one of the solvents of the line between private and public life was TV. In the 1950s and 1960s another long-serving Prime Minister, Sir Robert Menzies, presided over a boom economy which for a while put Australia in the top ten growth nations in the world. And what did Australians do with this astonishing prosperity? Encouraged on all sides, by Bob Menzies and TV alike, they bought, built and beautified homes.

TV around the world came into its own during this period, as a response and a further stimulus to domestic privatization, gathering whole populations to its smudgy little black-and-white screen. Social life moved ever more decisively indoors. Emblematic of large-scale cultural changes – from public to private, open air to interior, crowd to family – is the transfer of domestic wet areas from the yard into the house. Even before television, the dunny, traditionally an *outside* toilet, had begun its historic migration from the back fence down to the veranda, thence inside the house, ultimately to be enthroned in the central *en suite* bathroom attached to the 'master' bedroom.

So rapid and pervasive was the impact of TV in the late 1950s and 1960s that it came to be seen, at least by its critics, as an irresistible force, and its audience as passive, an immovable object. But in fact the first viewers of TV in Australia had to put a lot of effort into their new role. It wasn't just a matter of getting hold of a set and switching it on. It was hard work. Jim Mayne (Broken Hill, New South Wales [NSW]) tells how in 1962 he bought a Healing 26-inch TV set, the first big-screen model. To get a signal on it he had to put a fully rotating Hills antenna on a 50-foot mast, and

Figure 4.3 Healing 26-inch TV set (Jim Mayne)

101

look for something that might catch the elusive TV beams from distant Adelaide:

> We found if there were heavy banks of rain cloud formation in the North we got the rebound of the signal beam & received good picture, also I live near a hill with two large water storage tanks for our town supply & depending on atmosphere & wind conditions we could turn our antenna in that direction with good results. One unusual event we had was one night we were getting an under average picture, when a large aluminium passenger aircraft flew over the town & believe it or not while it was in range of the town we had a perfect picture for a few minutes.

And so these different emblems of modernity – signal beams, aluminium aircraft and domestic TV – coalesced over the heart of Australia. Small wonder that people were pleased with themselves when they got everything going; so pleased that they marked the event with a photo of the TV picture, a kind of 'video recording' technique invented by users long before VCRs.

Viewers' efforts didn't stop at improving reception; Jim Mayne also wanted to do something about transmission: 'We formed a TV committee of which I was secretary, & we got a petition up to send to the government to get a TV station here, we eventually got Channel 2 relay station & in 1968 a commercial station BKN7.'

Public looking

There was nothing passive about these efforts to get into the picture in TV's early days. W. Anderson (Kojonup, Western Australia) writes that: 'The television purchase caused great excitement especially to me who lived and worked 160 kilometres away in the country where there was no TV at all. Hence the photo I took of this valuable object on my next visit home', and note the ghostly figure of TV's first photographer-viewer reflected in the screen (Figure 4.4). Noel Blundell (Dudley, NSW) writes that TV was actively preferred over other valuable household objects: 'I was learning piano up to 1955 and had gone off the whole idea, so my parents asked me if I wished to continue or to have a TV. The piano was soon sold – the proceeds going towards the TV.'

The TV in question could be very impressive. Susan Lloyd (Cairns, Queensland) was on holiday in Chatswood from New Guinea in January 1963, and neither she nor daughter Tracey had seen TV before, so 'Grandma's new television was certainly a highlight', not least because it was 'very swish' – one of the first with remote control, attached by a long lead.

Watching TV was something of a cultural event. Susan Lloyd recalls

Figure 4.4 'This valuable object' (W. Anderson)

Figure 4.5 'The piano was soon sold' (Noel Blundell)

Figure 4.6 'Grandma's new television' (Susan Lloyd)

'people gathering around shop windows – some with portable stools'. Allan Chawner (Cooks Hill, NSW) does too:

> Before we had the local station we could only get Brisbane – with plenty of 'snow'. So Dad said we would wait for the local to arrive, 1962. We used to see the Brisbane channels by going down to Casino Road TV shop & sitting down with everyone else outside on the footpath to watch TV. Common sight in those days to see a group of people with deck chairs etc. camped outside the local shop – used to get a bit cool sometimes – but anything to watch that 'snow' paint picture of 20th Century technology.

Meanwhile, the habit of watching TV as if it were a public medium, more like cinema, spilled from the footpath right into the home. Susan Lloyd remembers 'several relatives (who were TV less) came to watch a Special Event about China'. Allan Chawner writes: 'We would gather as a clan on Saturday particularly to view *Bonanza* – or Bananas as we called it – upwards of twenty people in the room, with my sister's kids, aunties' kids etc.'

But Jan Pukallus (E. Mackay, Queensland) points out that having a lot of people wanting to sit down together to watch TV put a new strain on the existing household arrangements: 'As a family of 6, for some reason we only had four chairs, so two had to sit on the floor to watch TV. As kids, I remember fighting for a chair.'

Figure 4.7 'Four chairs for six viewers' (Jan Pukallus)

TV could also put a strain on friendship. Esmé Therdor (Coonabarabran, NSW) had a daily visitor who watched her TV – and enjoyed her tea and Arnott's biscuits. In the end, she writes, 'I do not want to lose my friend but enough is enough.' She had to tell the persistent caller that the TV was broken down, and move it to her bedroom!

An honoured guest

Once the TV set and the audience were installed, more or less happily, it was still hard work to watch. Jan Pukallus writes about early TV in Melbourne:

It was always on the blink. The TV sat in a corner on its own, and we had wires coming off it everywhere.They were strung up to a curtain at one side and out the window on the other. We were forever stamping our feet to stop the program from rolling over. When it went fuzzy we would walk up to it, fiddle with the wires and reposition them in a precarious fashion, then walk *very* gently away (as if it were a baby and might wake up!). Many times we would do this, and *just* as you sat down ever so gently, it would play up again. Even though we went through this drama to watch TV, I don't recall ever asking for a new or better one. You just accepted it.

Figure 4.8 'Its space is loungeified' (Jean Grice)

So TV came into people's homes as a guest, with its own tactfully tolerated quirks and foibles, and it was usually placed in the most formal room, the 'public' or social lounge, not in the 'private' family kitchen. If a TV set did find its way into the kitchen, it had to wipe its shoes and tidy its hair, so to speak. Jean Grice (Southport, Queensland) sends a photo in which the TV stands among tiles and units in the middle of the kitchen, but even so, its space is 'loungeified' by a little mat under its legs, and a dressing of lamp and ornaments on top. One reason why the kitchen setting did not catch on more widely, perhaps, is that, as W. Anderson reports, 'I remember we kept the light off to watch the TV so all other occupations ceased in that room.'

As for where to position the big, spindly-legged, awkwardly shaped set with its power and antenna wires, people experimented with TVs in corners, along walls, and even standing out in the room itself, with perhaps a small table behind, or in front of a built-in bookshelf. Very few looked 'comfortable' in their new environment. Doreen Gilbert's (Echunga, South Australia) ingenious husband solved the problem by making a base with casters so the whole thing would be mobile: 'It was along a wall in the centre of the loungeroom but light from the window used to shine on the screen, so we pushed it under the window and used to arrange our chairs in appropriate places, to watch it.'

But most people let the cumbersome set stay in one place, where it

Figure 4.9 'Showpiece'
(Doreen Gilbert)

caused some disruption to the existing arrangements of furniture; chairs had to be realigned and the fireplace lost its visual predominance, as it was unsafe to put the TV too close to it (much later the fireplace revived when people renovated the house and put the TV set *in* it).

Underdressing

Housing layout and furnishings took a while to catch up with the altered lines of sight and relationships of looking occasioned by TV, and most designers simply ignored it. After the initial flurry of press coverage when it was launched, there was little interest in it as a physical, tactile object – it is rarely shown in magazine spreads on interior decorating, for instance (though it has enjoyed a more recent vogue as an accompanimment to those languid, self-absorbed and unaccountably underdressed models whose poses are meant to illustrate the psychobabble self-improvement articles in *Cosmo*-style monthlies; perhaps TV sets have at last achieved symbolic status, unexpectedly, as images of self-identity). But while readers and viewers have had relentless advice on how to dress and look at themselves from the glossies, they were left pretty much to their own devices when it came to dressing the TV and designing the looking environment.

They soon learnt to treat TV more familiarly, especially by having their meals while watching, despite rearguard opposition from the food-providing member of the household. Jan Pukallus recalls: 'Our TV was a sore point with mum as she was forever calling us to have dinner in the middle of a program, *Bugs Bunny* I think. Since Dad liked cartoons, we usually ate cold dinners.'

Now presented by Sophie Lee, famed for her own variety of power dressing – and underdressing – on the show, *Bugs Bunny* is still a favourite with some parents I know well. But houses, and family roles within them, have changed since the early 1960s. Houses have become more open, with central kitchens, informal family rooms and integrated eating areas (the separate dining room has virtually disappeared). The 'private' part of modern houses is not the kitchen but the parental 'master' bedroom. So there are fewer barriers to looking, and even while working in the kitchen parents can keep an eye on the family *and* Sophie Lee's latest eye-catching outfit (see Figure 4.2).

Top-dressing

In fact eye-catching looks are the essence of TV, and not just on screen. Although people treat it casually, the set has never quite lost its public, formal status as a physical object. It is a focus of visual attention, perhaps the most important one in the house. The top of the set performs different functions for different households, but I have never seen a photo of an early TV without some adornment on it; they're all 'dressed'.

Often their polished wooden tops were shrines of family remembrance, with photos of absent children, wedding pictures or formal portraits, enhanced by an assortment of flowers, ornaments, trophies and doilies, neatly arranged into a votive altar. W. Anderson recalls: 'As was usual the lounge room of those days had photos of all the families around (and portraits not snaps), and two of the family daughters are pictured here (Figure 4.4) with a flower arrangement including dried wood for effect.' Some people overdid the flowers or pot plants, so much so that early TV suppliers had to warn customers about the dim view that TVs take to being watered by the over-enthusiastic home gardener.

A virtually obligatory top-dressing for early TV sets was the lamp, frequently justified on technical grounds as a balance to the light emanating from the screen (to avoid eye strain), or as an alternative to the main ceiling or standard lamp which would be ceremoniously switched off to enhance the picture quality – and the ambience of the home theatrette. Some of these TV lamps were quite ornate, taking fantastic exotic

Figure 4.10 'The pet' (V. Shephard and Bouncer)

forms, emblems of the 'wild viewer' right on top of the box. There was a vogue for naked, black, kneeling, plaster female figures holding scarlet lampshades of plastic taffeta; there were bizarre miniature ship's wheels with illuminated coral inside; or painted porcelain figurines of crinolined ladies, to add the respectable glow of Enlightenment Society to the technological icon of contemporary popular culture.

Altaring the look

Once established as the centre of attraction, the TV set marked the physical place where other visual ceremonies were undertaken. It was the spot where you put the baby, the bride, or the pet for an intimate portrait, and you might put the Christmas prezzies under it, or the birthday cards on it. Anneliese Kern (South Brighton, South Australia) has a Christmas 1961 photo showing her children Sieglinde and Roland framing the TV set, which is itself decorated with a Nativity crib. Many of the surviving photographs of early Australian TV sets are in fact pictures of something more personally significant.

The same goes for the knick-knacks on top of the set. These were often displayed not for their intrinsic aesthetic charm, but because they were a present from or reminder of someone special. Each TV programme may be the same for all the millions of its viewers, but what's 'on TV' – literally

109

Figure 4.11 'The Christmas prezzies' (Dawn Livingstone)

Figure 4.12 'The
birthday cards'
(Alison Muir)

on it – is never the same; it's always personal, private and significant.
Doreen Gilbert writes:

> I was surprised when I found the photo just how much I used it [the
> TV] as a show-piece. The flowers in the crystal vase are artificial (an

Figure 4.13 'In the migrant hostel' (Renee Stacey)

old fad now), standing on a doyley, with two golf trophies alongside. My husband had made a base with rollers on it so we could move the TV more easily, & I see I even used that base to put a tray & an icebucket on it (this time bowls trophies) [Figure 4.9].

One variation on the theme of personalization is that people who were not at home were able to use the TV set itself to domesticate their rooms. In 1958–9 Renée Stacey (Wollongong, NSW) lived in the local migrant hostel. She has a photograph of herself, her two daughters, TV set, table and chairs, taken by her husband who 'was laying on the divan, that opened up and which we slept on. As you can see he managed to get his feet into the picture.' In this cramped and transient setting, where bedroom, lounge room and dining room were all in one, the TV was a focal point, and it left a lasting impression:

> The set was an H.G. Palmers set, black and white of course. We had such good service from this one that we bought another from the same people; it had to be on HP then as there wasn't much money about. That's a long time ago, though I look back on our time there with fond memories.
> P.S. We still have the lamp that was on the TV. It's a black lady and the shade is bright red.

Figure 4.14 'Our first set' (Ron and Joyce Elbourn)

First impressions

One surprise to me when reading through these letters is how clearly people remember their first set, and how much they valued it. One or two have even hung on to it for thirty-odd years. Here's Ron and Joyce Elbourn (Parramatta, NSW), whose loyalty to their 1957 Astor was sorely tested:

> But the shock we got after three months or so was one night it broke down sending out smoke and sparks from the back. The service man said it would have to go back to the factory. After that it went well and I still have the old set on hand with very little wrong with it.

Similarly, Allan Chawner writes of his 1962 Kreisler: 'It was an icon of great importance for many years. In fact Dad could not stand to throw it out after it died and still has the cabinet today.'

People remember the name, size, price and supplier of their first TV sets, though W. Anderson's 1959 Astor wasn't about to let anyone forget who made it, with the brand name blazoned across the top of its screen.

Luckily, 'the set was very reliable and was not replaced until with a colour set many, many years later (Figure 4.4)'.

People often remember getting and watching the set, but not always *what* they saw. Perhaps that's because, like Mrs D. Anderson (Burleigh Heads, Queensland), they were so inspired by its novelty that 'we even rushed to view the commercials', or, like Doreen Gilbert, they gazed interestedly at the screen: 'when we first bought the TV we would sit & watch the snow on it!!!' Some proud owners, like Jim Mayne in Broken Hill, even took snaps of the test pattern to celebrate good reception, and D. Schulz (Ottoway, South Australia) recalls that: 'The talking point at the time of TV was "It's a really good picture," "Gee the sound's good," "It fits in with the lounge," and always the topic of conversation was "Gee it's got a good picture."'

But others weren't allowed to watch much at all. Pamela Beveridge's family (Traralgon, Victoria) had one of the very first sets in late 1956 or early 1957. However: 'As children we were not permitted to watch Television at all. Only on weekends when supervised as to what was considered suitable viewing. About the only show I can remember watching frequently was *Disneyland* on Sundays.' Jean Grice's young son 'was only allowed to watch wholesome shows. He was always in bed by 7pm.' Mrs Grice adds, as if to comment on the lasting effect of this sensory deprivation: 'Strange even to this day he will doze off around 7pm!' (Figure 4.8).

In other words, early viewing was not a habit at all, but a kind of wobble between over-policing and indiscriminate interest, and it took place most intensively when adults and children were at home together, so programme choices were rarely individual ones and the shows most often mentioned are cartoons. Broadcasters remember the cartoons with gratitude too: it was *Disneyland* that persuaded many undomesticated viewers of the day to abandon the practice, uneconomic to Channel 9, of watching TV in shop windows, and finally get round to hiring or buying their own sets. So Channel 9 reckons its financial viability – and its attractiveness to advertisers – not from the date of first transmission but from the launch of *Disneyland*.[31]

Private/public space (and heat)

Later, TV sets migrated out of the formal lounge room, and formal adornments went somewhat out of favour. The set is still personalized, but not as a family icon; more a familiar resource, often propped up in bedrooms, kitchens and studies, with more than one set per household. More sets are integrated into sound/screen systems, though this idea isn't new; Joy Ferrie (Lane Cove, NSW) had a Calstan '3 in 1' (TV–radio– record player) in 1963, itself only a formalized version of the even earlier bakelite radio sitting on top of her 'very old' 17-inch HMV.

Figure 4.15 'The Calstan "3 in 1" . . .' (Joy Ferrie)

Figure 4.16 . . . and a 'very old'
do-it-yourself version (Joy Ferrie)

Figure 4.17 'In the open spaces' (Allan Mitchell)

Joy and her husband 'were in the TV business and I remember he built his first TV in 1956 & we saw transmissions being sent from Petersham Town Hall before real transmissions started'; from even before the start TV was a link between civic and private space. As it began, so it continues: TV is still dissolving the line between public and private space, with TVs in fashion stores, clubs, surgeries and shopping malls.

It has spilled into the wide open spaces of Central Australia too. Allan Mitchell (Anula, Northern Territories) sends a 1984 photograph taken in Ali-Curung (formerly Warrabri), showing an Aboriginal way of watching TV without having to personalize it in the familiar, private, domestic, suburban manner. Here the (unadorned) set is invited outside to join the community, taking its place in public, social space, where a sizeable group of people can gather together to watch. Perhaps this picture of 'outside broadcasting' is not as outlandish as it looks at first sight, for the incorporation of hi-tech communications into existing Aboriginal modes of social and spatial organization points the way to new configurations of the TV viewing environment, appropriate to the Australian landscape. Already, in fact, broadcast TV's pre-eminence as a screen in many suburban households has gone; the computer and the VCR both compete with it for eye and time. And the combination of hot summers and more portable sets means that many Australians have invented for themselves this 'Aboriginal' mode of viewing in their own backyards, or at picnics and

Figure 4.18 'Warmth'
(Freda Thur)

sporting events. TV is coming out of the closet, viewing is ever more Australianized, and the history of looking is going through another change.

But one thing remains the same. Freda Thur (Gorokan, NSW) reminds us that the most abiding feature of TV from 1956 to today is its *warmth* – cats still love to sleep on it.

Part II

THE PICTURES OF POLITICS

5

THE SMILING PROFESSIONS
From a sea monster to synchronized swimming

Glasnost has brought Western films and news reports into every living room [in the Soviet Union]. All of them depict a brighter, more prosperous but, above all, happier world than people see around them. The television program about [Yuri] Gagarin's space flight showed a roll call of Soviet and US astronauts in chronological order of their flight. All of the Russians looked stern and dutiful. All of the Americans were smiling.

(*The Australian*, quoting *The Times*)[1]

Institutions of reason – the public and their picture

Media audiences have often been subjected to strategies designed to turn them into something else, something more organized, more recognizable as a community, more responsible, responsive, biddable. Chief among these is the attempt to turn the audience into the public.[2] The public, conversely, has been subjected to a campaign, initiated more than 300 years ago, to turn it into an audience.

This chapter considers the philosophical rationale of that campaign, where what was known in the seventeenth century as the 'common-people' were brought into the purview of the first modern political philosophy, in the guise of blank sheets of paper on which government would print its own authorized opinions. This print metaphor presumes, of course, that the common people will stand still long enough to receive clearly enough the impressions designed for their edification. How to persuade them to stand still? What media to use? Who or what institution could be trusted with the job? These technical problems overwhelmed a more fundamental one, namely that people are not sheets of paper, an error which has never really been corrected in the three centuries it has taken to imagine, institute and popularize media capable of calling the public into being not as a self-regulating assembly, but as a product of publicity.

Because the public as such is as elusive as the audience as such, the belief in the public's existence is much more real than the public is. Some

119

mighty institutions have been built on the strength of that belief – the most important being government, education and the media. All three have been organized around the belief in the public as blank sheets of paper on which moral, political, religious, commercial and other knowledges are to be impressed. In all three institutions it is harder to find a belief in the public as a sovereign assembly which may act and decide on its own behalf and produce those or any other knowledges. Government, education and the media are among the chief sites on which the public is built, each holding up a different part of the overall superstructure. The old, mutually sustaining, classical civic virtues of democracy, didactics and drama have been dis-integrated; education gets the didactics, the media take the drama, government gets the democracy, and the public gets taught, entertained, governed, apparently independently, and often without much consultation.

The contemporary media, as components of public life, did not suddenly appear on the social landscape as a result of technological invention, but were imagined, in terms of their social purpose and political function, long before their technology was invented. Popular media like television, cinema and the press, which seem not only to symbolize the twentieth century but also to mark it off decisively from previous times, are not best understood by being treated as endlessly present tense, self-generating and unconnected with previous social realities. Such a treatment is nevertheless quite common, being itself an updated nostalgia for a supposedly more organic, authentic 'golden age' of social harmony which always seems to be located in a period just prior to the moment when its proponent was born.

Alongside the twentieth-century expansion of popular media, an uncomprehending moral outrage has continued, based on golden-age nostalgia, of the kind that regrets the very existence of the supposedly trivial, corrupting, sensationalist media. This discourse circulates publicly, not only in institutions of education and government, but even in the media, as an obvious kind of common sense. It serves, however, to cut off popular media from history, leading to mystifying dreams about how much nicer contemporary society would be if only we didn't have them, endlessly distorting our pristine innocent consciousness. It also results in recurrent cultural commentaries, published as respectable and serious studies, under the banner of academic neutrality, which are in effect exercises in the social diffusion of fear: fear of popular politics and popular culture, fear of cultural debasement, moral decline, political manipulation, aesthetic banality, psychological influence and social disintegration, fear of competition.

A full century after the popular picture press and cinema were first launched, it seems the media are still understood (if that's the right word) ahistorically. So it is still worthwhile to argue that the popular media are not nightmarish aliens visiting curses upon our otherwise warm and glowing century. Instead, they are social institutions whose purpose was being reasoned out in the seventeenth century, and whose development was not in response to the sudden massification of the newly industrialized modern world, but, on the contrary, was a planned and necessary component of that development, continuously overseen by (though not entirely under the control of) the very forces of order whose latter-day supporters are most vocal in regretting the whole enterprise. Thus, I would argue, the politics of pictures is not a newfangled symptom of a postmodern world, but a continuing and central feature of modernity, taking 'modern' to refer to post-medieval western history. In short, television as a social institution was invented in the first half of the seventeenth century; the perfection of the technology took a while longer.

The popular media may be better at their historic job of public-creation than they are commonly given credit for. While this chapter traces the philosophical rationale and the social mechanisms for creating the public, underlying it all is a contrary sense that of the three main institutions of 'publicity' – government, education and the media – the media have retained and refined the strongest sense of integration of the three Ds of democracy, didactics and drama. Meanwhile, and perhaps even for this reason, the most popular media are themselves subjected to powerful campaigns, mounted most notoriously by the other two institutions of education and government, which are designed to discipline them, to wipe the smile off their faces, to make them do their civic duty of educating the '*impression*able' public along the lines authorized by government.

So there's a politics of pictures which is also a politics of knowledge, a political history of technologizing the premodern oral function of preaching, and turning it to secular ends, that is to preach Correct Ideas to the people and make them assent to ideologies which are not of their making and not necessarily to their advantage. Given that the public, elusive at the best of times, has a historic tendency not to stand still and take impressions that are deemed good for it, but simply to walk away, the media's efforts at popular instruction (whether the object of the exercise is didactic or democratic, disciplinary or disruptive), are strikingly successful. With drama, entertainment, pictures and pleasure as their stock in trade, the media are the first and greatest of the 'smiling professions', and the public they create out of these raw materials is the envy of education and government.

It transpires, as the latter part of this chapter discovers, that there is a new development in the history of looking: the public has slipped, perhaps decisively, from the disciplinary grasp of educational and governmental authorities into the gentler hands of the smiling professions. Smiling has become one of the most important public virtues of our times, a uniform that must be worn on the lips of those whose social function it is to create, sustain, tutor, represent and make images of the public – to call it into discursive being. Meanwhile, both government and education have had to take a leaf out of the media's book, learning that smiling is not incompatible with either politics or knowledge, but that Correct Ideas, whether civic or civilized, are only ever as good as the media through which they're communicated. Smiling, in fact, is now the 'dominant ideology' of the 'public domain', the mouthpiece of the politics of pictures.

A sea monster

There is a commonplace evaluative distinction between 'public' (hooray!) and 'publicity' (boo!), which suggests that there is also, still, a widespread and uninspected acceptance of the ancient, Platonic, philosophical distinction between reality and illusion, where the public is seen as an authentic, original, natural organism, while any communicative attempt to reach it (i.e. publicity) is tainted, manipulative, false. The idea that the public may be a *creation of publicity* is not therefore very popular. This idea does circulate quite widely too, but only in the most negative and pejorative sense, where commentators lament the 'influence' (on otherwise prelapsarian, natural, innocent, childlike members of the public) of advertising and propaganda campaigns, whether commercial or political.

Is it possible that 'the public' is a creation of publicity, and that publicity is a necessary social institution which calls the public into being and doing, and gives it a local habitation and a name? The quest for the public is not, or not only, a quest for a 'real' collective of human bodies or organized populations; it is a quest for the discourses, imaginings and communicative strategies by means of which those populations might be recognized, organized, mobilized and 'impressed', or even congregate to take collective action in their own name, the name of the public.

To address these questions it is useful to retrieve, forensically, some historical sense of where the public came from. It may even be useful to begin with the historical moment when, it may be said, the 'real' public was *abolished* – in favour of private individuals and sovereign states, between which two extremes there was little room for a classically conceived public of active citizens participating in their own legislation, government, jurism and military defence. This moment was, in general terms, the early modern period; specifically, in the English-speaking world, it occurred in the seventeenth century (bracketed by 'medieval' Elizabeth I who died in 1603 and 'modern' William and Mary who were parliamentarily instated after the Glorious Revolution of 1688–9); a century which saw the transformation from feudal to bourgeois politics and economics. In the middle of that century, the Commons of England abolished monarchy and episcopy, kings and bishops, decapitating the twin peaks of medieval politics. Exactly at this momentous time, in 1651,

Thomas Hobbes abolished the public too, putting in its place a very large fish.

'Mortall God'

> This is the Generation of that great LEVIATHAN, or rather (to speake more reverently) of that *Mortall God*, to which wee owe under the *Immortall God*, our peace and defence.[3]

Leviathan (a name borrowed from a mythical sea monster) is the name given by Hobbes to the strong, sovereign state which is required to keep order among unsynchronized individuals who are otherwise free to pursue their own good by competition for dominion over one another.

Hobbes was the first political theorist of modern bourgeois society, and of the political theory of possessive individualism which underpins it. For Hobbes, *natural* human relations, and the competitive relations of the *market*, are one and the same. As C.B. Macpherson puts it:

> Hobbes is assuming the 'anarchy' of capitalist society. The anarchy of the market . . . is only possible . . . if there is an authority, the state, to maintain the bourgeois freedoms (contract, labour, exchange and accumulation) against the demands of those who are dispossessed and against other national societies.[4]

Leviathan was published in 1651, before the self-regulating market economy was either fully established or fully understood; it stands over a fundamental break from previous conceptions of politics, both classical and feudal. From now on the main requirement of state authority was to maintain *bourgeois* freedoms; the theoretical and practical underpinnings of capitalist social relations, which are based on individual (private) not collective (public) freedoms, and which require in politics not participation but representation.

In the possessive market economy, each person's labour power is privately owned, and each is both free and compelled to sell it in the market for what it will fetch (wages), or, with capital, to buy it for what it will produce (surplus value). In the Hobbesian universe, free private individuals are so charged with competitiveness that they naturally repel one another; their natural tendency is towards atomization, not mutual attraction, and towards mutual destruction not collective community building. So for Hobbes there's no such thing as the public, a self-regulating social organism. Instead, there's incessant war. Hence, to enforce *market* freedom (of labour, contract, exchange and accumulation), *political* freedom must be taken from these intrinsically combative individuals and vested in a body which, armed with their collective powers, is strong enough to keep order between them despite their competitive struggle. Hobbes deemed that everyone's political powers must be dele-gated to the strong representative state, Leviathan, since it stood to Reason. As Macpherson has shown, this competitive, possessive indi-vidualism allows infinite accumulation for property owners (property as command over people, resources and production, not property as consumer goods), and progressive dispossession for everyone else, by means of what he calls the 'net transfer of powers'.[5]

The populace in general transfers its political sovereignty to Leviathan, the body politic: 'that great LEVIATHAN called a COMMON-WEALTH, or STATE . . . which is but an artificiall Man'.[6] Leviathan was conceived by Hobbes as a social simulacrum of the human body, a product of Reason conforming to Nature, a body imagined as containing all the powers of the public but one in which the public as such had no place. The 'artificiall Man' *represents* all, but not in the sense of representing a substance which remains itself, located elsewhere. On the contrary, Leviathan is given life by completely taking over the powers of those represented, leaving nothing behind. Any power henceforth exercised by civil subjects (private individuals) are those that Leviathan 'authorises' or devolves back on to them. In short, the public transfers its sovereign powers to Leviathan, and Leviathan is thence *author* of the public.[7]

An author(iz)ed public

The idea that authority and authorship are literally coterminous, and thence the idea that the public is a text written by government, may seem to be ultra-postmodern notions, but they are both explicit in Hobbes:

> The Common-peoples minds, unlesse they be tainted with depen-dance on the Potent, or scribbled over with the opinions of their Doctors, are like clean paper, fit to receive whatsoever by Publique Authority shall be imprinted in them.[8]

To show how easy it is to write on that blank paper Hobbes merely points out that if 'whole nations' and 'millions of men' can be made to believe the mysteries of religion, which are 'contrary to reason', then it shouldn't be too hard to persuade them to receive instruction in their obligation to the sovereign state, because the principle on which that duty is based is 'so consonant to Reason, that any unprejudiced man, needs no more to learn it, than to hear it'.[9] Hobbes recognizes the capacity of the common people to understand what is consonant to Reason, but only if their minds are not already tainted by the rich (Potent) or scribbled over with the opinions of the learned (Doctors). Such a condition is historically unknown; one might say that all social divisions of labour are founded on the taint of dependence and the scribble of opinion, such being what the rich and the learned, historically, are for.

Hobbes is well aware of this, appealing to the common people's natural, prelapsarian reason, over the heads of the established institutions of power and learning, in order to circumvent social relations and ideologies with which he does not agree. He proposes a programme whose purpose is to scribble *rational* opinions on the clean paper of the people's minds, using the device of a secularized set of ten commandments,[10] including a version of the sabbath, when the people are regularly to be assembled to 'hear those their Duties told them, and the Positive Lawes, such as generally concern them all, read and expounded, and be put in mind of the Authority that maketh them Lawes'.[11] (This authority is Reason.)

Hobbes here invents a function which his possessive individualist market society needs if it is to secure the obedience or acquiescence of the whole community, even before the means to discharge that function have been invented: telling, reading, expounding, putting in mind; here is the invention of modern political publicity. Hobbes's print metaphor for people's minds, paper to be imprinted by authority which is also authorship, is startling; Hobbes is inventing a function for the mass media, before those media were technically possible or even imagined, and before there were masses to mediate. In fact, Hobbes is promulgating the first modern theory of ideology, the need to secure popular assent – to gain hegemonic leadership – if the polity based on the rationality of the market is to succeed, not only for the beneficiaries of the net transfer of powers, but for those whose powers, both economic and political, are traded and transferred. Only if this is done can Leviathan truly *represent* the whole society, with 'laws' that 'generally concern' all classes, which means that the market economy of possessive individualism was imagined from the very start as being dependent upon publicity, political pedagogy and ideology to generalize, neutralize and communicate its otherwise far from popular mechanisms.

However, with something like the mechanism Hobbes has imagined in place, something magical occurs: the strong state, Leviathan, which has often been equated with *absolute monarchy*, becomes the polity under which *democracy* is possible. This is because political *participation* has transformed into *representation* on the abolition of the public. One representative (Leviathan) can stand for, and govern in the name of, any number of millions, so a representative sovereign can just as easily be a parliament as a king, and a parliament can represent the public directly (by election), where monarchs can only do it symbolically. It wasn't Hobbes who thought this through to its conclusion, but any such outcome would have been unthinkable without his authorized but abolished, sovereign but impressionable public. It follows that the idea of a sovereign parliament which can be progressively democratized (it took nearly 250 years) comes both historically and philosophically after the invention of 'publicity'.

A sprinkler system

Hobbes recognizes fundamental class division, describing 'two sorts of men' which 'take up the greatest part of Man-kind': on one side are 'they whom necessity or covetousness keepeth attent on their trades, and labour'; and 'they, on the other side, whom superfluity, or sloth carrieth after their sensuall pleasures'. These two classes can be glossed as labouring poor and idle rich, or as producers and consumers; but Hobbes was not primarily interested in the distinction or division between them.[12] What interested him was the need for an intermediary to communicate his rational political theory (ideology) to both of the classes he had identified. Having no time for 'deep meditation' themselves, both sorts 'receive the Notions of their duty, chiefly from Divines in the Pulpit, and partly from such of their Neighbours, or familiar acquaintance, as having the Faculty of discoursing readily, and plausibly, seem wiser and better learned . . . than themselves'.[13] The diffusion throughout the population of notions of duty is not a personal attribute but a social function, performed at that time 'chiefly' by the church (Divines) and 'partly' by the educated gentry (Neighbours). What Hobbes is looking for, in such a social set-up, is an institutional mechanism to ensure this social function is properly performed.

However, the only approximation to an institutionalized mass medium in his time was the established church. It follows that: 'the Instruction of the people, dependeth wholly, on the right teaching of Youth in the Universities'. But here there is a problem; the mixture of 'false doctrines' and 'contradiction of Opinion' in the universities offers small hope to Hobbes that they are up to the job. The kind of knowledge he seeks to popularize is not the kind that the higher branches of learning can teach. Hobbes is not interested in the extension of knowledge for its own sake; he concludes *Leviathan* with the suggestion that his book 'may be profitably printed, and more profitably taught in the Universities', but not for the benefit of the learned themselves; he sees the universities strictly as *media* through which to popularize the principles 'of which no man, that pretends but reason enough to govern his private family, ought to be ignorant':

> For seeing the Universities are the Fountains of Civill, and Morall Doctrine, from whence the Preachers, and the Gentry, drawing such water as they find, use to sprinkle the same (both from the Pulpit, and in their Conversation) upon the People, there ought certainly to be great care taken, to have it pure.[14]

Hobbes's warning about the need for 'great care' in the production ('fountain') and circulation ('sprinkling') of ideology ('civil and moral doctrine') shows that although he had a sophisticated understanding of the need for pedagogic public media in the service of politics, he had no confidence in the existing sprinkler system. Leviathan must be kept wet, but the 'Means, and Conduits, by which the people may receive this Instruction' (i.e. the media),[15] are left as an unsolved problem at the end of *Leviathan*. Hobbes was certain that the universities were dangerous, both politically (their knowledge is no more than the 'handmaid to the Romane Religion') and epistemologically (based 'onely' on Aristotle, their 'study is not properly Philosophy, (the nature whereof dependeth not on Authors,) but Aristotelity').[16] The universities were the only available social institution of knowledge which also had access to the common people, but for Hobbes they could not be trusted with either truth or propaganda.

Reason

Hobbes's successor John Locke was just as keen to instruct the common people, but less inclined than Hobbes to criticize the educational establishment for its failures in this respect. Instead of blaming the universities, Locke pointed the finger at the capacities of the common people themselves, blaming the victims for their lack of leisure and habits of labour:

> The greatest part of mankind have not leisure for learning and logick, and superfine distinctions of the schools. Where the hand is used to the plough and the spade, the head is seldom elevated to sublime notions, or exercised in mysterious reasoning. 'Tis well if men of that rank (to say nothing of the other sex) can comprehend plain propositions.[17]

For 'the day-labourers and tradesmen, the spinsters and dairy maids', it follows, according to Locke, that 'hearing plain commands, is the sure and only course to bring them to obedience and practice. The greatest part cannot know, and therefore they must believe.'[18]

Locke's pedagogy is to *make* the people believe, instructing truths authorized from above. He takes common people's ignorance for granted, relying on a secularized divinity to invest teaching with unarguable, unsmiling power, using force and commandment, authority and monologue, wanting to immobilize the people in their ignorance in order to procure their obedience, which is itself seen as acceptance of knowledge they don't understand, of Reason whose reasonableness is not discernible to them.

Knowledge shorn of reason, political participation reduced to obedience, teaching boiled down to the issue of commandments; here is a manifesto for the popular press, as the social mechanism which must inculcate belief, communicating the ideology of Reason to the common people, to secure their unreasoning consent to the rational economy, whose only requirements of them are to transfer their labour power to the market and their political power to the state. The public has been abolished, instantly to be recreated in the image of the theory of possessive individualism. Hobbesianism (Locke's version) leaves the public, like King Lear, with only the 'style and additions' of its 'natural' sovereignty and, like King Lear, modern rational public politics 'divides in three' its erstwhile united kingdom, separating the public arts of pedagogy and performance from political participation. Democracy, didactics and drama have become dissociated. Democracy is authorized from above, having first been gathered up as the exclusive monopoly of Leviathan; didactics becomes the province of a secularized clerisy; drama, wearing an unseemly grin on its irrational mask, is exiled from the body politic altogether, ostracized to the south bank of city life, to the unlicensed, barely tolerable soft underbelly of Reason, where it survives as an informal popular social institution, no more politically significant than a picnic, where it performs unauthorized versions of didactic, democratic public service – in pictures.

Death

Despite its Reason and realism, the Hobbes–Locke pedagogic doctrine is counterproductive. In the end it works against its own principal aim of instituting an orderly commonwealth dedicated to ever-increasing economic productivity in order to beat natural scarcity. For increasing productivity requires an increasingly educated and self-motivating population. Hobbes foresaw that increased productivity would result in population growth, but he saw this increased population as a waste by-product, not as the precondition for further growth. Thus he proposed to deal with future excess population in three stages, none of which would include integrating the people into the commonwealth. Hobbes's prescription for dealing with increased popular mobility is to immobilize it by forced labour, transportation, and death:

> But for such as have strong bodies . . . they are to be forced to work;
> . . . The multitude of poor, and yet strong people still encreasing,
> they are to be transplanted into Countries not sufficiently inhabited:
> where neverthelesse, they are not to exterminate those they find
> there; but constrain them to inhabit closer together. . . . And when
> all the world is overcharged with Inhabitants, then the last remedy
> of all is Warre; which provideth for every man, by Victory, or
> Death.[19]

This is not a 'just' war, but a war imagined by Reason. No adversary is named; presumably the 'overcharged Inhabitants' are to cull each other, in which case victory and death are the same thing. Hobbes's Leviathan, representative of the people and guardian of their security, ends by

128

shipping them out and plotting their deaths, in the meantime overcharging all the world with multitudes of poor, strong (no mention of 'free') British subjects, transported beyond the seas to relieve unemployment. Such is the political philosophy of possessive individualism.

The astonishing thing about this modest proposal is not that it was ludicrous or unthinkable, but that history turned out (ludicrously, unthinkably) just this way (though not without popular resistance), down to the last remedy of Reason, namely war, in 1914–18, where the ludicrousness of equating victory and death was preserved for ever in the rousing chorus of the Tommies' song: 'The bells of hell go ting-a-ling-aling, for you but not for me. Oh Death where is thy sting-a-ling-aling, oh grave thy Victory?' So sang my uncle, until he was killed, at the age of seventeen, near Arras, and my father, who wasn't (which is some kind of answer to the question in the song, at least for me).

The only part Hobbes predicted wrongly was that indigenous people might not be exterminated but only 'constrained to inhabit closer together, and not range a great deal of ground, to snatch what they can find'. In both North America and Australasia, the gigantic but not empty continents where the British eventually conducted this rationalist experiment, constrainment and extermination turned out, like victory and death, to be the same thing, at least for most of the Aboriginal inhabitants.

It is clear (with hindsight) that the Hobbes–Locke doctrine is deficient in the very area of public policy that it was most designed to promote. It designated all as subject to the market relations of possessive individualism, and it promoted the activity of the most active classes of society as they were then recognized (merchants, farmers, manufacturers), but when it came to the common people (i.e. to the largest number of those subjected to the market), and to the increase in people produced by this activity, it could propose nothing more than immobility of mind and transportability of body. This is perhaps the inevitable end point for a political theory which awards agency to the big fish, the 'Artificiall Man' of Leviathan, and understands the commons only as objects of public policy, not actors in its formation; they were to be imprinted, sprinkled, commanded, transported and left to fight or die. It's a Gonzalan Commonwealth whose end, death, has forgotten its beginning, Reason. Small wonder that the people have a historic suspicion of theory, political or otherwise, and perhaps just as well for them that they are frequently deaf to the blandishments of Reason itself. But Hobbes gets the last laugh: the name of the hulk upon which convicts were huddled 600 at a time, fettered and 'rendered "tame as rabbits" by starvation and discipline' before being transported to Australia, was *Leviathan*.[20] Mocking the heroic memory of Nelson, 'a very little boy 13 years of age'[21] was seen creeping about the hulk in double fetters, for this was the same *Leviathan* that had fought in the van at Trafalgar. And so Hobbes's predictions of transportation and death came to pass in a ship that bore the name of his book.

Knowledge

Since Hobbes's time, the universities of which he was suspicious have continued as important cultural institutions, but they have never directly participated in the education of the public *qua* public. The higher you go in the world of learning, the less public becomes the knowledge; not only is it more specialized and arcane, but the highest branches of the tree of knowledge do not have an educational function at all. Since Hobbes's time, the social function of educating the citizen according to his pre-scriptions has devolved upon the media. Meanwhile institutions of educa-tion themselves, especially at the highest levels, have taken on a quite different social role; they are institutions of the leisure class, as Locke recognized, attributing to them 'superfine distinctions . . . sublime notions . . . mysterious reasoning', in short, knowledge as conspicuous waste.

Thorstein Veblen, in *The Theory of the Leisure Class* (1899), analyses a society that is by now fully industrialized, and politically constituted around the market and bourgeois freedoms: American society at the turn of the twentieth century. He divides its various processes and products into two broad types: the serviceable and the honorific. He recognizes the Hobbesian doctrine of possessive individualism: that is, infinite desire within an economy of scarcity, which is an infinite desire to consume. In such a social set-up, consumption is culturally honourable, in inverse proportion to its utility or serviceability. Productivity, industry, science and the 'instinct of workmanship' are serviceable but (therefore) dis-honourable; leisure, conspicuous consumption and 'higher learning' are all wasteful of time, goods and resources and are (therefore) honourable.

Socially reputable knowledge in such circumstances is knowledge which displays the greatest waste of time in the getting, knowledge which is non-productive, archaic and personal (as opposed to productive, progressive and social). It is reputable precisely because such knowledge declares its holder to be leisurely; its wasteful, archaic disutility is its value, and its value is the higher the more it consumes time and goods, the more it advertises the wealth required to sustain its uselessness. Says Veblen:

> The habits of thought which characterize the life of the [leisure] class run on the personal relation of dominance, and on the derivative, invidious [comparative] concepts of honor, worth, merit, character and the like. The causal sequence which makes up the subject matter of science is not visible from this point of view. Neither does any good repute attach to knowledge of facts that are vulgarly useful.[22]

Such is the 'higher learning' for Veblen, that is the learning taught in universities. Of the lower learning he has this to say:

Science, in the sense of an articulate recognition of causal sequence in phenomena, whether physical or social, has been a feature of the Western culture only since the industrial process in the Western communities has come to be substantially a process of mechanical contrivances in which man's office is that of discrimination and valuation of material forces.[23]

Veblen maintains that science is a 'by-product of the industrial process', while the higher learning is a 'by-product of the priestly office and the life of leisure'. Hence, science and higher learning are inimical to one another, and science has gained ground both against the humanities and within the institutions of higher learning only as an intruder, and in the face of resistance. But leisure is still the mother of philosophy (science), for Veblen as for Hobbes:

The higher learning owes the intrusion of the sciences in part to . . . aberrant scions of the leisure class . . . and in a higher degree, to members of the industrious classes who have been in sufficiently easy circumstances to turn their attention to other interests than that of finding daily sustenance.[24]

Self

It seems that there's a politics of knowledge, spanning the centuries, in which 'higher learning' (institutionalized in universities, the more ancient the better) is prey to the honorific regime of the leisure and priestly classes, while scientific or philosophical knowledge (understood by both Hobbes and Veblen to be the study of 'causal sequence' in bodies both natural and social; that is, materialism) still requires leisure, but is conducted *in opposition to* formally institutionalized knowledge as such.

Where Veblen differs from Hobbes most radically is in the attribution of causal sequence to scientific knowledge itself. Hobbes recommends a method founded on looking, but on looking inwards, metaphorically, to see the self as book, as author of Reason; a method that is itself a statement of possessive individualism, founding not only that particular theory but the entire enterprise of philosophical investigation on the possession (and legibility) of the self:

Read thy selfe: which was not meant, as it is now used, to countenance, either the barbarous state of men in power, towards their inferiors; or to encourage men of low degree, to a sawcie behaviour towards their betters; But to teach us, that for the similitude of the thoughts, and Passions of one man, to the thoughts, and Passions of another, whosoever looketh into himself, and considereth what he doth, when he does *think, opine, reason, hope, feare*, &c, and upon what grounds; he shall thereby read and know, what are the thoughts, and Passions of all other men, upon the like occasions.[25]

Struggling manfully to distinguish self-knowledge from selfishness, Hobbes is clearly faced with problems about the material, biological bases of consciousness; it can be read as rational, but equally it can be read 'as it is now used', as barbarous and saucy. Veblen, on the other hand, bases his materialism in social, not individual practices, ascribing scientific knowledge explicitly to the productive processes of the community as a whole: 'the habits of thought enforced upon the community, through contact with its environment under the exigencies of modern associated life and its mechanical industries'.[26] Those who pursue scientific knowledge from the basis of 'associated life' are for Veblen what Gramsci was later to call organic as opposed to traditional intellectuals. The work of such intellectuals is the 'vehicle' not the source of science.

Here, then, Veblen marks a decisive shift from Hobbes, recognizing the agency of the community as a whole in the productive process, and in the social production of knowledge. Where Hobbes would imprint his achieved doctrine on the clean paper of the common people's minds, Veblen makes those minds ('habits of thought') the source of science. But though 'modern associated life' is the source of knowledge, it is not self-represented either politically or in formal knowledge; on the contrary it is represented by leisured specialists.

Media

Norwegian American Thorstein Veblen is exactly contemporary, and of one mind, with Russian Count Peter Kropotkin, whose anarchist politics was also both performative and pedagogic. Kropotkin too holds that theory follows practice; for instance the theory of steam and the science of aeronautics follow the practical invention of steam engines and flying machines. Formal, pure knowledge (university science) is not only parasitic upon but destructive of the progress of knowledge for Kropotkin. Like Veblen, he concludes that knowledge of historical utility springs from the actions of those within the factories, farms and workshops at large, operating outside institutions of higher learning.[27] Here also is Gramsci's more familiar distinction between organic and traditional intellectuals.

But Gramsci, Kropotkin and Veblen alike were not much further forward than Hobbes with one problem: the 'means and conduits' through which social knowledge is communicated, i.e. the media. Although all of these theorists were critical of the traditional intellectual functions of higher learning, none of them theorized the socialized production of public knowledge designed for communication across classes, so their theories did not extend to consideration of the popular media as institutions of discursive production which create and sustain the public not served by traditional institutions of knowledge. Indeed, these precursors of contemporary cultural theory were not very interested in the popular media at all; Gramsci pinned his hopes on the Party as a medium of mass communication, Kropotkin on decentralized work-based schooling, and Veblen on renegade members of the industrious classes who had leisure enough to codify and objectify their social knowledge.

Meanwhile, untheorized, the popular media were developing as a good example of what Veblen, Kropotkin and Gramsci were pointing to. In the realm of symbolic and social knowledge, beyond the purview and beneath the contempt of formal learning, the popular media were in the business of practical public creation, of communicating truths across classes, the organic intellectuals of the popular classes, the populist party of the proletariat, the schoolroom of the industrious. But the methods they developed were nothing like the instructional, institutional, disciplinary, secular preaching imagined by Hobbes, Locke, and their successors. The media used the methods traditionally associated with art: 'To teach, to move, to delight'.

Competition

Fredric Jameson, a leading contemporary Marxist cultural theorist, has written this about art:

'To teach, to move, to delight': of these traditional formulations of the uses of the work of art, the first has virtually been eclipsed from contemporary criticism and theory. Yet the pedagogical function of a work of art seems in various forms to have been an inescapable parameter of any conceivable Marxist aesthetic, if of few others.[28]

This contention needs some explanation, because there is one sense in which Jameson is right. In fully fanfared theoretical and critical work, as in the 'high' arts, a refusal to teach is quite evident in the later twentieth century; the 'tyranny of lucidity' is resisted, popularization is contemptible, concepts and arguments are comprehensible only to the initiated (and initiation takes a very long time), while the commitment to referentiality or indeed to anything that might be understood as real is condemned. In short, the most advanced contemporary theory and criticism has retreated into monastic scholasticism, communicating only fear and loathing to the outside world. That such a refusal to teach is most prevalent in universities is worthy of note, though, after Hobbes, Veblen and Kropotkin, perhaps not so surprising. In this sense Jameson is right.

But Jameson's contention that the teaching use of art has been eclipsed can only hold if the entire output of the media of this century and the last is disbarred from the category of 'art'; or, alternatively, if contemporary criticism and theory confines itself to that art which is produced in and for the institutions of higher learning (in which case it confines itself to performing the task of demonstrating honorific values for its practitioners by virtue of its conspicuous disutility and waste).

For 'to teach, to move, to delight' are between them the *sine qua non* of contemporary popular media, if not of contemporary criticism and theory. *What* they teach may not be to the liking of any conceivable Marxist aesthetic, but that's not Jameson's point (and it's certainly not inconceivable that Marxist or post-Marxist aesthetics may find something pedagogically instructive in popular art). Presumably it is not his point either to confine criticism and theory to what postmodernist critical theorists in universities have to say to each other, but that is the effect of his formulation of the problem he addresses. Either that or he must presume that the popular arts (drama and journalism) are neither critical nor theoretical – an untenable position – and in addition that popular criticism in the popular media is not criticism. For such criticism (such as guides, previews, reviews, features, editorials, letters), is *strictly* pedagogic.

Higher learning and popular media are not separated by watertight seals even if universities are circumvallated like medieval monasteries. Umberto Eco recognizes what few 'high' critics make theoretically explicit, namely the reciprocity between two very different worlds:

> the sophisticated elitist experiment coexists with the great enterprise of popularization (the relationship between illuminated manuscript and cathedral is the same as that between MOMA [the Museum of Modern Art] and Hollywood), with interchanges and borrowings, reciprocal and continuous.[29]

In such a world, the 'either/or' binary (*either* the sophisticated elitist experiment, *or* the great enterprise of popularization) is no longer theoretically tenable, even if there are still plenty of practical impediments to trade between these two historic blocs of knowledge. In particular, the domain of scholastic debate, coexisting with (and learning from) the great enterprise of popularization, but not constituting it, is not exempt from the general social politics of knowledge, nor are the popular media beyond the pale of theory. It is precisely at the point when such ambiguity in the historically erected binary distinction is observed by commentators such as Eco (whose own work straddles those ambiguities), that the popular media and higher learning can be seen not as chalk and cheese, but in respect of creating publics and producing public knowledge, they share the same social functions. At that point, they also become *competitors*.

Professional smiling

The smiling professions – jobs where work, preparation, skill and talent are all necessary but hidden, where performance is measured by consumer satisfaction, where self is dedicated to other, success to service, where knowledge is niceness and education is entertainment. Such professions are often associated with women, and often enjoy less than perfect social prestige, with marginal rather than centralized power. Historically, the smiling professions were attached to service industries, especially those with public (bodily) contact, from sex and nursing to cleaning and acting.

Smiling is now an honourable public accomplishment for men, and roles previously private, performed by mother or sex partner, have become professionalized. But the historic binary distinction (taboo) between mother and sex partner has not survived this transition from private to public; motherly there-there care is now rented out by visually attractive people; wiping up mess and not minding is a sexual not a maternal service. Functions are feminized; even if they're not occupied by women, opposites are ambiguated, which indeed appears to be the general cultural function of the smiling professions.

Meanwhile, they have expanded and, as so often happens, both their public prestige and their internal career structures have improved coincidentally with their penetration by men; you can get ahead and achieve public approval on the strength of your smile. The smiling professions include all the various onscreen media glamour jobs: anchors, presenters, newsreaders, actors, journalists, host(esse)s. They include teachers: from global intellectuals in universities to neighbourhood self-help circles gathering in sitting rooms for knitting classes. The list is not endless but it is long; religious and other proselytizers (the whole New Age is smiling), therapists and care-givers (from bar staff to psychologists), are all professors of smiling.

Despite these historic transformations, some professionals continue their disciplinary, classical, clubby and institutionalized maleness, as bastions of older notions of power, enemies of smiling, last of those who hate the public even if it is the object of their professional practice or the source of their income, protectors of binary opposition and clear boundaries between authority, access, truth, and their opposites, or at least their others, outside(r)s. The law, medicine, science (militant professions dedicated to acting on the world's body) have retained a straight-faced craggy-jawed masculism, especially in their higher echelons. So the distinction between smiling and non-smiling professions is not watertight; both types may appear within the one institution, distributed, as in teaching and medicine, along a scale of public contact (smiling) to seniority (non-smiling). Meanwhile, in white-collar, clerical and bureaucratic professions, especially those handling (other people's) money, from banking to social security departments, the opposite scale seems to hold – public contact (po-faced) to higher echelons (grinning from ear to ear, at least in TV publicity).

The curious world of education has its taxonomic roots in classical

(Aristotelian) Greece and its institutional branches in medieval Europe. Across its whole contemporary canopy there's a systematic institutional prejudice against smilers. Research, publication, the expansion of the field and the maintenance of disciplinary purity are not smiling professions, but teaching is. Teaching as such has never been fully accepted as a branch of learning in itself, and the teaching profession is one of the clearest examples of an institution whose hierarchy is both feminized and lip-synced; the 'lower' you go towards primary teaching, the more women you encounter and the more they must smile as part of their professional skill. Conversely, the higher up the professional ladder you go, the more you encounter men whose smiles are of the Dylan Thomas variety, like razor blades. In institutions of higher learning teaching is done as a necessary evil without training or professional reward, while at the 'lower' end of the scale teaching is fully trained but of insecure status as a profession; conditions, work practices, unionization and social prestige indicate that teaching functions socially as a proletarian art.

In institutions of 'higher' learning there is also a disciplinary hierarchical distinction between Faculties of Education and Departments of Philosophy, whose object of study is identical (knowledge), but whose institutional prestige is in inverse proportion to the utility of the activity. High-prestige philosophy is an unsmiling profession with few students, no social utility and few women in senior posts. Education is a smiler and a teacher of smiling, with many students, mostly female, and proportionally more senior women. It is of enormous social utility but it enjoys little collegiate prestige. So there's an institutional difference between 'learning' and 'teaching', where (higher) learning is prestigious but teaching is not; where learning means the body of knowledge held to be prestigious, not the processes of finding it out or transmitting it to disciplinary disciples. Similarly, the upholders of learning are venerated, while the popularizers of teaching are vulgar.

Aesth-letics

The representative, competitive success of smiling in the public eye has at last been recognized as a sporting achievement, reaching Olympian heights, albeit under water. Synchronized swimming is the emblematic sport of the age, a new chapter in the history of looking. But it displays few of the traditional sporting values. It is not dedicated to speed, nor is it derived from combative, male, team games of the kind where scores determine success. Its ancestry belongs to the motion picture industry, a spectacular invention to show off the bodily and athletic talents of Esther Williams; appropriately for the postmodern age, its origin is a simulacrum. Only women compete in it, at least on television, and one of its most peculiar features, for a sport, is the requirement of smiling. Whether this is appropriate for the post-feminist age remains to be seen; it is certainly emblematic not only of femininity but also of the contemporary politics of pictures.

It is clearly very hard to stay upside down with your legs sticking straight out of the water as far up as your thighs for as long as a minute and come up breathing, let alone smiling. Even when your body is right way up, it must be equally hard to perform the strange robo-dance arm routines, both arms out of the water, without sinking like a stone. Add to these the perfection of repetition, two bodies (sometimes eight) rendered one, simultaneous simulation, each of the other, add too the wonder of the turns and flips, bodies as Busby Berkleian flowers and fish, rhythmical and robotic but sleek and sensuous, and you have invented not only sport but also spectacle, not only maximum but also theatrical performance.

Synchronized swimming may be fun to do but it has no history as a participant sport, nor was it evolved out of utilitarian concern for the functional enhancement of the swimmers' own bodies and skills. Its genesis comes not from doing but seeing, its explanation lies in the visual desire of its viewers to gaze upon the bodies of desirable, dolphinian others. So it is not like other sports, being dedicated entirely to the point of view of the spectator, to winning and holding an intensity of gaze not distracted even by comprehension. The moves and accomplishments do not belong to the competitors themselves; their bodies hardly make sense as their own, head a metre under water, upside down, arms working powerfully but elegantly to control movements that can only be seen by the unseen spectators looking down from above at legs agape in inverted balletic splits, movements appreciated for the beauty of posed wet skin, trained prowess hidden by regulation, selfhood split in two (or eight), the measure of success being the extent to which each swimmer is indistinguishable from her partner, the delight of the spectators consisting in not knowing which one to look at, the whole edifice kept triumphantly aloft by that fixed but necessarily convincing smile.

Like netball it's an all-women sport, but while netball is noteworthy for mass participation despite minimal media coverage and exclusion from Olympian heights, synchronized swimming is characterized by the reverse. Like gymnastics it has been popularized by the screen media, but unlike the barely pubescent anorexic waifs of gymnastics, synchronized swimmers can be any age from fourteen to forty, even at national competitive level, dedicated to the body powerful, sporting neither the gymnast's girlish pigtail nor the bald head and rubber cap of the swimmer, but coiled hair, sophisticated spangled hats and nose-plugs worn like jewellery, teaching men and women alike how to look on female sexual maturity as admirable and respectable, and giving telegenic visibility to the only sport which rewards co-operation within the team rather than giving points to individuals or allowing competing teams to score against each other.

Synchronized swimming was hardly invented as sport before it was aestheticized even further as text; not action but art, the art of television, in the finale of *Making a Splash*, a half-hour wordless video-clip made by Peter Greenaway for Channel 4 TV in Britain in the mid-1980s. The craftsman's contract, to make film art for TV, takes the traditional subject of art, the nude, and turns it into TV art by means of his own authorial name, achieving unity, or at least continuity, by editing and music, foregrounding time itself as form, stripping away the usual TV content of character–dialogue–narrative. Most of the 'nudes' in Greenaway's film are in fact swimsuited, updated and progressively multiplied; *Making a Splash* distinguishes between natural and technological bodies, so the traditional female nude is encountered in the sea, while the modern techno-nudes appear, coated in their techno-lycra skins, in the pool. The indoor, artificial environment of the pool is itself the technology whose productive capacity is exploited by synchronized swimming, which cannot be done in the sea. It is a sport of technological visualization, not of the 'natural' capacities of the human body; appropriately, Greenaway borrows a technique from twentieth-century modernist art, to visualize it from all angles at once, above and below the surface together, cubist style, making the body of water (the pool itself) as much the subject of the text as the bobbing bodies of the swimmers. Greenaway's combination of human form, light and water may be quoting David Hockney, but synchronized swimming, in this art context, is not celebrated; this is not futurist or vorticist passion for techno-bodies, but sophisticated mannerism, using television, the most popular art, to ironize popular culture, focusing on the Betjemanian allusiveness of suburbanity, or the knowing, naive ludicrousness of Beryl Reid at bowls.

There's nothing new about bodies as art, a form of communication in which shape is legible and concepts are borne by colour. There's nothing new in women as writing, as bodily texts, moving messages. But to make an Olympic sport of such moving pictures is postmodern, if not new. Sport, like learning, traces its taxonomy back, via Olympia, to classical Greece, where naked free men pursued the martial arts of throwing, running, heaving and so on out of sight of the women. These athletes honoured Mars, nudity and young boys (they who put the 'ped' in 'pedagogy' also put it in 'pederasty'). What they'd make of synchronized swimming, which honours not war and masculine self-regard but Hollywoomanly *aesth-letics*, is hard to say, but why synchronized swimming is a spectacle of post-modern global culture is worth trying to fathom out. It isn't necessary to go back as far as Olympus, but a detour through the history of looking (Chapters 6–8), via the smiling professions, will show that something fishy is going on. Aesthletics is the latest lesson in civics for a public which no longer exists.

A witty television commercial (TVC) for Carling Black Label lager, screened in Britain in 1991, takes the theme of synchronized swimming as civic education one step (one stroke?) further. It opens with an ethereal arm rising from a lake to grant (as everybody knows) the sword Excalibur to King Arthur. But the TVC transforms the Lady of the Lake into a dazzling display of synchronized swimmers, prompting one of the attendant Knights of the Round Table, by way of an explanatory remark to account for this aesthletic feat, to utter the product's catchphrase (which everybody knows): 'I bet they drink Carling Black Label.' The TVC also offers an explanation of how Excalibur got *into* its stone – in a continuation of the motion of jaw-dropping astonishment of one of the knights as he leans on it to watch all this. It so happens that the legend of King Arthur represents two fundamental political myths (in Henry Tudor's sense)[30] about the foundation of the British polity. Arthur himself, as the figure who (according to legend, i.e. *narratively*) brought together the post-Roman Britons into a single realm for the first time, is the personalization of *national unity*, while the story of Excalibur signifies the conferring by magical (i.e. divine) agents of *legitimate sovereignty* on the monarch. So the TVC is a national foundation myth; the Ladies in the Lake put synchronized swimming at the very source of Britishness, bestowing their magical powers not only on Arthur but also on Carling Black Label (and not vice versa – that being the joke). The updated myth of nationhood places the public in the public bar, pedagogic performance in the public baths, and participation in the ethereal realm of publicity, but that's OK. The humble TVC is just the place for the anthropological pervasion of commonalty, the construction of a community of viewers whose identity depends upon the witty allusiveness of intertextual knowledge, in this case at least letting the disreputable and often grotty form of the ad rise above its murky surroundings to make synchronized swimmers stand (literally, in/on the water) glamorously for the essence of 'usness', representing the magic moment when the national narrative begins, but cheerfully displacing that origin (which in the authorized version has no forum, no public and no spectators) into the postmodern time frame of simultaneity, smilingly making a spectacle of themselves for the delight and edification of the public, who are thereby invented in front of their very own eyes.

The water is enticing; the great enterprise of popularization – of constituting, imagining, educating and mobilizing the public – is the prime social function of the two great lip-synchronized professions of contemporary public life: journalism and drama production, the smiling professions, teaching the public how to synchronize with each other and with the global economy. But one question does remain. Will Leviathan, the 'artificiall Man', simulacrum of the public called into being by media, ever learn to perform *for itself* the aesthletic feat of walking on water? As King Arthur put it in his TVC, stripping off before jumping in the lake to join the Ladies: 'I'm going in to find out.'

6

HELIOGRAPHY
Journalism and the visualization of truth

If there is no history, except through language, and if language . . .
is elementally metaphorical, Borges is correct: 'Perhaps universal
history is but the history of several metaphors.' Light is only one
example of these 'several' fundamental 'metaphors', but what an
example! Who will ever dominate it, who will ever pronounce its
meaning without first being pronounced by it? What language will
ever escape it? . . . If all languages combat within it, *modifying only*
the same metaphor and choosing the *best* light, Borges . . . is correct
again: 'Perhaps universal history is but the history of the diverse
intonations of several metaphors.'

Jacques Derrida[1]

Choosing the *best* light

Journalism is the art of tele-visualization; it constitutes, then renders
visible, distant visions of order. The fundamental test of newsworthiness
is disorder – deviation from any supposed steady state – and the most
important metaphors of journalistic method, used by journalists themselves to make sense of what they do, are metaphors of sight: eyewitness
news, watchdogs, in the spotlight, insight, discovery, revelation – metaphors of bringing to light or looking. The classic *OED* general definition
of 'truth' – 'that which exists in fact' – is commonly verified by taking it to
refer to 'that which can be seen', even when seeing is itself metaphorical,
as in the case of 'seeing' by reading. Thus the founding *medium* of
journalism is not the material verbal speech or print of which it is literally
made (just as 'the media' are not the material paper and screens upon
which news is carried); the medium of journalism is *vision*, seeing
what the words say, and not literal sight but imagined; journalists are
visionaries of truth, seers of distant order, communicated to their communities by a process of photographic negativization, where the image
of order is actually recorded as its own negative, in stories of disorder. Journalism is a philosophical discourse on what Derrida has

140

called the *heliological metaphor*.[2] It is therefore the social practice of heliography.

It is important to clarify what is going on here, for the process of visualization involves two sense-making moves, which may be parallel but which are certainly moving in opposite directions. Richard Ericson, Patricia Baranek and Janet Chan open their study of news organization, *Visualizing Deviance*, with some observations which help to identify the opposing tendencies in journalism.

First they characterize journalists as 'playing a key role in constituting visions of order, stability and change, and in influencing the control practices that accord with these visions':

> In effect, journalists join with other agents of control as a kind of 'deviance-defining élite', using the news media to provide an ongoing articulation of the proper bounds to behaviour in all organized spheres of life. Moreover, journalists do not merely reflect others' efforts to designate deviance and effect control, but are actively involved themselves as social-control agents. . . . In sum, journalists are central agents in the reproduction of order.[3]

The sense-making component of this process of social visualization and control, it should be noted, is not *reporting*, if by that is meant observation and recording of a thing or event; sense-making is rightly identified by Ericson, Baranek and Chan as 'ongoing articulation of the proper bounds of behaviour'; it is an exercise in disciplining social activity ('organized behaviour'), by means of discourse ('constituting', 'defining', 'articulating'). The social function of journalism has at this general structural level nothing to do with the reality or truth of pre-discursive events in themselves, but with the diegetic world imagined inside reporting; a world verified by constant and militant reference to the real, to be sure, but one in which the real is secondary to the vision, for it is the visualization of order/disorder that is authenticated by reference to actuality, not vice versa. Journalism, in short, makes sense by inventing the real in the image of vision.

Second, this characterization of journalism as a social discourse of disciplinary vision leads to the parallel but contrary observation that truth, as *that which exists in fact*, has already been toppled from its pedestal; journalism seeks verification in *that which can be seen*, but it needs to be understood that what is being verified in such moves is not the truth of factual existence but the plausibility of the discursive vision. The method of journalism, as described by Ericson, Baranek and Chan, draws it in the opposite direction from reporting that which exists in fact at a very great rate of knots:

> Using their sources, journalists offer accounts of reality, their own versions of events as they think they are most appropriately

141

visualized. The object of their accounts is rarely presented for the viewer, listener, or reader to contemplate directly. This is so even in television news, where the pictures are most often of the reporter and his or her sources giving a 'talking head' account. Rarely shown are the documents, behaviours, or other objects that are the subject of the account. And even when they are shown, it is usually to represent indexically or symbolically, rather than iconically.[4]

In other words, the 'reality', whether it be a person, an event (behaviour) or a document, does not mean what it says, at least for the viewer of news. It means: *You can see with your own eyes that I symbolize reality*, because seeing is believing; but what the viewer actually sees is the journalist and his or her account, anchored to reality by visual evidence, which however is not evidence for viewers to read directly (iconically), but to use as verisimilitude (the simulation of truth). Journalists are engaged in producing realist logic of the order of *thus it can be seen that . . .* , but what can be seen is the 'account', the 'version', not the 'reality', even in its textualized form ('documents').

A real surprise

Such logic will come as no surprise to students of discourse and textuality, for whom it is axiomatic that reality is a socio-discursive construction, beyond which it is impossible for our sense-making species to go. But these students do not as yet comprise a majority of those who 'contemplate' news as viewers, listeners or readers, even though journalism, using the methods described, now pervades whole populations and entire continents with its visions of order, photo-negativized into stories of disorder. For journalism as a social agency of visualization and control to work, it seems that the vast populations it converts into contemplators of order must not associate truth with *that which exists in fact*, but with *plausible stories*, packed with diegetic visual verisimilitude.

Perhaps the success of this enterprise is historically unsurprising too, for notions of truth as generated by militant nineteenth-century modernist science, presuming that truth exists independently of the observer (but that it can nonetheless be revealed by observation), are not as influential in popular culture as at least one alternative, which finds truth not stranger than fiction but the direct product of fiction. This popular theory of truth is not necessarily 'of' the people, but it does have a long history of being 'for' them. It is in fact a pedagogic strategy developed before the contemporary popular media were technologically or socially established (but after the people who would form the audiences for contemporary media were already being formed by industrialization, urbanization and mass mobility). The literature of popular instruction of the nineteenth-century social engineers, who built bridges of ideology over the yawning chasms between intellectual knowledge and popular reality, used fiction as their mainstay. Here for instance is one of the most prolific of them, R.M. Ballantyne, whose popular *Miscellany* series of cheap books, illustrated with proto-photos, was issued in the 1880s to place 'interesting information' in the hands of those, 'especially the young', who could not otherwise afford access to it. Ballantyne's 'plan' for the *Miscellany* gives this as its general strategy:

> Truth is stranger than fiction, but fiction is a valuable assistant in the development of truth. Both, therefore, shall be used in these volumes. Care will be taken to ensure, as far as possible, that the *facts* stated shall be true, and that the *impressions* given shall be truthful. As all classes, in every age, have proved that tales and stories are the most popular style of literature, each volume of the series . . . will contain a complete tale, the heroes and actors in which, together with the combination of circumstances in which they move, shall be more or less fictitious.[5]

It is worth recording that the volume from which I'm quoting was awarded to its first owner as a 'REWARD FOR PUNCTUAL ATTENDANCE' by the Sheffield School Board, whose proud device is printed with the date 1870: the year of the Forster Education Act in Britain, which inaugurated free compulsory elementary education for all. So the first generation of literates called into being by universal education were taught that fictitious tales which give a (Hobbesian) *impression* of truth are *in fact* true.

What is really surprising, perhaps, is that the global-social pervasion of journalism in the second half of the twentieth century is using the time-honoured method of visionary storytelling to popularize its epistemological opposite: the ideology of militant nineteenth-century scientific modernism. The heroic eyewitness, out there in the dark continent of reality, piercing the tangled undergrowth of jungly ignorance with the steady eye of the dispassionate observer, is no longer the destiny of scientist explorers like Speke (see Chapter 3), but of reporters, from top-of-the-range foreign and war correspondents to humble local juniors standing in front of doorways, the visionaries of our times whose stories are authenticated by *being there*, but whose accounts are rendered truthful by, well, faking.

Face values: faking, truth

How can truth result from faking? Late in their study of newsroom culture, Ericson, Baranek and Chan turn to the question of faking in news stories. They suggest that 'fake words' (like 'political terrorism' to describe an *unexplained* bombing incident) are 'required to invest these matters with significance, to make it apparent to common sense that what was being visualized was worth attending to'. Fake words are 'important in filling the

143

gap between a random event in the world and what most people find meaningful'. They continue:

> The need for order, coherence, and unity also motivated other practices commonly referred to in the newsroom as 'fakes'. . . . The term 'fake' within newsroom culture was not used to refer to intentional deception or forging. Rather, it referred to simulation devices, and fictions that would add order, coherence, and unity and thus make their items, segments, and entire newscasts more presentable and plausible.[6]

Such professional fouls are not a fabrication of events to deceive the public; on the contrary they are designed to help public understanding of the world by rendering it meaningful at a structural level, as a whole. Part of the sham actually has nothing to do with the stories as events, but with the presentation of them *as true*:

> Something deeply ingrained in the plausibility structure of newscasts is that the outlet's journalists have been 'everywhere' to cull the news and to produce first-hand accounts of their discoveries. Hence, references are dropped in at appropriate places in the script to the effect that the outlet's journalists have overextended themselves to ensure that they are on-the-scene witnesses of reality for their audiences.[7]

This ideology of eyewitness authenticity is much stronger than the actuality of newsgathering practices. It's a case of form being out of sync with content.

Neither reporters nor their subjects are always where they appear to be. A direct-to-camera stand-up in front of a building is not the same as, but does signify, the reporter's 'being there', the newsworthy event itself presumably unfolding behind his or her back as we watch. Celebrity faces (the current hero-villains of a given tale) are illustrated whenever they are mentioned in a story, using whatever footage is available, which may be months or years old and out of context; the same 15 seconds used night after night in a running story, usually showing the hapless personality endlessly entering or leaving a building or doorway, caught on the cusp between public and private space. Footage is not dated, so news is always 'news', present tense, even when it isn't. The story of a report criticizing police violence against Aborigines is visualized with library footage of an unidentified police/Aboriginal stand-off, in which what is actually shown is an Aborigine striking a police riot shield. Sound effects are added to mute or even still pictures, or conversely a stock shot of a tycoon addressing an AGM is shown mute under a voiceover about a different matter entirely. Editing deftly guides viewers as to what a story means (emotionally, not intellectually). A shot of a war-injured/famished/refugee child is held longer than the information requires, deferred to the 'moment of truth', which is when the close-up victim looks up directly into the camera (at which point several million lumps rise into several million throats, and a proud professional editor can cry 'Gotcha, you sentimental bastards!'). Non-diegetic music and even slow-motion photography are used to emotionalize a homecoming. A single interview with stock-footage cutaways is used to signify a complex event/controversy, while in fact being the visualization of a preconceived news angle commissioned in advance of the event by the news editor of the day. All this is faking, but all the stories thus faked are true.

Meanwhile, as Ericson, Baranek and Chan say, 'good television news has visuals to show what the reporter has visualized in his script' – it is the script, not the event, that is primary. Their example is of a shot of a woman looking up at a burning building with a horrified expression, used to illustrate the truth of the reporter's voiceover: 'relatives waited anxiously for news of the trapped victims'. No doubt they did, but it so happened that the only 'relative' this *particular* woman had in the building was her cat. It doesn't matter; it's the 'truthfulness' of the story, narrated by fictitious devices, that matters. Ericson, Baranek and Chan conclude:

> Editors and producers are compelled to imaginatively construe, alter, and even forgo the facts in order to sustain news as a form of fiction. Concerned as they are with news as theatre, it is impossible for them to 'reflect the essential truth without distortion', or to avoid having 'production techniques . . . distort reality'. . . . The fact of fiction is too central to the news genre for it to be otherwise.[8]

Journalism, then, pervades society with visualizations of order, coherence and unity, which are verified by reference to the eyewitness ideology of newsgathering, and by the ocular proof of visual evidence, but which use that ideology and that evidence in a semiotic struggle between 'random events' and meaningfulness (a struggle which for journalists themselves takes the form of the endless war between picture and soundtrack, sight and sense), in the course of which truth becomes the textual product of fiction, 'theatre' and faking.

It would be easy to conclude that journalism is flawed, making truth claims that are at odds with its ability to deliver; it would be easy to charge journalism with professional hypocrisy or at least wilful blindness to its own shortcomings. But such a judgmental response to some of the contradictions inherent in journalism:

fake v. truth
fictional form v. factual content
script v. event
narration v. information

emotional response v. dispassionate record
meaningless pictures v. voiceover interpretation
random events v. coherent stories
reports of disorder v. visualized order
picture v. sound

would be playing the same game, trying to resolve the contradictions one way or the other ('should we have raw footage or cooked books?'), preserving a belief in (overvaluing) truth, coherence and order, while stigmatizing (undervaluing) fake, random, disorder. Such a procedure ignores the very obvious characteristic of journalism, which is to hold these oppositions in tension, constantly negotiating a relationship between the two sides, expending really prodigious effort and considerable professional skill on holding the line between them.

Trying to 'decide' *between* these opposites is mere holier than thou self-deception by the critic, and it has at least one general and immediate effect – it limits truth to the coherence/order/eyewitness side of the equation, and denies it to the fake/random/disorder/fiction side. This limitation of truth may explain why journalists are respectful and high-minded about 'facts', which belong to the province of order, but simultaneously cavalier and duplicitous in their use of the very words and pictures that give literalism to their visualizations of order. Unfortunately, it seems that journalists themselves insist on making this ideological binary choice, in order to make sense of, and to be able to continue with, the execution of their social function: to 'provide an ongoing articulation of the proper bounds to behaviour in all organized spheres of life' (Ericson, Baranek and Chan's phrase, quoted p. 141; proclaiming the truthfulness (credibility) of their visions, but hiding both their own presentational fictionality and the world's inchoate chaos. The professional ideology of journalists, in codes of ethics, editorial manifestos and informal reflection, 'chooses' truth. But because of that ideology's binary distinction between imagined facts (sacrosanct) and their actual textual realizations (mere tools and tricks of the trade), the choice is one that restricts truth to facticity, exempting from its sway the very vehicle that conveys it to the public.

To make matters yet more difficult for journalism, even the choice to restrict truth to the domain of facts is no longer such an easy one to make. For facts are not what they used to be.

Two faces: Janus (journalism/science); twin peaks (truth/communication)

The physical sciences are beginning to theorize, with chaos or catastrophe theory, the possibility of randomness, chance, uncertainty and disorder within the very substance of the universe of things that had previously been imagined as working like clockwork – accurate, interconnected,

146

predictable, reliable, and very well made out of lovely materials. The metaphor is so elegant, in fact, that it takes over; the universe becomes evidence to support the metaphor, transformed into an invention of eighteenth-century rationalist-materialist expansionism, not so much cosmos as chronometer. Meanwhile, certain social, cultural and textual theories (let's call them postmodernist) are beginning to challenge the scientific concept of truth with suggestions that the belief in revelation of truth is as mystical as belief in other kinds of (religious) revelation, that visions of order, coherence and unity are 'totalizing fictions', and that fiction itself, far from being the poor relation of mighty imperial truth, is in fact the characteristic human mechanism for knowledge production, and not just in fairy tales, news or popular miscellanies. The implications of such theories of uncertainty and semiotic productivity are that journalism ought not to be put on trial for being untrue to its own eyewitness ideology; instead it ought to be investigated forensically and historically to see why as a social institution it has maintained for several hundred years the twin but incommensurate commitments to hard, empirical, countable, observable facticity on the one hand, and to fakery, fictionality, tales and 'truthful impressions' on the other.

It is my own hunch that the problem, if it is one, arises out of journalism's twin commitment to truth and communication.

Ever since Newton, science has developed institutionally on the premise that the world is knowable, that observation is the means of knowledge, and that observation will lead not merely to information but to a revelation and understanding of the underlying 'laws' of physics (Newton), of nature (Darwin), and of society (Marx). Journalism is committed to the same metaphysical belief in underlying laws (order), but in addition to this it is committed to generalizing (i.e. making generally available to the general public) these militant scientific realisms (laws of order) through the form of its own methodology of eyewitness visualization; its credibility depends not only on veracity but also on popularity, which in this case doesn't necessarily mean 'well-liked', but does mean 'ubiquitous'.

Journalism, however, actually predates the physical, natural and social sciences as a profession and a discourse, so its twin peaks of truth and popularization are not, historically, mere vulgarized, inverted reflections of a philosophy of knowledge whose summits are found somewhere else (the snow-capped pinnacles of pure science). Historically, in fact, as Chapter 4 has noted from Hobbes, news was classically coterminous with philosophy, being a feature of the same Athenian idleness ('loytering and prating') out of which western philosophy was born. Interestingly, modern philosophy, arising from the works of Francis Bacon and Thomas Hobbes in the early part of the seventeenth century, is also coterminous with the first English news, permitted by royal licence (though only foreign news) in 1622. In May of that year appeared Nicholas Bourne and Thomas

Archer's *Weekely Newes*, and on 15 October *A Relation of the late Occurrents which have happened in Christendom, Nouo 1*, and *A Continuation of the Affaires of the Low Countries, etc., No. 2* were published together by Nathaniel Butter.[9] The professional organization of rationalist materialist science, on the other hand, in the form of the Royal Society, did not occur until after the Restoration, in 1662. (One of the Royal Society's founding members was the prattling sticky-beak gossip John Aubrey, whose *Brief Lives* is a marvel of journalism if not science, and whose antiquarianism, presumably the 'scientific' reason for his membership, was just as founded on tales, speculations, and on reading order into the chaos of evidence, not least through the mechanisms of astrology, as is any journalism.)

No, journalistic truth is not the foundling child of scientific truth, though there may be some evidence for the contrary view; instead, scientific and journalistic knowledge are entangled and mutual, reciprocating methods, epistemologies, personnel and prejudices. But there are differences, chief among which is the orientation of the two professions' *gaze*. The speculum of science is trained on the material world, the speculations of journalism are addressed to the social world. This is not the moment to criticize the implied binarism of such a distinction (that the social world is material, and so on); what's important here is that the epistemological Janus of journalism/science, while being connected, actually does look out in opposite directions. Whereas science as a discourse is addressed to 'knowledge', to other scientists and to action upon the bodies analysed, journalism as a discourse is addressed to 'common sense', to the general public and to action upon society. Science, especially pure science, *must not* communicate directly with the general social formation (its truths, its entire institutional structure, could not survive such an encounter); journalism *must*. That's the difference – communication. But the difference is not separation; january journalism and science are still facets of *knowledge*, which is two-faced. And we all know what that means.

So as the following short history of truth will reveal, the journalistic twin peaks of truth and popularization are just that: twins, not mutually exclusive binaries. Right from the start, visualizations of journalistic truth were concerned not only with its own immanent form but also, and crucially, with its diffusion, and so they were just as concerned with instruction as with information. This concern, although pedagogic, does not visualize the *writer* of journalism as being in possession of the truth, but places the 'moment of truth' at the moment of reading, in the *readership*, who are obliged to work it out for themselves on the basis of the evidence and arguments offered – truth is seen as the result of adversarial forensics. Such a position emphasizes the readership, creating a demand for its enlargement and enlightenment in order to bring the whole of society, not just its literate leadership, into the purview of truth.

The job of the journalist in these circumstances is above all to unify, to make common, the community of readers; it's a job of generalization. This enterprise, the creation of the 'common reader', characterizes journalistic theory up until the three revolutions of the eighteenth century, the American, French and Industrial (what happened at that point is the subject of Chapter 7).

A virgin birth

Traditionally, seers are blind; they cannot see this sublunary world owing to the intensity of their vision of afar (they have tele-vision). The freedom of the press in the English-speaking world was first promulgated by the blind English visionary poet and political pamphleteer, John Milton, whose *Paradise Lost* is a spatial visualization of the cosmos in verse. His *Areopagitica*, a pamphlet addressed to parliament in 1644 in opposition to the licensing of the press, is the first fully argued case for press freedom. In it, Milton visualizes truth thus:

> Truth indeed came once into the world with her divine Master, and was a perfect shape most glorious to look on: but when he ascended, And his Apostles after hime were laind asleep, then strait arose a wicked race of deceivers, who . . . took the virgin Truth, hewd her lovely form into a thousand pieces, and scatter'd them to the four winds. From that time ever since, the sad friends of Truth, such as durst appear . . . went up and down gathering up limb by limb still as they could find them. We have not found them all, Lords and Commons, nor ever shall doe, till her Masters second comming; he shall bring together every joynt and member, and shall mould them into an immortall feature of lovelines and perfection. Suffer not these licencing prohibitions to stand at every place of opportunity forbidding and disturbing them that continue seeking, that continue to do our obsequies to the torn body of our martyr'd Saint.[10]

Over the torn body of an imagined prelapsarian virgin, this is a strictly visionary view of truth. It neatly solves the philosophical problem of the *incommensurate* nature of different truths (i.e. that scientific, religious, philosophical and poetical truths are different from each other and not interchangeable). It does so by making them dismembered parts of a virgin whose 'body is *homogeneal*, and proportionall',[11] or would be but for the deceivers who have torn it apart. This body will be whole again at the teleological final cause of the second coming. So the seeker for truth, in Milton's view, is one who finds bits of that body and sticks them together. This metaphor of truth as a vulnerable female body simultaneously homogeneous and dissected is the founding metaphor of journalism, producing in turn a methodology that is to go in search of bits which may not even be recognizable when first discovered, proceeding from the known to the unknown in the manner of a jigsaw puzzle, until a more complete picture is pieced together.

What is progressive and modern about Milton's argument is that his metaphor of vision, and his explanation of the incommensurate nature of truths, is both political and indiscriminate; if truth is strewn around in dismembered bits and pieces, who is to say *in advance* what is true and what is not? Milton argues for the 'liberty to know, to utter, and to argue freely according to conscience, above all liberties',[12] which must include the liberty to be wrong. Furthermore, Milton takes this liberty to be general; the licensing of the press is 'an undervaluing and vilifying of the whole Nation', including 'the common people', who are reproached by such regulations because

> if we be so jealous over them, as that we dare not trust them with an English pamphlet, what do we but censure them for a giddy, vitious, and ungrounded people; in such a sick and weak estate of faith and discretion, as to be able to take nothing down but through the pipe of a licencer.[13]

If licensing be the means to order for printing, says Milton, in what he clearly offers as a *reductio ad absurdum*, then to preserve order 'we must regulat all recreations and pastimes, all that is delightfull to man', including music, song, dancing, eating ('household gluttony'), drinking, clothing, talking ('mixt conversation'), and mixed company ('idle resort').[14] Unfortunately for his *reductio* virtually all of these activities have in fact been regulated, both before and since Milton's time, precisely because governments have displayed a historic distrust for the 'common people', and have sought to regulate their every move, especially moves associated with the ungoverned ('licencious') disposition and display of their bodies.

The alternative for Milton is to preserve order by guarding the freedom to choose: 'for reason is but choosing'.[15] Compulsory virtue is no virtue, and the greatness and strength of the nation, for Milton, is thus to be measured precisely by the amount of 'disputing, reasoning, reading, inventing, discoursing' that 'the people, or the greater part' are taken up with even at times of national danger and war. Freedom to engage in controversy and 'new invention' leads, says Milton, to prosperity, honour and greatness for the nation, while regulation leads back to the state of former ignorance, 'brutish, formall, and slavish'.[16]

But how is such a policy to be implemented? For freedom of the press in this vision is not freedom *from* restraint only, it is freedom *to* seek knowledge. The answer is journalism; it performs the function of preserving order by disseminating to the people the power of choice, which is reason. But without official control and government guidance, how would the people, restored to bodily health by freedom of speech (having been made sick in the first place not by their own giddy viciousness but by the 'pipe of a licencer'), know how to recognize the fragments of truth among the detritus of deception? The method that follows from Milton's model of truth, choice, reason and freedom is still the mainspring of journalism: in order for people to exercise reason there must be alternatives from which to choose, and to make choice itself clearer the alternatives must be as extreme as possible, a requirement that inevitably pushes journalism towards binarism – both sides of the story. Journalistic method is not to describe the world as it is, but to visualize extremes, both positive and negative, visions of disorder, deviations from the line, binary polarities. Without having to determine or define in advance what constitutes order, or what truth's fragmented body looks like, such a method visualizes order and truth negatively by assigning each case or event to one side of a line or the other. By such a method the public can recognize and reconnect for itself the thousand pieces of truth's 'lovely form', a kind of skiamorphic ('shadow-form') silhouette seen not directly, perhaps, but in outline, and order can be 'calculated' by triangulating between the various disorders that surround it and thus define its boundary. Journalism thus gives the public something to do; to choose, according to reason, the shape of their own truth.

A spectator . . .

Appropriately for the art of visualizing order, one of the earliest regular journals was called the *Spectator*. It will serve to show that some of the preoccupations of journalism are very persistent. Number 567 of the *Spectator* for Wednesday, 14 July 1714, for instance, opens with some comments which illuminate both the style of journalism at that time and the relations between journalists and their readership:

> I have received private advice from some of my correspondents, that if I would give my paper a general run, I should take care to season it with scandal. I have indeed observed of late, that few writings sell which are not filled with great names and illustrious titles. . . . A sprinkling of the words 'faction, Frenchman, papist, plunderer,' and the like significant terms, in an Italic character, have also a very good effect upon the eye of the purchaser; not to mention 'scribbler, liar, rogue, rascal, knave, and villain', without which it is impossible to carry on a modern controversy.[17]

Although tongue in cheek, this is an account of what would now be called news values, first among which is audience maximization – giving the paper a 'general run' by making it appeal to 'the eye of the purchaser'. 1714 news values are based on the same tenet as now: bad news is good news. Scandal, elite names, adversarial controversy, accusations of corruption (liar

. . . villain) in the same breath as the creation of external enemies (Frenchmen . . . papists), are still the standard visualizations of disorder, served up in what passed for sensationalist style at the time – italic typeface, together with 'the secret virtue of an innuendo' conveyed by dashes, asterisks and etceteras, so that 'the reader casts his eye upon a new book, and, if he finds several letters separated from one another by a dash, he buys it up and peruses it with great satisfaction'.

The following edition of the *Spectator*, No. 568 for Friday 16 July 1714, carries on this theme by relating how such journalism was actually consumed, and by what type of reader:

> I was yesterday in a coffee-house not far from the Royal Exchange, where I observed three persons in close conference over a pipe of tobacco; upon which, having filled one for my own use, I lighted it at the little wax candle that stood between them; and, after having thrown in two or three whiffs amongst them, sat down and made one of the company. I need not tell my reader that lighting a man's pipe at the same candle is looked upon among brother smokers as an overture to conversation and friendship. As we here laid our heads together in a very amicable manner, being entrenched under a cloud of our own raising, I took up the last Spectator [the issue quoted above], and casting my eye over it, 'The Spectator', says I, 'is very witty to-day.'[18]

The wit is in fact a practical joke being played by Mr Spectator for the amusement of his readers; he uses the ensuing conversation to provoke one of his interlocutors, an 'angry politician' with a 'contemptuous manner', into declaring that the asterisks and dashes inserted in the previous day's *Spectator* clearly referred to himself. The moral of this story is that they did not:

> At my leaving the coffee-house, I could not forbear reflecting with myself upon that gross tribe of fools who may be termed the over wise, and upon the difficulty of writing any thing in this censorious age which a weak head may not construe into private satire and personal reflection.[19]

In the meantime there are a couple of sociological facts to be gleaned from this pleasant fiction. The journalist addresses his readers as a community united by the etiquette of pipe-smoking in coffee-houses, where it is taken for granted that the *Spectator* is found, and the readership comprises men who are not personally acquainted but who may converse as intimates – that is, men of the same class, a class moreover whose members may expect not only to read the *Spectator* but to appear in it, if only by innuendo, and even if they are fools. This glimpse into the public–private, clubby atmosphere of the then fashionable coffee-houses reveals

152

the first, very upper-crust, home for journalism, where it appears as a discourse on politics, manners, writing and wit, for a readership of leisured gentlemen.

The society visualized by Mr Spectator is by no means archaic. The closed, inward-looking, gentlemanly, mutual contempt of his coffee-house encounter is still familiar, having become a kind of emblem of British 'upperclassness', mythologized for a mass readership in detective thrillers (Wodehouse, Christie), where a civilized but murderous community gathers in some conveniently sequestered stately home or hotel to bump each other off, observed by a Poirot–Marple–Spectator outside/insider who can see, under the polish and politeness, a tribe of fools and a censorious age. The difference is of course that Agatha Christie's society is fully fictional, consumed most avidly by those whose social circumstances render 'high' society a remote fantasy, while Mr Spectator's vision of coffee, pipe and paper pretends not only to reality but also to influence, construing his readers as the very same community of top people that appears in his story. But that apparent difference hides the fact that both of these worlds are rendered visible (real) to the *reader* by the devices of *writing*, which in both cases connect the reader to society by putting into suspenseful narrative the actions and dialogue of an isolated, self-absorbed group of characters, whose deeds and words are not even legible to themselves, let alone to the public, without the help of a spectator–participant. Journalism, in 1714, was already *fictionalizing* the world of affairs, placing itself in a *forensic* relation to society; the 'spectator' is no innocent bystander but an active agent in the *representation* of the imagined public to itself: it actually doesn't matter whether or not the coffee-house conversation reported by Mr Spectator ever took place, or the 'angry politician' ever existed, for their function is precisely representative, and any truth-impression results not from their existential status but from the plausibility of the anecdote in relation to the reader's experience.

. . . in a Fog

News values and the creative spectator–journalist are not the only aspects of journalism to have persisted from the eighteenth century. The stories are pretty much the same too. *Fog's Weekly Journal* of 20 November 1736, for instance, contains five distinct sections: Foreign Affairs, Country News, London, a feature story from a correspondent in Cairo (a lively mixture of history and myth, gossip and speculation), and advertisements, which take up the still customary proportion of the paper, just under 50 per cent. The layout and presentation is unfamiliar, with the feature coming first, the advertisements gathered together at the back, and the stories running on from one to the next without much formal differentiation. There are no pictures (apart from a device calling attention to the largest display

FOG's WEEKLY JOURNAL.

NUMB 41

SATURDAY NOVEMBER 20, 1736.

Caire, Aug. ——.

I Have not yet spoken of the famous Pyramides of *Egypt*, built by the antient Kings of this Country, who rais'd these Monuments for their Tombs. Some People of little Learning, and others of much Prejudice, look upon these magnificent Works, as meer Heaps of Stones, piled up without Beauty or Art, but when by Examination we find that the favourite Passion of the *Egyptians* was to build stately Tombs, wherein their Bodies might be kept uncorrupted and unmolested: A Man would not be astonished that Kings as powerful as those of *Egypt*, should cause eternal Monuments to be built, to procure that fancy'd Repose they were so fond of after their Death.

The Names of these Monarchs, who rais'd such magnificent Tombs are not known; tho' one *Psammaticus* is reckon'd of the Number, but without any Reason given, that can render that Opinion probable. Some have pretended that the three greatest Pyramides were built by Mercury; others maintain that the most considerable of them, was erected by *Pharoah*, the Persecutor of the Children of *Israel*, who was drown'd in the Red Sea. They thought to have found the Proof of this Notion in opening the Pyramid, but then they saw themselves grosly mistaken, as supposing the Pyramid had been ever clos'd to that Day. When with Attention they examined it, they could perceive that it had already been opened, and that with no little Labour and Art.

Some antient Writers impute the Construction of one of the principal Monuments to a famous Courtesan called *Doriche*, to whom others give the Name of *Rodope*. *Heredotes* pretends, that the Woman who built this Pyramid by the Favours of her Lovers, was the Daughter of a King of *Egypt*, whose Name was *Cheopes*, which Prince had ruined himself by building the other Pyramids. However, this Story appears absolutely fabulous, and I can give no Credit to it, altho' the Author assures us, that he had taken the Fact from the *Egyptians* themselves. He says as follows, *The prodigious Expences that must have been laid out upon this Edifice, was the Cause of* Cheopes's *want of Money, thro' which Necessity he suffer'd himself to fall under the Ignominy, of prostituting his Daughter in a certain House for Hire. The Daughter not only executed her Father's Command, but thought of celebrating her Fame to future Ages, by leaving some Monument of her Life. It was therefore she desired each of the Lovers that visited her to give her a Stone, to raise the Building she design'd. They told me that with those Stones the middle of the three Pyramids was built.*

I do not comprehend, how *Heredotes* could relate a Story of so little Probability, with so serious an Air; for tho' he writes but what he had been told, yet he ought to have given the Fact as a vulgar Tale, and refuted it when he had done. What Appearance is there, that a Beauty common enough to amass such a Quantity of Stones, as might serve for the Foundation and Basis of the Pyramid, should continue so precious in the Eyes of her Lovers, as to make them importunate enough to lavish the Expences necessary in this superb Building. Indeed at first View, a Stone seems no extraordinary Matter for the Purchase of a fine Lady's Favours; I believe our modern *Beaus* would not desire them cheaper, tho' they were to fetch them out of St. *Paul's* Cathedral, but if we consider this Stone as a Marble Granite brought from a Quarry at 200 Leagues distance, it will be thought, that they who furnished Stones of this Sort, paid dear enough for the Interest they had in so known a Mistress. Perhaps the antient *Egyptians* were not so delicate in their Love, and yet it cannot be deny'd, but the Lady's Admirers were generous to excess.

These Pyramids were heretofore cas'd with Marble, according to all Appearance, but they are not so now, for the Sovereigns who wanted Marble, chose rather to strip these Monuments, than be obliged to send for it so far off.

The *Arabian* Authors account pleasantly enough, for the original of these Pyramids. They assure us that they were built a long while before the Flood, by a Nation of Gyants, each of them transporting a Stone from the Quarries, to the Place where they were erected of about 25 or 30 Foot long, as a Man might carry a Book under his Arm. In this Case, there must be as little Trouble to build up a Pyramid, as a Child raise a House of Cards. It happen'd however that one of these Gyants met with an unlucky Accident, for bringing along the famous Column of *Pompey*, the biggest and highest in the Universe, he tired by the Way, and was forced to shift it from one side to the other, in doing of which, he managed his Affairs so ill, that he broke a Rib, this Misfortune nevertheless did not hinder his Business, he came Home with his Burthen, and got his Rib set again, by an able Surgeon.

I like *Heredotes's* Story better than that of the *Arabian* Authors, but I would have Men keep up more to the Dignity of their Character, and not think human Nature contemptible enough, to give Credit to such ridiculous Tales: The greatest Part of Writers seem to abuse the Priviledge of handing Facts to Posterity, for they so disguise them by the Dresses of their own Fancy, that they leave to future Times a Heap of Chimerical Ideas, rather than a real Exposition of Things. All Nations give Breath to a Number of insupportable Historians, Reporters of Things more strange than true, Compilers of Fables; the *Turks* have their Expounders of Laws, the *Jews* their Rabbins, the *Roman* Catholicks their *Monks*, and we our *Fanaticks*, or *Whigs*. Whoever would study History, cannot be too attentive in the Choice of the Authors they take to guide them; the first Prejudices we receive in Historical Matters are difficult to root out. It is as vicious to give heedlesly into what *Heredotes* adopts for his Sentiments, as blindly to believe all the Tenets of *Aristotle*. A Man must have Judgment and Discretion in reading over the best Books, for there are none which do not in some Places, make us sensible of the Weakness of human Nature. All one can do is to endeavour to discover the Places, and supply the Defects as those Occasions happen.

A Merchant of *Marseilles*, who forwards my Letters hither, has given me in one of his own, a Relation of an Adventure that lately happen'd in his own Country; it seems to me a pleasant Story enough. I'll transcribe it to you in the Terms he wrote it.

" You won't be sorry Sir, if I inform you of a comical Event, occasioned by a celebrated Procession, " made here some Days ago. The *Monks* built an Altar in the Street, to repose a Shrine, which was carry'd thro' the Town; they rais'd a kind of Dome, " supported by Pillars of Wood, and wreath'd with " Boughs; under this Dome was form'd a Grotto hung " with Greens, in which they were to place the Figure " of St. *Mary Magdalen*, but that it might have as near " a Resemblance as possible with the Original, they " undress'd a young Virgin of fifteen Years of Age, " and put her in a Posture to represent the expiring " Saint; she was lain on a Bed of Grass Turf, and her " Hair was so artfully dispos'd, that few Places of her " Body were left naked, and expos'd to the Eye of " the Beholders. This animated Statue was charg'd " to lie still without Motion, till the Ceremony was " over. The Procession in short defiled before the " Altar, but when the Bishop in passing by, was going to rest the Relicts of this Saint for some Moments, the Statue forgetting the Part she was to act, " and touch'd with a Fit of Devotion, started up and " put herself on her Knees in her Grotto, before the " Shrine. Her fine long curled Locks which cover'd " her, fell down behind her; and the Damsel remaining in the pure State of Nature, offer'd to the " Sight of the Spectators, such lively Beauties that " appear'd nothing like those of a dying Person. The " Bishop, a truly pious Prelate, was really scandaliz'd " at the Impertinence and Folly of the *Monks*, who, " to punish them for having executed so stupid a Project, interdicted the Community, and is so much " provok'd at the Farce that has been acted, that in " all likelihood it will be a long while e'er he grants " them the Powers he has lately taken from them.

I know not what you may think of this Adventure, but to me, it is a very ridiculous Transaction. The Coptic Priests in this Country, do something much like it every Year, to the Honour of one of their deceas'd Patriarchs whom they regard as a Saint. A Man quite naked appears on a Tomb, and there delivers a Discourse in Praise of him. All the Successors of this *Coptic* Pontiff hold him in great Veneration, whose Manners they say were as pure as those of an Angel.
If so, the Patriarchs they choose in these Times, ha
scarce any Thing in common with this Saint. Th
abuse the Religion, of which they are the Deposi
ries, make sale of all Permissions or Dispensati
granted by them, and refuse nothing for Money,
there is nothing a *Coptic* Priest may not authorize
the Credit they have with the People; Divorces
very common here; when a Man is discontented w
his Wife, or when a Woman complains that she c
not accommodate Matters with her Husband, the
triarch separates them, without searching into
Cause of the Disagreement, or endeavouring to rest
the Union that ought to subsist between Man and W
He is afraid it seems of losing the Fees, which such
separation brings with it, for a good Part of the Re
nues of this Right Reverend Person is founded u
the Misunderstandings between Women and their H
bands.

The *European* Priests would certainly be far ricl
than they are, if this Priviledge belong'd to
Functions of their Office. What Treasures wo
rowl into our Clergy's Coffres by broken Marriag
if they were possess'd of that Power! I imagine
Pontiff of *Rome* might renew the antient Croisades,
he would but grant the Adventurers a License to thr
off the Wedding Cloak. On these Terms, more
merous Armies might be assembled, than that wh
Xerxes conducted against the *Greeks*. It appears to
the only Method now practicable, for carrying o
successful War against the Enemies of Christianity,
tho' in former Times, the *Europeans* run in Crow
and abandon'd their own Land to get their Thro
cut, and their Brains beat out in a Country which
was impossible to keep. The Fury of these Wand
ers were so warm, that the Women even clap'd
their Helmets, and buckled on their Armour, to ta
a Share of the Fatigues of the Holy War. The
were particularly at *Genoa*, a Number of Ladies
Figure and Rank, who got into a Military Harn
and resolv'd to depart for *Egypt*, having a Monk
their Head for their Officer, who himself raised t
charming Recruit. The Pope was pleas'd to hear of
beloved Regiment, and wrote a long Letter on
Subject, address'd in these Terms, *To the noble* [illegible]
Daughters in Christ, the Noblewomen Carmendius C
fulsi, Grimaldi, &c. *We have learned by your Lette*
and to those written to us by our dear Son, Phillip of S
vona, *Lecturer of the Order of* Minor Fryars, *that*
and many other Genoese *Women, animated with a Sp*
of Sanctity, had resolv'd to pass into the Holy Land, &c.

FOREIGN AFFAIRS.

From *Naples, Oct.* 17. That the Delay of the Pub
cation of Peace is now owing to a Punctilio of H
nour not of Fact, for the Emperor, by his Act of C
sion, makes Don Carlos Master of the two Kingdo
of Sicily; but Spain don't care that the Prince shou
hold it by Treaty or by Right, that of Conquest
look'd upon as the most glorious Title, and will ha
it so incerted in the Emperor's Renunciation, and th
the Conquest was made too *by Spanish Arms.* ——An unfo
tunate Accident has happen'd here to the young Ma
quis de Genzano, the Cardinal Spinola's Nephew, w
being in a Balcony to see a Procession pass, a Battali
made a Discharge of their Fusils by Way of Salu
tion, in one of which was a Ball, which shot the M
quis thro' the Head, so that he fell dead on the Sp
The King, as soon as he heard of the Misfortune, s
two Gentlemen to his Father, with Compliments
Condoleance in the most obliging Manner possible, a
let him know that he had assigned an annual Pensi
upon another of his Sons, of 500 Ducats a Year.—
Cardinal Coscia is yet here, and notwithstanding wh
has been said of his appearing again in the Gay Worl
he cannot prevail with the Pope to let him quit alt
gether his old Habitation in the Castle of St. Angel
where, on the Forfeiture of his Hat, he is to go a
surrender himself.

From *Rome, Oct.* 27. The other Day two Rogues
Archers, disguis'd themselves in Fryars Hoods, and a
rested a Man at Trajan's Pillar, near the Duke of S
Aignan's Palace, but the Governour of the Tow
hearing of the Matters, he clapt the pretended Fry
into Prison, for which Complaisance to the Duk
the Ambassador sent a Gentleman to thank the Gov
nour, and at the same Time, beseech'd him to [illegible]

Figure 6.1 Fog's Weekly Journal, 20 November 1736

Archers at Liberty. A Courier arriving from Madrid, as ſoon as the Cardinal Belluga had read his Packet, he went to Cardinal Aquaviva, and had a long Conference with him, relating to the Situation of Affairs, between this See and the Courts of Spain and Naples, which we ſuppoſe will be accommodated along with the General Peace.——At the Celebration of the Feaſt of St. Tereſe, in the Church of Notre Dame della Scala at the Expence of the Infant Cardinal of Spain, the Spaniſh Miniſters put on the Church Gate, the Arms of the Pope, and thoſe of the ſaid Cardinal of Bourbon; but becauſe they would not joyn thereto the Arms of the Roman Senate, the Conſervators of the Roman People would not preſent to the Church the Calice and four great Candles, as has been uſual every Year. Here will be new Buſineſs cut out; it is ſuch Things as theſe, which embroil us with all Europe. We are always careful to guard the Shell of Religion, the Kernel we ſuppoſe to be ſafe, and therefore don't trouble our Heads about it.

Bolognia, *Oct.* 30. The Marquis de Monti, who was Ambaſſador of France in Poland, is now in this Town, but he has been aſſured, that the King of France will name him for his Ambaſſador at Vienna when the Peace ſhall be publiſhed, as the ſaid Marquis is perfectly acquainted with the Affairs of thoſe two Courts; therefore he will ſtay here in his own Country, and prepare his Equipage to make his Embaſſy with the greateſt Magnificence.

From *Milan*, *Nov.* 4. Count Traun, our Governour, is expected here about the Middle of this Month from Vienna, he is alſo to have the Government of the States of Parma, Plaiſance and Mantua. The Court brings with him Seignior Zajas, a Spaniard, in Quality of his private Secretary for the War Affairs, who is an able Man, and one that underſtands the Trade well. Our ſaid Governour is to be attended alſo by Count Corodor, a Man capable to aſſiſt him in his Labours.

From *Florence*, *Oct.* 31. The Imperialiſts who lately departed from the Neighbourhood of Lucca, were gone into Cantons at Borgo, not being able to ſupport longer, the Rigour of the Seaſon under Tents. The Duke de Montemar, who was thought to have been gone for Barcelona, was yet at Piſa, where according to all Appearance, he would paſs the Winter, having propos'd a New Opera there, for his Entertainment, and has not made any Sort of Diſpoſition for evacuating Tuſcany.

From the *Independant Tartary*, by the Way of Venice, we hear that the Provinces of Perſia, ſituated on the Mogul's Frontiers are riſen in Arms, againſt the Uſurper Koulikan, and have put the old Sophy of Perſia at Liberty. By the Aſſiſtance of the Great Mogul, the People of the ſaid Provinces have declared aloud for a Reſtoration.

From *Madrid*, That the Act of Ceſſion, made by the Emperor of the Kingdoms of Naples and Sicily doth not yet pleaſe his Catholick Majeſty, and that he will have ſome Changes made in it, which is the Thing that has put off the Publication of the Peace, and hinders the Execution of the Preliminaries.

From *Vienna*, *Nov.* 7. The Dukes of Lorraine are here return'd from Presburgh, which is the Reſidence of the eldeſt. The eldeſt Arch-Dutcheſs is indiſpos'd of a violent Cold, ſo that ſhe cannot go to the Publick Devotion, nevertheleſs ſhe advances happily in her Pregnancy, and they are now in Treaty for a Bed of State, ſhe is to make uſe of after her Lying Inn; they talk of 20,000 Florins for providing it, but to be ſure, it muſt be embelliſhed at another Rate. The Aulick Chamber find a great Want of Money, and thoſe who apply for it, and are obliged to go without it, is a Number very conſiderable.——There is nothing talk'd now of the Evacuation of Tuſcany, there muſt certainly be ſome hidden Views, that Spain holds on for ſo long a Time, her Obſtinacy, and makes ſo many Shifts as ſhe has done, from Time to Time, to hinder the Concluſion of the Peace.——The Count de Metſch, Vice Chancellor of the Empire, has treated all the Envoys of the Proteſtant Powers here, and they ſay the Revocation of the 4th Article of the Treaty of Ryſwick has been approv'd of by our Court, and yet this may be but a Finneſs to ballance ſome certain Matters, thrown into another Scale, for Politicians weigh the minuteſt Scruple in theſe Times.——We ſee here a vaſt Quantity of Spaniſh Piſtols, and the Imperial Court pays in nothing elſe at preſent, this gives an abundant Matter for Reaſoning.

Petersburg, *Oct.* 26. We underſtand that the Negotiations of Peace go on at Conſtantinople, between our Empreſs and the Turks, managed chiefly by the Plenipotentiaries of the Maritime Powers. The Walachians have ſent hither a Deputation to put themſelves under the Protection of the Czarina. But the new Kam is fortifying Little Tartarie, and putting it in a State of Defence, in caſe our Army ſhould march that way again.

From the *Danube*, *Nov.* 7, That the News from Hungary adviſe, that the Ottoman Porte is preparing ſtrongly for a War againſt the Chriſtians. The Raſciens, the Morlaques, and the Croatians have received Orders from the Emperor to mount on Horſeback to guard their Frontiers againſt the Eruptions of the Turks and Tartars, whoſe Number very much augments in Boſnia.

From *Heidelberg*, *Nov.* 9, That the Peace was look'd upon there as doubtful, and the French continued to conduct Proviſions from Alzace to Phillipsburgh; there reigns however a perfect Harmony between the Courts of Vienna and Paris, and they talk now again, that a Congreſs will he held ſhortly at the Hague.

From the *Hague*, *Nov.* 16, His Majeſty, K. George, will at leaſt ſtay all this Month at Hanover, where arrives a Number of Couriers from Vienna and Paris, whoſe Diſpatches concern the aſſembling of a Congreſs ſo much deſired by the two Maritime Powers; but if the ſame ſhould take Place, it will be but with this Proviſion, that *nothing ſhall be treated of but what is abſolutely neceſſary to the principal End, and that nothing new be brought on the Tapis.*

COUNTRY NEWS.

From *Dublin*, That a Piece of Iriſh Holland, or Linnen, was bought for 40s. per Yard. *If our foreign Trade could be reduc'd, which is at preſent ſo flouriſhing, and Induſtry encouraged at Home in numberleſs Branches of Buſineſs, our Wants would be likewiſe reduced, our Poor better fed, and an Infinity of People better employ'd.*

From *Dundalk*, That the young Woman in Priſon for the Murder of her Child, daſh'd her Head againſt a large Nail, ſhe found in the Dungeon, which pierc'd her Brain and kill'd her.

From *Gallway*, That ſeveral Veſſels have been caſt away on the Coaſt, and the poor Sailors barbarouſly uſed by the Country People. From *Beerhaven*, In the County of Cork was caſt away the Mazarine from Virginia, with Pipe Staves and 365 Hogſheads of Tobacco, the Captain and two Men drown'd. Two other Ships alſo of Liverpool.—Great Damages done by Thunder and Lightning in ſeveral Parts of Ireland.

From *Edinburgh*, That a Guard was mounted in the Royal Palace of Holy-rood-Houſe by the Authority of her Majeſty's Warrant, without which Power Acceſs had been deny'd, by the Servants acting under Duke Hamilton as Keeper of the Palace. —— A Fire broke out in General Wade's Lodgings in Cannongate, and conſum'd all his rich Cloaths and Equipage. —— Great Induſtry is uſed in diſcovering the Perſons concern'd in executing the Sentence of John Porteous contrary to Law.———The Law concerning retaling Spirituous Liquors is ſtrictly put in Execution in this Kingdom. And Detachments from the Independant Companies are order'd to the Coaſt of Nairn, Cromarty, &c. to check the great Tide of Smuggling on that Coaſt.

From *Exeter*, That the Loſs of Capt. Skinner, with ſeveral of his Men, and a Cargo of 20000 *l.* is confirm'd: And likewiſe the Convicts, ſhipp'd at Biddeford for Tranſportation; but the Thimble-Men from Ilcheſter Gaol went in another Veſſel, which arrived ſafe.

From *Norwich*, That the Sacrilegious Rogues who robb'd Weldon Church were apprehended at the Crown in St. Stephen's, viz. John Hall, alias Painter, and James Blead, alias John Johnſon, alias Black Jack of the Weſt; the Surplice and other Things were found upon them, alſo Arms and Ammunition, Picklock Keys, and ſeveral Implements, which but ill ſuited with the Veſtments they pretended to belong to them. They both broke out of Bury Goal a little before the laſt Aſſizes, at which they were to have been try'd for different Robberies.

LONDON, *Nov.* 20, 1736.

We hear great Complaints from Carolina of the Georgians, who whether out of Neceſſity, or a rapacious Deſire of what is none of their own, have plunder'd and taken under Colour of Authority, the Goods of lawful Traders in the upper Cherokee Nation, far North of any Part of Georgia Colony. It ſeems alſo that the Spaniards from the Havanna, have taken upon themſelves to demand a ſtricter and more confin'd Reſidence from the Georgians, and require them to evacuate the Country they are now poſſeſs'd of, to the Southward of St. Helena's Sound.

Four Months Proviſions are order'd to be ſent next Month to our Fleet, under Sir John Norris at Liſbon, and they talk that eight Men of War will be put in Commiſſion early in the Spring to joyn that Fleet in the Tagus.

Our Affairs at Home run much in the ſame Road this Week as the laſt, Hopkins a Hop Merchant, was attack'd between Tooting and Clapham, by two Foot-Pads, who knock'd him off his Horſe, and robb'd him of 16 l. his Watch, Great Coat, Hat and [illegible] &c. Mr. Marſton of Ruſſel Street, and another Gentleman attack'd in a Chariot, near Paddington by two Highwaymen, and robb'd; and ſoon after, two Gentlemen on Horſeback were robb'd near the ſame Place, by the ſaid Highwaymen, the Job came to about 18 l. in all.

Laſt Wedneſday Se'night the Rev. Mr. Capon, of Low-Layton in Eſſex, went from his Houſe to tranſact ſome Buſineſs in London, and with an Intent of returning Home the ſame Evening; but has not ſince been ſeen or heard of by any of his Friends. He is a Man of a middling Stature, ſwarthy Complection, and had on when he went from Home, a black Cape Coat, a black Callimanco Waiſtcoat, Iron-grey Breeches and black Stockings, and had two Mourning Rings on his Fingers, viz. one a Joynt Ring with a Cipher, and this Name, Mag. Pluymert, ob. 5. May 1733. Ætat. 75. the other had Mrs. Thorp on it. As he was never accuſtom'd to lie from Home without the Knowledge of his Family, it is fear'd ſome Accident has befallen him. If any Perſon will give Notice of him, dead or alive, to his Family at Low-Layton aforeſaid; or to the Printer of this Paper, it will be gratefully acknowledg'd.

We hear that the Right Hon. the Lord Chief Juſtice Reeve, having on Account of his Bodily Infirmities, deſired his *Quietus eſt*, is to have a Penſion of 1,200 per Annum, allowed him during Life.

That Alexander Denton, Eſq; one of his Majeſty's Juſtices of the Court of Common Pleas, is to be appointed Lord Chief Juſtice in his Stead. And

That Sir William Chapple, Knt. one of his Majeſty's Serjeants at Law, and Member of Parliament for the Town of Dorcheſter, is to ſucceed Mr. Juſtice Denton, as one of the Judges of the ſaid Court.

The Eaſt-India Company's Ship the Darby, Capt. Anſelm Commander, which lately fell into the Hands of Angria the Pyrate, had on Board when taken 30 Cheſts of Silver, for Account of the Company; beſides ſome others on Account of private Perſons, the whole Cargo being valued at about 100,000 l Sterling.

The Inhabitants of Red Lyon Square have agreed to apply to Parliament in the next Seſſions, for a Bill to make an Aſſeſſment for cleaning, encloſing, and beautifying the ſaid Square, after the Manner of Lincoln's-Inn-Fields, &c.

The Rt. Hon. the Earl of Arran hath wrote to Dublin, to forbid the printing and publiſhing a Book containing (as hath been advertiſed) an Hiſtorical Account of the late Duke of Ormond and his Anceſtors, &c. becauſe the ſame is in Prejudice to a Gentleman who is doing it in this Kingdom, by the ſaid Earl's Permiſſion, conformable to a ſtanding Order of the Rt. Hon. the Houſe of Peers, made upon Edmund Curll's printing the Poſthumous Works of John Duke of Buckingham without Leave of the ſurviving Family.

Yeſterday Mr. Brittle, one of his Majeſty's Meſſengers arrived here, Expreſs from Hanover, with News of her Royal Highneſs the Princeſs of Orange being ſafely delivered of a Prince, to the Joy of the Court. Her Majeſty order'd the Meſſenger fifty Guineas.

Yeſterday at Noon there was a fine Appearance of Nobility, Quality and Gentry at St. James's, to compliment the Prince and Princeſs of Wales, on the Anniverſary of her Royal Highneſs's Birth. About Three o'Clock the Queen and the two youngeſt Princeſſes went back to Kenſington to Dinner. In the Afternoon there were four open Tables for the Company, furniſh'd with great Delicacies at his Royal Highneſs's Expence, and at Night a Ball,

The Death of Don Joſeph Patinho is univerſally regretted in Spain, who went thro' all the Branches of the Adminiſtration, with that Zeal, Capacity and Succeſs, as is ſcarcely to be parallel'd; it is true, he apply'd himſelf wholly to the Publick Affairs, and brought them under an admirable Order and Management, whilſt his own were entirely neglected, or left to Perſons that wanted the Prudence, Ability, or Integrity of the Miniſter. He found Means to anſwer the vaſt Expences during the Wars of Spain in Africa and Italy, beſides the great *Treaſures* made Uſe of in the ſettling Don Carlos on the Thrones of the two Sicilys, without any extraordinary Tax upon the King's Subjects; and yet with the Profits of all the Chief Places of the Kingdom, could ſcarce maintain his own Houſehold. He was *Governour of the Council of the Finances*, and of the *Independant Tribunals*; *Superintendant General of all the Revenues*, *Secretary of State*, *and Secretary of the univerſal Diſpatches*, concerning *the Indies*, *the Marine*, and *the Finances*. Don Patinho, inſtead of leaving great Eſtates, and great Legacies to his Family at his Death, order'd in few Words, his Plate and Furniture to be ſold to pay his Debts, and that was all the Care he took about his own Affairs, which the King hearing of, gave the ſmall Perſonal Eſtate in Queſtion to his Relations, and took upon himſelf, both

... and Funeral Charges of this great Miniſter ... faithful Servant. It might be imagin'd, that the Miniſter now deceas'd, liv'd a moſt voluptuous Life to make ſuch Expences; it is true he kept a Houſe of great Hoſpitality, the Grandeur of which, ſuited the Condition of his high Station, but for himſelf, he was contented with the meaneſt Dinner that could be ſet before him, nor could he be charged with the moſt faſhionable Vices. He was look'd upon to be a Native of Spain, tho' born in Italy, as he came of Spaniſh Parents. The vacant Places are not fill'd up, tho' ſeveral Gentlemen are appointed to execute in the Interim the ſeveral Offices, but the Principal Direction the King has taken upon himſelf, and has gone thro', ſince his Miniſter's Death, a vaſt deal of Buſineſs; and therefore it is not yet known, whether or no he will be ſucceeded in the Prime Adminiſtration, by any other Perſon than his Catholick Majeſty himſelf.

Our Brethren certainly dream of the Yachts and of Hanover, we ſay again, that no Yachts are ordered, nor is his Majeſty expected over yet a while.

A Cauſe is at Iſſue in Weſtminſter Hall, between a Gentleman who has dealt much in Beauty, Plaintiff, and a young Lady of particular Virtue, Defendant, on Account of a Miſtake concerning three Yards of Lace, of above 20 l. a Yard. The Fair receiv'd it as a Preſent, but the Gentleman deſign'd it for a Pair of Ruffles, and has therefore brought his Action of Trover and Converſion.

Mr. Kelly embark'd at Broad Stairs in the Iſle of Thanet, landed near Calais, ſpoke privately to a Friend at Boulogne, and took Poſt-Horſes the next Morning for Paris.

South-Sea-Stock 99 1 qr. Ditto Annuities 111 1 half. Bank 148 3 qrs. India 178.

MATTHEW BLAKISTON, Grocer,

Oppoſite the One Tun Tavern in the Strand, Hereby gives Notice,

THAT he will ſell the beſt double refin'd Loaf-Sugar at Sevenpence Three Farthings a Pound, which is cheaper than the ſame is now ſold by any Grocer in London; and ſo in Proportion for all Sorts of fine Teas, Coffee, Chocolate, Cocoa Nuts, and all other Goods ſold in the Grocery Trade.

BENJAMIN WILLIAMS, *Grocer,*

At the Blue Bell over-againſt Charles Court near York-Buildings in the Strand, hereby gives Notice,

THAT he will ſell the beſt Loaf-Sugar, commonly call'd Treble-refin'd, at Seven Pence Three Farthings per Pound, which is cheaper than the ſame is, or has been ſold by any Grocer in London; likewiſe in Proportion all Sorts of the fineſt Teas, the beſt of Chocolate; and Coffee freſh roaſted every Day, with all Sorts of Grocery Wares.

This Day is Publiſh'd, Price 1 s. 6 d.

THE Hiſtory of AUTONOUS. Containing, a Relation how that young Nobleman was accidentally left alone, in his Infancy, upon a deſolate Iſland; where he lived Nineteen Years, remote from all human Society, till taken up by his Father. With an Account of his Life, Reflections and Improvements in Knowledge, during his Continuance in that ſolitary State. The whole as taken from his own Mouth.

Printed for J. Roberts near the Oxford Arms in Warwick-Lane.

This Day is Publiſh'd,

Containing Eight Sheets in Folio for 1 s. No. CVIII. being the 20th Number of, The Fourth Volume of

MR. Bayle's Hiſtorical and Critical Dictionary, carefully collated with the ſeveral Editions of the Original, in which many Paſſages are reſtored, and the whole greatly Augmented, particularly with a Tranſlation of the Quotations from eminent Writers in various Languages. Reviſed and corrected. By M. Maizeux, F. R. S.

N. B. By the Advice of ſeveral learned and ingenious Gentlemen, the Undertakers of this Tranſlation determine to preſerve Mr. Bayle's Works entire. But for thoſe who ſhall deſire it, they intend to print (by way of Supplement) the Lives of the moſt eminent Men not mentioned by Mr. Bayle; which will be delivered upon the ſame Terms with the preſent Undertaking.

N. B. The next Volume will finiſh this Work.

This Day is Publiſhed,

In Two Vols. Folio, with the Original Copper Plates,

MR. LE BRUYN's TRAVELS into Muſcovy, Perſia, and the Eaſt-Indies. Containing an accurate Deſcription of whatever is moſt remarkable in thoſe Countries; and embelliſh'd with above 320 Copper Plates, repreſenting the fineſt Proſpects, and moſt conſiderable Cities in thoſe Parts; the different Habits of the People; the ſingular and extraordinary Birds, Fiſhes and Plants, which are there to be found: As likewiſe the Antiquities of thoſe Countries, and particularly the noble Ruins of the famous Palace of Perſepolis, call'd Chelminar by the Perſians. The Whole being delineated on the Spot, from the reſpective Objects. To which is added, An Account of the Journey of Mr. Isbrants, Ambaſſador from Muſcovy, through Ruſſia and Tartary, to China; together with Remarks on the Travels of Sir John Chardin and Mr. Kempfer; and a Letter written to the Author on that Subject. Tranſlated from the Original French.

Printed for A. Betteſworth, C. Hitch, and C. Davis, in Pater-Noſter-Row; S. Birt, in Ave-Mary-Lane; J. Clarke, under the Royal Exchange; S. Harding in St. Martin's Lane; D. Browne and A. Millar, without Temple-Bar; J. Shuckburgh, in Fleetſtreet; and T. Oſborne in Grays-Inn.

These are to give Notice,

To all Ladies of Quality, and Others,

THAT there is a great Choice of wav'd, curl'd, flower'd and plain feather'd Hats of different Sizes, as well for Young Miſſes as Gentlewomen; all after the neweſt Faſhion. To be Sold at reaſonable Rates by the Maker, JAMES MOTHERSALL, at the Golden Angel in Cranbone Alley, the Corner of Leiceſter-Fields. Where may be had all Sorts of Turnery Wares at the loweſt Prices.

This Day is Publiſh'd,

In Two Volumes, Octavo,

THE Hiſtory of Marſhal TURENNE. The First Volume contains the Life of the Marſhal, written (originally in French) by the Chevalier Ramſay, Author of the Travels of Cyrus.

The ſecond contains the Authorities for the preceding Hiſtory; the Memoirs of the Marſhal's Campaigns, written with his own Hand; Memoirs written by the Duke of York, afterwards King James II. &c.

Printed by J. Bettenham; and ſold by A. Betteſworth and C. Hitch in Pater-Noſter-Row, and T. Woodward in Fleetſtreet. Of whom may be had,

The Political Works of Andrew Fletcher of Saltoun, Eſq; in one Vol. 8vo.

This is to give Notice,

To all GENTLEMEN, and Others,

THAT they may have good Druggets, Sagathie, and Duroy Suits made well and faſhionable, for the firſt ſize Men at 3 l. 10 s. a Suit, and the larger Size at 4 l. Cloth Serge, commonly call'd by the Name of German Serge Suits for 4 l. and 4 l. 10 s. Livery Suits for 4 l. and 4 l. 10 s. Coloured and black Cloth Suits for 5 l. and 5 l. 10 s. At the Two Golden balls the upper End of Southampton Street, facing the Market, Covent-Garden.

Alſo Horſemens great Coats to be ſold ready made at 20 s each, blue Cloak-bags ready made at 16 s. each, blue Rockers ready made.

On Saturday the 29th of November will be Publiſhed,

THE Salisbury Weekly JOURNAL: Containing the moſt Material and Authentick Occurrences, both Foreign and Domeſtick; and to render this Paper more uſeful to the Publick, the written London News Letters will always be inſerted, and likewiſe what is moſt material in the London Daily Poſt, London Evening, St. James's, Gazette, and many other London Papers not frequently ſeen in the Country. This Paper will be publiſh'd every Saturday; by William Collins Bookſeller in Salisbury; by whom all Perſons in Town and Country may be ſupplied with the ſame at two Shillings a Quarter. Advertiſements are taken in at the Place of Sale, and by T. Aſtley, Bookſeller, at the Roſe in St. Paul's Church-yard, London, and alſo by E. Thornton, Bookſeller, in Dorcheſter.

On Wedneſday the firſt of December next will be Publiſh'd, Curiouſly Printed in four Volumes in Octavo.

THE GENERAL HISTORY of CHINA, Chineſe Tartary, Corea and Thibet, being an Hiſtorical, Geographical, Chronological, Political, and Phyſical Deſcription of thoſe Countries; done from the Celebrated Work of the PERE DU HALDE,

By R. BROOKES, A. M. Rector of Aſhney in Northamptonſhire.

N. B. This Work not only contains a Hiſtory of theſe Countries, and a Deſcription of the ſeveral Parts and Inhabitants of them, as well as a View of their Government, Religion, Laws, Cuſtoms, Trade, &c. but likewiſe a great many Tranſlations and curious Extracts of Chineſe Books upon moſt of the Arts and Sciences, viz. Moral Philoſophy, Phyſick, Hiſtory, Muſick, &c. Among other Particulars, a complete Chineſe Tragedy, and a Piece of their Muſic Engrav'd. Thro' the whole are caſually interſpers'd, the entertaining Travels and Adventures of ſeveral of the Jeſuit Miſſionaries, and others in thoſe Countries: The Author of this Noble and Curious Work ſpent twenty Years in compiling it, which was done chiefly from the Accounts ſent him by the Miſſionaries then in China.

The Work is adorn'd with large and beautiful Maps of the ſeveral Countries, together with the Plans of the principal Cities, and the following Curious Plates, Engrav'd by Mr. Gerard Vandergucht, viz.

The Effigies of Confucius.
The Effigies of P. Verbieſt.
The Effigies of P. A. Schaal.
The Effigies of P. M. Ricci.
A Plate of the ſeveral curious Chineſe Shrubs and Plants, viz. The Leaf, Root, and Flower of Gin ſeng. Ou tung chu, or the Varniſh Tree Fou lin. The Tea Shrub. Two Sorts of Cotton-Trees Two Sorts of the Bamboo. Jaca. Betel. Li tchi.
A curious Draught of the Plant of Rhubarb.
A Chart ſerving to conduct a Ship up the River into the Port of Canton.
The Effigies of Paul Sin, Prime Miniſter of State.
The Effigies of Candida, Grand Daughter of the Colao, Paul Sin.
A Figure of the Croſs commonly put into the Grave with the Chineſe Chriſtians.
The Attendance of the Viceroy of a Province whenever he appears in Publick.
The various Habits of the Chineſe and Tartars, viz. The Emperor of China in his Robes of State, and in his ordinary Dreſs. Mandarins of Letters in their Summer and Winter Habits. Chineſe Mandarin of War. Tartarian Mandarin of War. A Bonze. A Countryman. Chineſe Ladies. A Tartarian Lady. A Bonzeſs. A Maid Servant. A Countrywoman.
A Repreſentation of a Chineſe Wedding.
The Proceſſion at a Chineſe Funeral.
A Draught of the Chineſe Ships and other Veſſels. An uncommon Method of Fiſhing, and catching Wild-Ducks.
Three Plates of the Chineſe Money.
The whole Proceſs of the Silk Manufactory, with the Management of Silk-worms.
The Obſervatory at Peking.
A Map of a new Diſcovery made by Capt. Beerings by Order of the late Czar of Moſcovy, in a Journey from Tobolk to Kamskatska.

Printed by and for John Watts at the Printing Office in Wild Court near Lincoln's-Inn-Fields: And ſold by the Bookſellers both of Town and Country.

GAMALIEL VOICE,

Operator in TEETH,

Removed from Whale-bone-Court, behind the Exchange, to the Mitre in St. Paul's Church-yard, on the North-ſide.

SEtteth in ARTIFICIAL TEETH in the moſt exact Manner, which, are ſo fitted and ſet in, that they may be taken out and put in again by the Perſons themſelves, and are not to be diſcerned from the Natural; they not only preſerve the Speech, but alſo preſerve the Teeth next to them from looſening or falling out; but thoſe who have Stumps to ſet them on, may with the greateſt Security, depend upon it, that they will anſwer the Ends of natural Teeth.

N B. Thoſe that are at a Diſtance, and have not Opportunity of coming to Town, may be furniſhed with any Number that are quite out in Front, if the next be faſt; this muſt be done by ſending a Pattern, which he will direct 'em to do if they pleaſe to ſend a Letter to him, paying the Carriage by Poſt, or otherwiſe.

To be Lett,

From Michaelmas laſt, and enter'd upon immediately,

THE FARM late in the Occupation of John Hugget Cowkeeper; containing about 56 Acres of Paſture Land, ſituated at Pimblio Gate behind St James's Park Wall, which lies very convenient for both the upper and lower Liberties of Weſtminſter; together with the Farm Houſe, and the Cowhouſes, which have good Lofts over them, and hold upwards of Eighty Cows, beſides a very good meaſuring Place, and alſo a Seven Horſe Stable, with a Cart Houſe and other neceſſary out Buildings, and a very good Layer well fenced in, all the Buildings lately built, and in good Repair, and in every Reſpect very commodiouſly adapted for the Buſineſs of a Cowkeeper.

Enquire of Mr. Andrews, at his Houſe in Groſvenor-Street.

N. B. A Part of the Land only if required, will be let with the Houſe and Buildings.

This Day is Publiſh'd,

The Ninth Volume of

THE ABRIDGMENT of the STATUTES from the Beginning of the fourth Year of King George II. to the End of the ninth Year of King George II.

Printed for R. Goſling, at the Crown and Mitre againſt Fetter-Lane in Fleet-Street.

Where may be had,

The former eight Volumes. And alſo

A compleat Collection of all the Statutes relating to the Poor.

The Statutes at Large concerning Bankrupts.

———— For the Preſervation of the Game.

———— Concerning Elections of Members to ſerve in the Houſe of Commons.

The Penal Laws againſt Papiſts and Popiſh Recuſants, conformiſts and Nonjurors, &c.

This Day is Publiſh'd,

LAW TRACTS, Containing, 1. A Propoſition for compiling and Amendment of our Laws. 2. An Offer of a Digeſt of the Laws. 3 The Elements of the Common Laws of England, containing a Collection of ſome Principal Rules and Maxims of the Common Law, with their Latitude and Extent. 4 The Uſe of the Law for Preſervation of our Perſons, Goods and good Names, according to the Practice of the Laws and Cuſtoms of this Land. 5. Caſes of Treaſon, Felony, Præmunire, Prerogative of the King, of the Office of a Conſtable. 6. Arguments in Law in certain great and difficult Caſes, viz. Of Impeachment of Waſte. Low's Caſe of Tenures. Of Revocation of Uſes. The Juriſdiction of the Marches. 7. Ordinances in Chancery for the better and more regular Adminiſtration of Juſtice in the Chancery, to be daily obſerved, ſaving the Prerogative of the Court. 8. Reading on the Statute of Uſes.

By Francis Bacon, Baron of Verulam, Viſcount St. Alban, and Lord High Chancellor of England.

Printed for R. Goſling, at the Crown and Mitre againſt Fetter-Lane End, Fleet-Street.

This Day is publiſh'd,

(In One Volume Octavo, Price Six Shillings)

The Second Edition, with Additions, of

A New General Engliſh DICTIONARY; peculiarly calculated for the Uſe and Improvement of ſuch as are unacquainted with the learned Languages; wherein the difficult Words and Technical Terms made Uſe of in

Anatomy,	Grammar,	Mathematicks,
Architecture,	Hawking,	Mechanicks,
Aritmetick,	Heraldry,	Muſick,
Algebra,	Hiſtory,	Navigation,
Aſtronomy,	Horſemanſhip,	Painting,
Botany,	Hunting,	Poetry,
Chymiſtry,	Husbandry,	Rhetorick,
Divinity,	Law,	Sculpture,
Gardening,	Logick,	Surgery, &c.

Are not only fully explained, but accented on their proper Syllables, to prevent a vicious Pronunciation; and mark'd with initial Letters, to denote the Part of Speech to which each Word peculiarly belongs.

To which is prefix'd,

A Compendious Engliſh Grammar, with general Rules for the ready Formation of one Part of Speech from another; by the due Application whereof ſuch as underſtand Engliſh only, may be able to write as correctly and elegantly as thoſe who have been ſome Years converſant in the Latin, Greek, &c. Languages.

Together with a Supplement of the Proper Names of the moſt noted Kingdoms, Provinces, Cities, Towns, Rivers, &c. throughout the known World; as alſo of the moſt celebrated Emperors, Kings Queens, Prieſts, Poets, Philoſophers, Generals, &c. whether Jewiſh, Pagan, Mahometan, or Chriſtian; but more eſpecially ſuch as are mentioned either in the Old or New Teſtament.

The whole alphabetically digeſted, and accented in the ſame Manner, and for the ſame Purpoſe, as the preceding Part; being collected for the Uſe of ſuch as have but an imperfect Idea of the Engliſh Orthography.

Originally begun by the late Rev. Mr. THOMAS DYCHE, Schoolmaſter at Stratford le Bow, Author of the Guide to the Engliſh Tongue, the Spelling-Dictionary, &c. And now finiſh'd by W. PARDON, Gent.

Printed for R. Ware at the Bible and Sun in Warwick-Lane, Amen-Corner.

advertisement), and the headlines, such as they are, indicate the generic sections of the paper not the content of the ensuing story. But the stories themselves are surprisingly familiar, from the range of topics and subject matter to the content of individual items.

FOREIGN AFFAIRS comprises a round-up from the major European capitals (and from '*Independant Tartary*'), comprising updates on government business and anecdotes about illustrious individuals. COUNTRY NEWS opens with a story which could have come from today's business section:

> From *Dublin*, That a Piece of Irish Holland, or Linnen, was bought for 40s. per Yard. *If our foreign Trade could be reduc'd, which is at present so flourishing, and Industry encouraged at Home in numberless Branches of Business, our Wants would be likewise reduced, our Poor better fed, and an Infinity of People better employ'd.*

They're still working on that one. Around the country, the newsworthy stories are: 'That the young Woman in Prison for the Murder of her Child, dash'd her Head against a large Nail, she found in the Dungeon, which pierc'd her Brain and kill'd her'; there's a storm, a fire, an arrest, and, 'from *Exeter* . . . the Loss of Capt. Skinner, with several of his Men, and a Cargo of 20000 1. is confirm'd: And likewise the Convicts, shipp'd at Biddeford for Transportation; but the Thimble-Men from Ilchester Gaol went in another Vessel, which arrived safe.'

From LONDON:

> Our Affairs at Home run much in the same Road this Week as the last, Hopkins a Hop Merchant, was attack'd between Tooting and Clapham, by two Footpads, who knock'd him off his Horse, and robb'd him of 16 1. his Watch, Great Coat, Hat and Wig.

They're still working on that one too, though nowadays footpads are called muggers. There are also the usual stories of the dressings-up and doings of the elite: the 'fine Appearance of Nobility, Quality and Gentry' at court; a judicial appointment; a royal birth; an overseas ministerial death. There's a miscellany of news items: the loss to 'Angria the Pyrate' of an East Indiaman and its £100,000 cargo; a proposal to beautify a London square; a summary of the stock market; and juicy titbits from the courts, already a news staple:

> A Cause is at Issue in Westminster Hall, between a Gentleman who has dealt much in Beauty, Plaintiff, and a young Lady of particular Virtue, Defendant, on Account of a Mistake concerning three Yards of Lace, of above 20 1. a Yard. The Fair receiv'd it as a Present, but the Gentleman design'd it for a Pair of Ruffles, and has therefore brought his Action of Trouver and Conversion.

It's not quite a case of *plus ça change*, but the treatment, preoccupations and prejudices of these stories are far from alien. This is remarkable not so much because of the passage of time but because of the persistence of journalism as a form of writing despite changes, almost an inversion, in its readership. Journalism still frequently reads like this gentlemanly digest, even though the readership is not now made up of gentlemen, but of those who appear in *Fog's Weekly Journal* only as subjects or outsiders: threatening (footpads), alien (convicts), disreputable (the Lady with Lace virtues), or pitiful (the prison suicide). Not to put too fine a point on it, popular readerships of today are closer in class to these unfortunates than to Hopkins the Hop Merchant, with whom the bewigged and hatted reader of *Fog's Weekly Journal* is being invited to identify. But the language of identification hasn't yet caught up with the democratization of readership; nowadays we're all addressed as if we're tut-tutting gentlemen deploring the criminal tendencies of the population (to which we belong), while joining in the business of the high and mighty (to which we do not).

Duty (and Desire), under Colour of Authority

Within a century of Milton's manifesto, journalism was sufficiently established to be recognizable as a distinct profession, separate from other branches of writing. In the meantime there had been a regicide, an interregnum, a Restoration, a 'Glorious Revolution' and the establishment of the bourgeois liberal parliamentary constitution, not to mention an empire, to which Britain was already sending convicts, and where rumblings were already ominous – the main item of metropolitan news in *Fog's Weekly Journal* for 20 November 1736 is this:

> We hear great Complaints from Carolina of the Georgians, who whether out of Necessity, or a rapacious Desire of what is none of their own, have plunder'd and taken under Colour of Authority, the Goods of lawful Traders in the upper Cherokee Nation, far North of any Part of Georgia Colony.

That problem would not concern the London press or public for very much longer, for the 'Colour of Authority' in the American empire was soon to change its stripe. But the varying fortunes of 'Necessity' v. 'rapacious Desire' were not only of import in the world of public affairs as such, they were of increasing moment within journalism itself as its practitioners struggled to keep up with all this. For the scribblers of Grub Street it was time to put their own house in order, to endow their profession with the respectability of its own code of ethics, its own 'Colour of Authority'.

What better than to plunder the neighbouring colonies of Literature and History? This was done, in 1758 (and republished in 1788), by no less a personage than Dr Samuel Johnson, the archetypal English 'man of letters', professional writer and journalist, codifier of the English language

159

in his *Dictionary*, of critical judgements in his literary writings and conversations, and 'Of the Duty of a Journalist' in this:

> A Journalist is an Historian, not indeed of the highest class, nor of the number of those whose works bestow immortality on others or themselves; yet, like other Historians, he distributes for a time reputation or infamy, regulates the opinions of the weak, raises hopes and terrors, inflames or allays the violence of the people.[20]

This vision of journalism has two theoretical underpinnings. First, popularization, communication, visualizing deviance: Johnson's journalist performs a series of up/down operations on presumed but unstated norms or steady-state conditions; the journalist distributes, regulates or raises by over- or undervaluing as appropriate – immortality/time, reputation/infamy, hopes/terrors, allays/inflames. Second, truth: the journalist, like the historian, is subject to law:

> He ought therefore to consider himself as subject at least to the first law of History, the Obligation to tell Truth. The Journalist, indeed, however honest, will frequently deceive, because he will frequently be deceived himself. He is obliged to transmit the earliest intelligence before he knows how far it may be credited; he relates transactions yet fluctuating in uncertainty; he delivers reports of which he knows not the Authors. It cannot be expected that he should know more than he is told, or that he should not sometimes be hurried down the current of a popular clamour. All that he can do is to consider attentively, and determine impartially; to admit no falsehoods by design, and to retract those which he shall have adopted by mistake.[21]

It's worth remembering that this is 1758, for these 'ethics' sound thoroughly contemporary, with the emphasis on a truth that is far from absolute, but is contingent upon deadlines, flux, uncertainty, lack of authority, unreliable sources, and the demands of demand (popular clamour); in these circumstances, Johnson's idea of the duty of the journalist is also contemporary, resting on the principles of impartiality and retraction.

It seems that some contemporary criticisms of journalists have been around for nearly a quarter of a millenium too, for Johnson goes on to castigate what is now called sensationalism, blaming it in 1758 on the very same causes:

> This is not much to be required, and yet this is more than the writers of news seem to exact from themselves. It must surely sometimes raise indignation to observe with what serenity of confidence they relate on one day, what they know not to be true, because they hope that it will please; and with what shameless tranquility they contradict

160

it on the next day, when they find that it will please no longer; how readily they receive any report that will disgrace our enemies; and how eagerly they accumulate praises upon a name which caprice or accident has made a favourite. They know, by experience, however destitute of reason, that what is desired will be credited without nice examination: they do not therefore always limit their narratives by possibility, but slaughter armies without battles, and conquer countries without invasions.[22]

It's tempting to read this prescient comment in the light of the Gulf and other modern media wars: Panama, Tripoli, Grenada, the Falklands . . . (but I refrain). What's important at this point are the terms Johnson employs to 'oppose' truth, for it is not direct *falsehood* that raises his righteous ire. He opposes truth with *pleasure*, reason with *desire*, making pleasure the opposite of truth, and making reason destitute the moment desire walks in. At one level this is common sense (of which more later), but at another level it is certainly open to question whether truth and pleasure, desire and reason, are mutually exclusive binary oppositions. This was not a problem that troubled Johnson, because he was sure of the answer. The opposition truth/reason v. pleasure/desire convinced him *bodily*; like Hobbes he was able to follow the materialist philosophical method of '*Reade thy selfe*', and what he read included his own considerable desires, which ran to gluttony, sloth and sex, which he recognized but struggled manfully to overcome. Refusing, for instance, an offer regularly to enjoy the backstage entertainments at David Garrick's theatre, he said 'I will never come back. For the white boobies and the silk stockings of your Actresses excite my genitals.'[23]

The common reader

Caprice, accident and 'the current of a popular clamour' are all, for Johnson, like sex, self-evidently beyond truth and reason; Johnson, journalism, and science are at one on this. But it's a risky discrimination, for it allows pleasure, desire, clamour, favourites, praise and disgrace to go unanalysed, explicable only as accident and caprice (fate), and it directs attention away from the dynamics of storytelling towards the facticity of information, hopeful, presumably, that narrative can be disciplined ('limited') by something that actually has nothing to do with it ('possibility'). Johnson sets up a form/content binary which valorizes content, but thereby lets form off the hook of reason and analysis.

Journalism is still Johnsonian in this respect. It is interesting to discover that the attributes that Ericson, Baranek and Chan identify as central to journalism's general social project have been isolated as the specific prose style of Johnson himself: Johnsonian prose 'is a use of language designed to give the raw, chaotic, disparate material of human life a quality of generalization, order and cohesion which will render it bearable, controllable, usable'.[24] Samuel Johnson's stature in the eighteenth century was such that his journalism, in the form of periodical essays from the *Rambler* (1750–2), the *Adventurer* (1753) and the *Idler* (1758–60 – to which 'Of the Duty of a Journalist' is a preface), was 'widely and deeply influential'.[25] This was partly because of Johnson's personal stamp; his prowess as a moralist, critic, poet and scholar resulted in the classic literary judgement, expressed here by one of his modern editors, that 'it will not seem excessive to claim that as *man of letters* no one in the English language can stand beside him'.[26] But Johnson's qualities were more than personal:

> The eighteenth century was the first age in which . . . the modern structure of the literary world, with its publishers and their establishments, its periodicals and their editors, all resting on the basis of the great anonymous public which pays for what it reads, was beginning to emerge. The whole structure, in turn, rested on a steady growth in population, urbanization, and literacy.[27]

The good Doctor presided over the invention, establishment and supply of that 'great anonymous public' during the period when it became not only a market, paying for what it read, but also an ideological construct, the naming of which has been credited to Johnson himself: 'Johnson's confidence rested, ultimately, on his faith in the "common reader". He invented the phrase; his age, almost, invented the thing – the anonymous, multitudinous arbiter of taste.'[28]

The anonymous 'common reader', whose judgement is expressed in (and *as*) the market, and for whom truth is thus a commodity or consumer good, is a novelty for Johnson, who nonetheless trusts it – he prefers commercial publication for a market ('learning itself is a trade') to the previous economy of knowledge, namely patronage ('what flattery! what falsehood!'), saying that 'the world always lets a man tell what he thinks, his own way', so under the regime of the common reader a writer 'throws truth among the multitude, and lets them take it as they please'.[29] This is not Edmund Burke's later and much more celebrated 'swinish multitude'; Johnson (himself a provincial of humble family) does not hold his imagined common multitude of readers in contempt, but is content to throw his pearls among them, with commercial journalism as the slingshot of truth, as it were. Boswell says:

> He had, indeed, upon all occasions, a great deference for the general opinion: 'A man (said he) who writes a book, thinks himself wiser or wittier than the rest of mankind; he supposes that he can instruct or amuse them, and the publick to whom he appeals, must, after all, be the judges of his pretensions.'[30]

Johnson is not concerned about the character of the reader (seeing the multitude not as swinish, but as the public). He is more concerned about the quality of writing; journalists should take care that what they throw are in fact pearls. To this end, however, regard for the truth is not enough. Journalists must keep faith with the humblest readers too. Johnson includes as part of the duty of a journalist communication *across* the demographic boundaries of class, gender and specialism, creating a 'common' sense out of restricted knowledges for the common reader, generalizing across the whole of society those visions of order which are the subject of journalism, but doing all this with due regard for the readership as well as the truth:

> A Journalist, above most other men, ought to be acquainted with the lower orders of mankind, that he may be able to judge, what will be plain, and what will be obscure; what will require a comment, and what will be apprehended without explanation. He is to consider himself not as writing to students or statesmen alone, but to women, shop-keepers, and artisans, who have little time to bestow upon mental attainments, but desire, upon easy terms, to know how the world goes; who rises, and who falls; who triumphs, and who is defeated.[31]

Here is a Johnson who has allowed a little ambiguity to creep into his own stern rationalist binarism; here the 'desire, upon easy terms, to know' is not desire *opposed* to reason and truth, but is presented as a reasonable demand by the public, which is itself socially pervasive (in eighteenth-century demographic terms). Johnson is at one with Milton, then, in assigning to the *general* public the power of choice, and in Johnson it is clear that the public means the 'reading public', the 'common reader'.

Already, in 1758, the public, deleted from the political stage by Hobbes, has been reconstituted not only into a fiction imagined by those who address it – the anonymous multitude of common readers – but also into a community, if that's the right word, whose relationship with politics is mediated by journalism. 'How the world goes; who rises, and who falls; who triumphs, and who is defeated' is an apt description of political activity, but here it is not a product of politics as such but the textual product of a kind of journalism which can judge, comment and explain it, in easy terms, to non-specialists, throughout society, through visualizations of disorder (rises/falls, triumphs/defeats). The duty of the journalist was to spread enlightenment throughout society, and with it the heliological metaphor of Enlightenment itself. Journalism has already achieved its contemporary purpose, which can be summarized as the production of 'common' sense.

However, as the next chapter will show, Johnson's common reader and journalism's common sense were no sooner imagined than invaded; the public domain of the common reader suffered a *coup d'état* from 'above', and a secessionist insurrection from 'below', simultaneously.

COMMON SENSE
Universal v. adversarial journalism

From readership to leadership

Samuel Johnson established an enduring set of criteria by which the social 'duty' of journalism could be understood as the provision of truth for the common reader, but matters were already afoot which would shatter the universalism and order of this Johnsonian vision once and for all. Neither truth nor a common readership was to survive the modernizing American, French and Industrial Revolutions intact, even though it was during these events that such innovations as the notions of *universal* truth and a *general* public underwent a period of vigorous self-invention and social promotion. The Milton/Johnson vision of the truth-seeking public was a secularized and updated version of the medieval Catholic concept of the laity, till then the largest 'imagined community' ever imagined, an all-inclusive, indiscriminate mixture of populations, indifferent to social hierarchies and bigger than nations, empires or language groups.

Such a model in its papist form was of course anathema to post-Reformation protestants like Milton and Johnson, but between them they hit on the perfect alternative in the guise of the common reader in search not of divine but of virginal truth. Their work marks an increase in the scope of the demographically imaginable, from the restricted readerships of 'high' society and its clerical/literary allies, right up to national populations and beyond. This process did not reach its high-water mark until 1956, 300 years after Milton, 200 years after Johnson, but in direct line of succession to their vision of a national popular citizen readership. That mark is Winston Churchill's *A History of the English-speaking Peoples*.[1] It is worth noting that a connection between Churchill's writing and Samuel Johnson's was made explicit in the early reviews of this history; fellow-historian Sir Arthur Bryant wrote in the *Sunday Times* that 'Sir Winston ranges the centuries with a flowing Johnsonian grace that holds the reader spellbound';[2] a style which is praised for its imagined, magical, Johnsonian effect on readership.

Churchill's title and theme explicitly call into being a global community based on the British Empire or Commonwealth (Churchill uses these terms interchangeably) together with the USA. It ought to be noted, however, that the diversity of varieties, dialects and accents of English speech are only unified, if at all, at the level of writing, so what actually connects Churchill's 'English-speaking peoples' is not speaking but publishing, and what he is invoking is a *readership*; he addresses his remarks to the Johnsonian 'common reader', and his cause is that of universalism and order, literally the globalization of English readership:

> we [the USA and the British Empire in two world wars] have become more conscious of our common duty to the human race. Language, law, and the processes by which we have come into being, already afforded a unique foundation for drawing together and portraying a concerted task. I thought [in the 1930s] . . . that such a unity might well notably influence the destiny of the world. Certainly I do not feel that the need for this has diminished in any way. . . . It is in the hope that contemplation of the trials and tribulations of our fore-fathers may not only fortify the English-speaking peoples of today, but also play some small part in uniting the whole world, that I present this account.[3]

Churchill writes as 'one not without some experience of historical and violent events in our own time';[4] his 'account' is presented as having a practical political impact. Thus his vision of an international community united by speech (English), writing (history) and order (law), whose 'common duty to the human race' includes a part in 'uniting the whole world', is a truly *catholic* statement of the *power of readership*; the Churchillian English-reading peoples become an imagined political con-stituency whose interests are visualized not only as internally 'common' but also as coincident with those of the human species, imagined as a unit.

Churchill's vision is not straightforwardly imperialist but it is totalizing – it *desires* the kind of universal truth and general public imagined by Milton and Johnson, showing the persistence in public writing over several centuries of the ultimate 'figure of speech' – a secular laity of common readers which is in principle the same size as the 'human race'. It is also noteworthy that Churchill's chosen genre is history, whose 'first law', according to Dr Johnson, is the 'Obligation to tell Truth',[5] and whose junior branch is journalism, which happened to be Winston Churchill's first profession. According to a memorial biography issued to mark his death in 1965 (and given to me in that year as a birthday present by my grandmother), Churchill combined journalism with military training and action; his first journalistic commissions were from the *Daily Graphic* in 1895 to cover a rebellion in Cuba, the *Allahabad Pioneer* and the *Daily Telegraph* to cover a 'punitive campaign' in India in 1897, the *Morning Post* to cover a campaign in the Sudan in 1898 (culminating in the Battle of Omdurman against the Dervishes in which he played an active military role). He was also commissioned by the *Morning Post* to cover the Boer War in South Africa in 1899, for which, having resigned his military commission in order to write two books based on the Indian and Sudan campaigns and to contest his first parliamentary election (unsuccessfully, for the seat of Oldham), he was 'offered the highest rate of pay ever given, up to that time, to a British war correspondent'. Of his first assignment in 1895 the biography has this to say: 'it initiated him into a practice of journalism which was ultimately to open to him a royal road . . . into national fame and public service'.[6] In other words, Winston Churchill himself stands as an example of the contemporary politics of pictures; a man whose public appeal is based on journalism, whose political career did not arise from imperial military service as such but from his own visualizations of it for a readership which is, only then, capable of being mobilized as a constituency.

From virgin to Virginia

But universal truth and the general public were neither universal nor general by the time Churchill came on the scene at the end of the nineteenth century; both truth and public were *adversarial*, so it is perhaps not inappropriate that Churchill's political career was founded on a style of journalism that held a revolver in the pen-hand. The universalism and order of Dr Johnson's common readership had been fragmented almost as soon as it was invented, tested to destruction by the events it was intended to describe if not control. Thus, the American Revolution fragmented the nascent 'English-speaking peoples' into two hemispheres. At the same time, however, that revolution also affords one of the clearest examples of the power of a Milton–Johnson–Churchill theory of journalism, showing just what could be done by addressing argumentation to a pervasive anonymous multitude of common readers, united across social divisions, in order for them to decide and act on the resulting truth for themselves.

The example, whose very title indicates the struggle over the meaning of 'common', was Tom Paine's pamphlet *Common Sense*, published in Philadelphia in January 1776.[7] 'Common' sense was suddenly revealed not to be 'common' to all in a given political readership, but adversarial, for the argument of *Common Sense*, written by an immigrant from the Old Country where Dr Johnson was still holding court as the 'great Cham of Literature', was against reconciliation with the constituted government of Britain, and for the independence of the American colonies.

Its publication was a sensation, its effect electrifying, its impact pervasive. *Common Sense* succeeded in uniting the general public of the colonies, transforming a minority in favour of independence in 1775 (estimated at perhaps as low as a third) into a decisive majority in 1776 among the entire community of colonists, including delegates to the Continental Congress meeting in Philadelphia. On 7 June 1776 a proposal was moved, by Richard Henry Lee on behalf of the colony of Virginia, to the effect that 'these united colonies are, and of right ought to be, free and independent states';[8] a proposal that neatly combined the incommensurate concepts of unity and fragmentation (but which was immortalized in the name of a country, which has itself been credited to Paine, even though 'united' and 'states' are strictly speaking mutually exclusive, contradictory terms). The proposal was eventually adopted a month later in the form of the Declaration of Independence of 4 July 1776.

Nothing like Paine's journalism had been seen before, not because of his arguments but because of *Common Sense*'s social reach. It 'burst from the press with an effect which has rarely been produced by types and papers in any age or country', according to one contemporary, an effect which can be gauged by its circulation – it sold 120,000 copies in the first three months of 1776, and perhaps half a million copies from 56 editions in that year alone, within a community of 1.6 million. Bearing in mind that each copy would typically be read by or to a household, not by an individual, this is the sort of audience for a single text that not even popular television can match today. *Common Sense* was 'written in a language that could be understood by any literate colonist, whether simple farmer or plain mechanic' – and not only *could* it be understood, it seems that it actually *was*. Contemporary comments on it, from Virginia to Massachusetts, from a New York 'committee of mechanics' to George Washington, credited it with turning public sentiment around: '*Common Sense* . . . is read to all ranks, and as many as read, so many became converted; though perhaps the hour before were most violent against the idea of independence.'[9]

Benjamin Franklin described its effect as 'prodigious'. Thomas Paine himself later wrote that 'the success it met with was beyond anything since the invention of printing',[10] and a later historian, George Macaulay Trevelyan, summed up its impact thus:

> It would be difficult to name any human composition which has had an effect at once so instant, so extended and so lasting. . . . It was pirated, parodied and imitated, and translated into the languages of every country where the new republic had well-wishers. It worked nothing short of miracles and turned Tories into Whigs.[11]

These are large claims; the transformation of Tories into Whigs is miracle enough, but to place *Common Sense* above 'any human composition' is to do honour not so much to the pamphlet itself as to its readership (and its timing); *Common Sense* demonstrated that journalism could mobilize a community (which it identifies spuriously but grandly with a continent) in ways that the official representative organization of politics could not match. Although the American colonies were colonies, they were *de facto* self-governing by this time and boasted a much higher participation rate from their citizens than did British politics at home. But still, it took the extension of readership to the whole community – that literal kind of 'common' sense – to unify their purpose at a crucial moment.

A sign that despite its pervasiveness *Common Sense* was nevertheless adversarial, not only in the sense of opposing to each other the nations of Britain and America but also in terms of its impression of truthfulness, is that it was soon answered by another pamphlet that deplored its stinging criticisms of the British (and hence colonial) constitution. Paine's adversary James Chalmers denounced *Common Sense* as 'an insult to our understanding', and claimed that the British constitution, 'with all its imperfections, is, and ever will be, the pride and envy of mankind', whereas with Paine's egalitarian proposals, abolishing king and aristocracy, 'our constitution would immediately degenerate into democracy'.[12] The name of this counterblast to *Common Sense* was . . . *Plain Truth*.

But, as everyone knows, it was another kind of truth that prevailed, and the 'truths' which the Declaration of Independence 'hold to be self-evident' were Painite. Placing the Americans as 'one people' in the general 'course of human events', and envisaging nationhood as arising from 'Laws of Nature',[13] the Declaration's appeal to unity, eternity and nature is a direct echo of *Common Sense*. Paine writes of the War of Independence as *continental* in scope: ''Tis not the affair of a city, a country, a province, or a kingdom, but of a continent'; as *eternal*: ''tis not the concern of a day, a year, or an age; posterity . . . will be more or less affected, even to the end of time, by the proceedings now'; and as necessitated by *nature*: 'there is something very absurd, in supposing a continent to be perpetually governed by an island. In no instance hath nature made the satellite larger than its primary planet, and as England and America, with respect to each other, reverses the common order of nature, it is evident they belong to different systems.' So, for Tom Paine, 'it is repugnant to reason, to the universal order of things, to all examples from former ages, to suppose, that this continent can longer remain subject to any external power'.[14]

With reason, eternity and universal order on his side, Paine clinches his adversarial argument with an appeal to desire, love and affection, which he places *within* the dictates of nature:

> There are injuries which nature cannot forgive; she would cease to be nature if she did. As well can the lover forgive the ravisher of his mistress, as the continent forgive the murders of Britain. . . . The social compact would dissolve, and justice be extirpated [from] the earth . . . were we callous to the touches of affection. . . . O ye that love mankind! Ye that dare oppose, not only the tyranny, but the tyrant, stand forth! Every spot of the old world is over-run with oppression. Freedom hath been hunted round the globe. . . . O! Receive the fugitive, and prepare in time an asylum for mankind.[15]

And so, like Milton, Paine visualizes the outcome of reason not as logical but as *desirable*, putting the final appeal to individual action in the guise of a man's 'natural' response to the rape and murder of his spouse; the lover becomes the agent and upholder of what makes nature nature. Milton's 'virgin' Truth has matured into Paine's 'mistress' Freedom. The sexualization of political language crops up again and again from Milton to the Melbourne *Truth*, as we shall see, but it is perhaps worth noting here that while 'our side' in this struggle was visualized by Paine as the protector of a mistress (freedom) from ravishment, 'their side' was characterized not only as the ravisher, i.e. rapist, but also, gender-bendingly, as another kind of mistress: Britain was described (not by Paine) as 'a vile imposter – an old abandoned prostitute – a robber, a murderer . . . a Jezebel'.[16]

The descent from the sublime to the familial is the same from Milton to Paine, and it is repeated (without the metaphors of sexual violence) in the Declaration of Independence, which makes a Painite move from universal abstractions to the individual's 'unalienable rights' to 'life, liberty, and the pursuit of happiness', which it was the business of government to secure. Like Paine, the Declaration was suspicious of government on principle, seeing it as a necessary evil, apt to 'become destructive' of the ends it is instituted to pursue; hence 'it is the right of the people to alter or to abolish it, and to institute new government'.[17] This is a direct echo of Paine's opening position in *Common Sense*:

> Society in every state is a blessing, but government even in its best state is but a necessary evil; in its worst state an intolerable one. . . . Government, like dress, is the badge of lost innocence; the palaces of kings are built on the ruins of the bowers of paradise. . . . *Wherefore*, security being the true design and end of government, it unanswerably follows that whatever *form* thereof appears most likely to ensure it to us, with the least expence and greatest benefit, is preferable to all others.[18]

For Paine, as for the Declaration of Independence, it unanswerably follows that when government is deemed intolerable by the governed, it must be transformed, which places sovereignty in the preferences of the populace.

Paine's work is important not because the founding document of the US constitution borrowed his ideas (the ideas are similar because Paine and Jefferson shared the same 'common sense'); what is special about Paine is his success in communicating those ideas to the populace whose rights were proclaimed in the Declaration, and whose preferences thenceforth had to be gauged, guided and governed.

Universalism v. adversarialism: Paine and anguish

At the very moment when a visualization of order derived from popular journalism was finding its way into the first-ever written constitution of a

New World, using truth as its self-evident pre-text, the concept of 'common' truth on which it was all based was, paradoxically, doomed. Henceforth, truth itself was restricted by adversarial binarism; opposing truths vied for popular assent, via the media of popular journalism, using the discursive resources of common sense. The common people, in the empirical form of popular readerships, were themselves constituted not as 'common humanity' but as 'we' identities in opposition to one or more 'they' outsiders.

However, Johnsonian universalist journalism continued as a discourse, even though it did not survive the eighteenth-century fragmentation of its (potential) social community. That is, the Johnsonian *vision* of a common readership united across political, demographic and economic divisions, participating in the production of truth by the exercise of reason, and connected to the political domain by the communicative apparatus of journalism, remained and is still active as an ideology, together with its apparatus of facticity, impartiality, retraction and popularization. But the kind of *community* imagined by Johnson, in which the pervasive anonymous multitudes judge for themselves the trustworthiness of journalism and its stories, was soon dismembered, disunited, if it ever existed beyond Johnson's own desire.

Pretty soon there was not one but at least two common readerships – popular and respectable – created and sustained by different conceptions of what constitutes the community, antagonistic to each other but both aspiring to social pervasion, and soon there were also different conceptions of truth which entailed different relationships between writers, journals and readers. Popular instruction also split into passive and active pedagogies; one version sought to instruct the populace in truths already decided upon, the other sought to broadcast the arguments and knowledges, theories and visions, which would not only teach their public but also mobilize it to action. Truth could not survive such oppositions; it was no longer possible to see it as Milton had done (in place of its medieval guarantor, God) as the outcome of public forensic argumentation with a claim on all, because after Johnson truth became not an outcome of adversarial *arguments* but a property of adversarial *parties*.

Tom Paine again exemplifies the transformation from universalism to adversarialism. After some years in America he returned to Europe where he played a significant role in the French Revolution and in the emerging class conflict in Britain arising from the Industrial Revolution. Johnson's 'duty of a journalist', and his own journalism, were both addressed to a common reader, but their social reach was restricted by the then scope of active participation in literate culture, which meant in effect that Johnson's commitment to the 'lower orders' of 'women, shopkeepers and artisans' was *intra-class* propaganda not *inter-class* communication (in practice he wrote about them, or even for them, rather than directly to them).

170

Johnson, in short, was a prescient theorist but not a practitioner of the popular-national as a readership community, united by journalism's societal visions of order. The creation of actual readers, in prodigious numbers, was not the achievement of Johnsonian universalist journalism, but that of the so-called 'pauper press' of the turn of the nineteenth century, an adversarialist journalism spurred into existence, at least in part, by Tom Paine's *Rights of Man* (1791).

The 'pauper press' was as distinct from the 'respectable' press in Britain at the end of the eighteenth century as America was distinct from Britain, and the difference between them was in its own (class) terms a 'war of independence'. The respectable press was at this time developing an interestingly ambiguous ideology. In terms of content and commentary it was both universalist and oppositional; that is, it began to find ways to attach abstract notions of truth to the reporting of news, which notions it could then use, as necessary, to oppose the government of the day or a given policy. However, the respectable press was not universalist in readership: it inherited from the coffee-house culture of the eighteenth century a model of public participation in politics that restricted its readership, and the scope of its understanding of public affairs, to what such a clientele could be presumed to find interesting and worthy of discussion. The archetype of this kind of journalism is *The Times*, launched under the (universalist) title of the *Daily Universal Register* on New Year's Day 1785, with the help of a grant of £300 a year from the government, by a printer, John Walter I, from his home in Printing House Square (where it remained for two centuries, until shifted to Wapping by a subsequent owner, Rupert Murdoch). As the 50,000th issue of *The Times* ruefully noted, it was not altogether an auspicious beginning:

> The first issue of the paper was not too well received. The news hawkers of the day apparently were not over-anxious to offer their coffee house clients a new sheet while eight other morning papers were already available. Before the change of title [three years later], the paper suffered innumerable casualties, and the denunciation of the morals and behaviour of the Royal Dukes by John Walter I led to his imprisonment.[19]

Under the editorship of John Walter II (1803), however, *The Times* became a commercial success and developed a stance of independence from government, while remaining steadily supportive of established interests in general. Thus it spoke out against the Peterloo massacre in 1819 (one of the formative events in the creation of working-class consciousness and the Labour movement), and it sided with the reformers in the great agitation for parliamentary reform in 1832, being dubbed 'The Thunderer' for its critical editorial stance, which at least once, later in the century during the Crimean War (1855), brought down a government.

171

The 'respectable' press was, then, caught up with the governmental affairs of the nation, but not necessarily with the government of the day. Its readership was small and politically active; *The Times* printed 2,000 copies a day in 1800, rising to 7,000 a day after the introduction of the first steam press in 1817. However, by comparison, the readership created by the radical press in the same period was of a different order, and the political activism it promoted among the unenfranchised was different in kind. The English pauper press began to develop in the wake of the libertarian ideas associated with the French Revolution – reason, enlightenment, equality, liberty – grafted on to the experience (which France had not had) of the accelerating Industrial Revolution. In this potent mixture Tom Paine's *Rights of Man* ignited a spark in 1791; in that year alone, despite its cover price of 3 shillings, the book sold 50,000 copies. Paine authorized cheap editions (as low as 6d.), and within three years *Rights of Man* had sold 200,000 copies, rising to perhaps 1.5 million before his death in 1809.[20] It became a manifesto for subsequent political radicals, who distributed its message in numbers, and at a price, that brought its political theory within the reach of the labourers, servants, artisans, industrial and agricultural workers who had hitherto been excluded from the constitution, most famously by Edmund Burke. He referred to them as the 'swinish multitude', and in the light of the discussion of learning in Chapter 5 it is noteworthy that he made this dehumanizing remark in relation to *knowledge*: 'Learning will be cast into the mire, and trodden down under the hoofs of a swinish multitude', with their 'muddy understandings'.[21]

The most celebrated radical to take up the cause of this multitude, and to devote himself to the Painite task of educating its political understandings, was William Cobbett. Cobbett clearly saw himself as Paine's intellectual heir, even going to the trouble, ten years after Paine's death in 1809, of exhuming his hero's body. The idea was to rescue him from his 'obscure grave on an open and disregarded bit of land' in New Rochelle outside New York, and return the remains to Britain for a suitably honoured reburial. Unfortunately, somewhere between the port of Liverpool and the City of London, Cobbett lost the bones.[22] Cobbett was much more successful with his Painite journalism, however. His *Political Register* (1802–35) was among the most influential of the pauper press, selling for 2d. and reaching estimated sales of between 44,000 and 60,000 copies weekly. His *Address to the Journeymen and Labourers* (1816) sold up to 200,000 copies, showing how Paine's *Rights* should be understood by the 'productive classes':

> The unfortunate journeyman and labourers and their families have a *right*, they have a *just claim* to relief from the purses of the rich. For, there can exist no riches and no resources which they, by their labour, have not *assisted to create*.

172

It is clear from this kind of rhetoric that while the pauper press espoused the art of adversarial journalism, building circulations that were an astonishment to onlookers, it was not in the business of what would nowadays pass for 'news'. The respectable press established very early some of the staples of news coverage, so that a copy of *Fog's Weekly Journal* from 1736, as detailed in the last chapter, contains easily recognizable news categories, stories, advertisements and news values (it's only the layout and lack of pictures that looks archaic). But the coffee-house press was not responsible for the social suffusion of journalism. This was achieved not because of a popular hunger for news but because of a popular agitation for enfranchisement, parliamentary reform and, eventually, fully self-conscious working-class politics. Thus, by 1801, the Tory *Anti-Jacobin Review* opposed newspapers not for their news but for their universality:

> We have long considered the establishment of newspapers in this country as a misfortune to be regretted; but, since their influence has become predominant by the universality of their circulation, we regard it as a calamity most deeply to be deplored.

So a clear split is already institutionalized by the end of the eighteenth century between a 'universalist' mode of journalism with a restricted readership, and an adversarialist mode of journalism with a 'universal' readership.

Mummery and monuments, idiots and cheats

The pauper press was not just creating and sustaining a readership bigger than anything previously imagined, it was doing so on the basis of a political pedagogy, teaching that readership some home truths. Two of the most celebrated 'pauper' publishers, after Tom Paine and William Cobbet, were Richard Carlile and Henry Hetherington, both active in the period leading up to the Reform Bill of 1832, and beyond that to the Chartist movement of the 1830s and 1840s. Like John Walter I, Richard Carlile fell foul of the law, but where Walter's *Times* opted for what might be called critical accommodation, Carlile's project was much more ambitious, much more radical; he was among those for whom *publication* meant *creation of a public*, which itself entailed *republican* politics. Carlile was an individualist, like Paine and Cobbett before him, opposed to 'clubs' (political parties) and 'association' (unions); in fact his position was straightforwardly Miltonic, believing in knowledge as the prerequisite of rationality, and therefore in freedom of knowledge as the primary means to political justice. He set about providing that knowledge; he republished several of Tom Paine's banned works, *Common Sense, The Rights of Man* and the anti-clerical *The Age of Reason* in 1817–18, and went on to produce the *Republican* (1819–26). Naturally Carlile's knowledge was the government's sedition; Carlile was to spend a total of nine and a half years in prison, suffer the loss of £10,000 in confiscated stock and £3,000 in confiscated bail, the imprisonment of his sister Jane and the prosecution of his wife, which misfortune, however, he saw as fuel for the fire:

> I hear from London that the prosecution of Mrs Carlile produces just the same effect as my prosecution did – it quadruples the sales of all her publications. . . . A prosecution becomes the grand impetus for reading a particular book, and in the language of Paine I say again: may every good book be prosecuted.

Despite his individualist unease about organized labour politics, but perhaps because of his individual heroism and that of his family, Carlile attracted to himself an organization of what was called 'General Carlile's Corps': volunteer vendors, drawn from the swinish multitude itself, who helped distribute and sell his publications across the country, including not just printers and shopkeepers but a cropper, a shoemaker, a weaver, a singer, a hatter and a carter, amounting at times to 150 people who between them notched up over 200 years of imprisonment for selling radical publications and defending the liberty of Carlile's press. Such was their contribution to Carlile's 'grand impetus': to 'quadruple the sales' and universalize the readership of a free press.

The increasing organization of radical readerships was taken a stage further by Henry Hetherington, one of Carlile's shopmen, whose *Poor Man's Guardian*, launched in 1830, was the most important of the pauper press. Hetherington and his vendors were also imprisoned, but still the *Poor Man's Guardian* achieved a circulation of 12,000 to 16,000 during 1830–4, with a readership that may have exceeded this number up to twenty-fold (i.e. up to 300,000 readers), given that such papers were often circulated in workplaces, shops, public houses and among families. Hetherington aligned the *Poor Man's Guardian* with the newly formed National Union of the Working Classes and Others. He refused to pay stamp duty (whose function was to price such papers as his beyond the reach of their intended readership); the *Poor Man's Guardian* went out at 1d. instead of the 7½d. or 8d. charged for a stamped paper. On its masthead, where the official imprint of stamp duty should have appeared, was a device showing a printing press over the slogan KNOWLEDGE IS POWER. Just in case of misunderstanding, Hetherington declared that the *Poor Man's Guardian* was 'published in Defiance of the Law, to try the Power of Right against Might'. Its launch editorial declared:

> It is the cause of the *rabble* we advocate, the poor, the suffering, the industrious, the productive classes. . . . We will teach this rabble their power – we will teach them that they are your master, instead of being your slaves.

In fact, the pauper press, especially the 'great unstamped' periodicals of the 1830s (of which there were over 560), were teachers of political theory at a time of unprecedented political agitation, culminating in the Reform Bill of 1832.

However, although the 'industrious, the productive classes' were active in the agitation, they were not enfranchised in the Act; reform was limited to about 250,000 new voters – men of property, still only one in six of the adult male population, and no women, making an estimated total electorate of 800,000 people.[23] However radical it may have seemed to its Tory opponents, the Reform Bill of 1832 was a continuation of the representational policy which in 1776 had led directly to the loss of America. In 1766 the Lord Chief Justice, Lord Mansfield, told the House of Lords how the 'greatest part of the people of England are represented':

among nine millions . . . there are eight which have no vote in electing members of Parliament. . . . A member of Parliament chosen for any borough represents not only the constituents and inhabitants of that particular place, but he represents . . . all the other commons of this land, and all the inhabitants of all the colonies and dominions of Great Britain.[24]

What was good enough for the member for the rotten or pocket borough of Old Sarum (population nil), was thought to be good enough for the American colonies and the inhabitants of industrial Manchester (representation nil) because this model of representation did not follow the arithmetical logic of democracy, but instead held to the idea that the *parliament* represents the whole *population*, whether they vote or not (so they don't need a vote).

In opposing the reform agitation of 1830 the outgoing Tory Prime Minister, the Duke of Wellington, defended the traditional view:

I have never read or heard of any measure . . . which can in any degree satisfy my mind that the state of the representation can be improved. . . . The representation of the people at present contains a large body of the property of the country, and in which the landed interests have a preponderating influence. Under these circumstances I am not prepared to bring forward any measure of the description alluded to.[25]

The Reform Bill increased the proportion of the electorate from one in nine to one in six, and the 'preponderating influence' of property in the House of Commons, and land in the House of Lords, remained intact. Nevertheless the measure was fought tooth and nail by the Tories and was defeated several times in the Lords, before eventually passing under a threat to create a flood of Whig peers to ensure its passage. Given what appeared to some as revolutionary agitation in favour of the Bill up and down the country, it is perhaps surprising to find that it was also opposed by the *Poor Man's Guardian*. In 1831 in its columns a handloom weaver addressed a letter to 'the Working People of England':

> People who live by plunder will always tell you to be submissive to thieves. To talk of *representation*, in any shape, being of any use to the people, is sheer nonsense, unless the people have a House of working men, and represent themselves. Those who make the laws now, and are intended, by the reform bill, to make them in the future, all live by profits of one sort or another. They will, therefore, no matter who elect them, or how often they are elected, always make the laws to raise profits and keep down the price of labour. Representation, therefore, by a different body of people to those who are represented, or whose interests are opposed to theirs, is a mockery, and those who persuade the people to the contrary are either idiots or cheats.

Despite echoes of the American Revolution, this position is far removed from Tom Paine's; his common sense was dedicated to getting representation out of the hands of 'a different body of people to those who are represented', certainly, but there's no word of the price of labour in *Common Sense*, or of profit, or that property might put the representatives in opposition to those whom they represent. The Industrial Revolution had spawned both capital and labour, but it was only now that their interests were seen as adversarial.

Thus, while the ascendant capitalist class was enfranchised in 1832, the pauper press was still struggling for *representation* of another kind. Still hounded by prosecutions for seditious and criminal libel, blasphemy, conspiracy and debt, they continued to find ways to represent the 'industrious, productive classes' in print. It was illegal to publish 'news, intelligence, occurrences and remarks and observations thereon tending to excite hatred and contempt of the government and constitution of this country as by law established', and steadily increasing levels of stamp duty on newspapers were designed to price the pauper press out of existence. The response was varied: some publishers like Cobbett and Carlile turned their newspapers into pamphlets, some like Hetherington defied the law openly, and one, Henry Berthold, tried to avoid the tax by contending that his product was not a newspaper because it contained no *paper*. In 1831 he issued the *Political Handkerchief*, printed on calico, which advised its readers:

> Your wives and daughters may become moving monuments of political knowledge. One shall be dressed in a description of kingcraft, another in a description of priestcraft, a third in a description of lordcraft. . . . The nakedness of mankind shall be covered both as to body and mind.

And in an early move to encourage recycling, Berthold advised thrifty customers that when the ink wore off they could return their *Political Handkerchiefs* for reprinting with new political knowledge. Getting in on the act, Richard Carlile also issued a *Coronation Handkerchief* on the day of William IV's coronation in 1831, for onlookers to wear as they watched the pomp. This is what Carlile put on, if not in, the heads of his readers:

> This coronation is an entire mummery, and a disgrace to the growing knowledge of the present time. . . . It is a festival at which the king, the priests, and the lords, celebrate their triumph over a conquered and degraded people . . . and send the bill of fifty thousand pounds to the people to be paid by them for their own degradation. . . . All the enjoyments of life arise from the productions of human labour; and these will be all the stronger, and all the better, as they are more diffused, and as they are left, as far as is desired, in the hands that produce them. They who labour should be the masters. . . . This is the rationale of society, and this will lead us all to exclaim, DOWN WITH KINGS, WITH PRIESTS, AND WITH LORDS.

From popular-radical to popular-commercial

The rationale of society was working against the pauper press. In 1833 Henry Hetherington could just about break even on sales of the *Poor Man's Guardian* of 3,000; his costs were £14 for 10,000 copies – paper £8, composing and printing £4 10s., ink, hire of type and placards £1 10s. If he sold 1,000 copies over the counter and 9,000 to vendors at a wholesale price of 13 copies for 8d., Hetherington's profit would be £24. The *Poor Man's Guardian* did not carry advertising, and Hetherington did not pay regular wages to his editors. The paper was printed on Stanhope presses, which cost £30 each.

However, it was Hetherington himself who showed how things were to change from these undercapitalized but self-sufficient beginnings. In 1834 he bought a Napier press. At 350 guineas, the machine was more than ten times the cost of a Stanhope, but it was capable of printing 2,500 sides of broadsheet an hour, and on it Hetherington began to print his *Twopenny Dispatch* in 1835, having advertised the new paper (with which the *Poor Man's Guardian* was amalgamated) in the following much quoted but deservedly immortal terms:

> It shall abound in Police Intelligence, in Murders, Rapes, Suicides, Burnings, Maimings, Theatricals, Races, Pugilism, and all manner of 'accidents by flood and field'. In short it will be stuffed with every sort of devilment that will make it sell. . . . Our object is not to make money, but to beat the Government.

In very large measure the pauper press had been a creation of its own readership, which meant that although circulations could be very high they were also tied to what the readership wanted to know about. This very pure form of 'demand' meant that sales fluctuated according to the excitement, crisis or emotion of the moment; Richard Carlile's *Republican* sold 15,000 copies on his arrest, the *Poor Man's Guardian* peaked at 16,000 during May 1832 when the Reform Bill was passed but, despite well-attested reader loyalty, all such papers were essentially ephemeral, likely to decline in circulation or fold altogether, perhaps to be replaced by another short-lived title from the same publisher, sparked into life by another issue, event or controversy.

The radical publishers were in business to 'beat the Government', but their social legacy was not straightforwardly political. There is no doubt that they did beat the government in the struggle for a free press, and all hail to them for that, and the long-term prospects for democratic reform were enhanced by their tireless and pervasive efforts, but such reforms took much longer than any individual radical publisher had time to wait; universal suffrage alone was delayed until 1867 (men) and 1918 (women). Meanwhile what the radical press had achieved was a popular readership for their 'cheap knowledge', and the next stage in the development of journalism was to transform this from intermittent flickerings (and failures) into an *institution*. The stabilization of popular readerships, and their habituation to long-term demand for routine supplies of standardized products, was the achievement of an offshoot of the radical press: Sunday newspapers.

Hetherington's 'every sort of devilment' to sustain circulation was not the first such combination of radical politics and a miscellany of sensational stories; John Cleave's unstamped *Weekly Police Gazette* was launched in 1834 and went on to achieve a circulation of 20,000. These pioneers pulled together the elements of what was to become popular journalism; a broad working-class readership, radical politics, and general news based on stories of crime and disorder. However, during the next phase of journalism, the Chartist decade from 1839 to 1848, two of these three elements were steadily detached from one another – the radical politics from the general news. Representing the former was the great Chartist newspaper, the *Northern Star* (1837–52), founded in Leeds as the champion and voice of Chartism, which was itself the first political movement of an organized working class seeking to represent itself as such. The *Northern Star* was established by public subscription, quickly became profitable, and achieved a circulation of up to 48,000 soon afterwards, becoming the nation's largest circulation newspaper despite its non-metropolitan origin. It dominated the Chartist movement, acting as a national forum (with the help of distribution by the new communications media of railways and the post), in which both regional struggles and sectional ones (i.e. those of different trades) could be seen as part of a larger, class movement. It was an agent in the formation of a national

Figure 7.1 Daguerreotype of the Great Chartist Crowd, 1848– the first picture of politics. *The Sunday Times* from original in the Royal Archive, April 1848. (Windsor Castle. Royal Archives © 1992 Her Majesty the Queen)

working-class consciousness; its editor Feargus O'Connor encouraged readers and supporters to send in reports of their actions from around the country, which had the incidental effect, in the history of journalism itself, of hastening the 'development away from publishing opinion towards reporting news',[26] and making the *Northern Star* the voice of a movement, not of an individual editor–publisher.

Chartism culminated in a huge (but unsuccessful) demonstration in 1848 in London, a rare and spectacular gathering of the urban, industrial public into an Aristotelian polity, assembled in single view of itself on a latter-day agora of its own making (Kennington Common), an occasion seen as historic enough at the time to warrant the taking of what has been claimed as the 'world's first crowd photograph' (Figure 7.1)[27] a daguerreotype by W.E. Kilburn, which was used as the source of a woodcut proto-photo published five days later in the world's first picture magazine, the *Illustrated London News* (15 April 1848). This event not only marks the appearance (literally) of popular democratic politics on the national stage, it also illustrates how thoroughly adversarial the popular and official polities actually were: 'two nations' at the representational as well as the economic level. For the crowd was treated as an external enemy by the government, and its plan to cross the Thames to present its Charter, which bore 2 million signatures, to parliament (which had one million electors), was taken as a declaration of war: the Duke of Wellington commanded a force which barred the entry of the Chartists to Westminster; there were 4,000 policemen on the bridges and along Whitehall, 8,000 soldiers on the Embankment, 1,500 Chelsea Pensioners to hold Battersea and Vauxhall, a dozen gun emplacements in the Royal Mews, and an astonishing 150,000 special constables sworn in as back-up. In a gesture of such perfect allegorical irony that it seems too apposite to be true, the windows of the Foreign Office were blocked to prevent the entry of bullets – using bound copies of *The Times*.[28] By such means was the established, respectable community protected by its own weighty truths from its own internal outsiders, who not surprisingly never made it across the river. The Charter itself was loaded into three cabs and taken to parliament. It called for universal male suffrage, secret ballots, payment for MPs, abolition of the property qualification for MPs, equal electoral districts and annual parliaments. The Kennington crowd quietly dispersed, the Charter was scornfully rejected, although, like many another socialist manifesto, all of its demands except annual parliaments eventually became Tory, even Thatcherite, policy. But Chartism itself couldn't wait for its sensible programme to be recognized as such by respectable hotheads from Finchley, and the movement soon fizzled out.

The time had come for a parting of the ways between popular-radical and popular-commercial. The political lesson of Chartism, both as a movement and as a failure, was simple: *organization*. Ever since, the specialist journals have concentrated on an organizing role for themselves, seeking both to encourage and supply it. Radical journalism was increasingly characterized by a retreat from the socially pervasive popular press it had founded towards a concentration on centralized party control mechanisms. Meanwhile, the vast popular readerships generated in the heat of emancipatory politics were still readerships, available for *disorganization*, as it were, into the atomized equality of a market.

Sunday newspapers, the bridge between organized radicalism and commercial populism, had already been launched – *Lloyd's Weekly News* in 1842 and the *News of the World* in 1843 – and both soon achieved massive circulations. The *Northern Star* declined in popularity, and was superseded by the most radical of the new Sunday papers, *Reynold's Newspaper*, founded in 1850. By 1854 the *News of the World* sold 109,000 copies a week, making it the world's largest newspaper at the time, a distinction it has repeated more than once in the twentieth century. It is now owned by Rupert Murdoch. *Lloyd's Weekly News* was the most successful newspaper during the latter part of the nineteenth century, reaching a circulation of over a million in 1896. It too survived into the twentieth century, as did *Reynold's News*, which had by then specialized into the paper of the Co-operative movement.

These three Sunday papers – *Lloyd's, Reynold's* and the *News of the World* – were all launched within the tradition of the pauper press, but they laid the foundation for the quite different 'mass' media, where the original means (social pervasion) became an end in itself. The *News of the World* proclaimed as much in its opening editorial (1 October 1843): 'It is only by a very extensive circulation that the proprietors can be compensated for the outlay of a large capital in this novel and original undertaking'.[29] Capital investment and 'very extensive circulation' were certainly novel priorities in 1842, but that was the shape of things to come, and in the process the steady dissociation between radical, organized, self-conscious class politics on the one hand, and commercial papers maximizing their readership by means of Hetheringtonian devilment on the other hand, became more and more pronounced. By the end of the century, capital investment, audience maximization and sensational journalism were so entrenched that their previous common cause with the pauper press would be hard to credit. But truth is stranger than fiction.

From leadership to readership

Popular journalism began as the 'mighty auxiliary' in the battle for democratic reform and self-representation by the 'labouring classes', as *The Charter* ('ESTABLISHED BY THE WORKING CLASSES') put it in 1839. Such journalism could not have been more adversarial, though the readership it established was approaching universality by the end of the nineteenth century.

The change that had occurred is perhaps measured by returning to the figure of the soldier–journalist Winston Churchill, and his successful use of the 'mighty auxiliary' of the press as a weapon for his own counter-revolutionary journalism and political advancement. His stories as a war correspondent made his own name and promoted imperial expansion as a kind of true-life adventure in the manner of Ballantyne's *Miscellany*. Here's the young aristocrat, holding his commission from the *Morning Post* in one hand and his revolver in the other, pushing into alien dangers in South America, India and South Africa, for the benefit of the cheering readers back home. Churchill's 'fantastically dramatic' escape from captivity in the Boer War 'is one of those true stories which are stranger than fiction', says his popular biographer: 'Small wonder if the British public, crestfallen with the reverses their arms were suffering at the moment, went wild with delight over this gay young champion whose courage, resource and good luck restored their national self confidence and seemed a pledge for victory.'[30]

By the beginning of the twentieth century it was possible, through the global operations of the British Empire, to imagine adversarial truth and an adversarial community as having universalist aspirations, and to claim popular journalism as an ally for imperial war aims without any reference to that journalism's own rebellious and democratic past. Small wonder that in the First World War, which Churchill entered as a Cabinet Minister, press barons like Beaverbrook and Northcliffe were active in producing and disseminating official propaganda. Times had changed; the use of the penny press to educate and democratize the general public had come a long way since the great unstamped of the 1830s. The government, the respectable press and the popular press became one and the same thing in the crucible of war; Lord Northcliffe was the same Alfred Harmsworth who founded the populist-imperialist *Daily Mail* in 1896, going on to buy *The Times*, whose price he dropped to a symbolically democratic penny in 1914, before becoming the Director of Propaganda in Enemy Countries (an official appointment he accepted instead of taking a ministerial post in what he saw as a 'wobbly' government).[31] From this perspective, he felt able to deliver himself of this opinion:

> You cannot carry on this war in the dark. No people in ignorance of the truth will consent to make the tremendous sacrifices which are going to be required. Journalists are more important to the winning of the war than generals.[32]

The revolver of truth was by now well and truly turned against its own manufacturers. It was nearly time for a little Russian roulette.

8

JOURNALISM IN A
POST-TRUTH SOCIETY
The sexualization of the body politic

'Read that then, said the Governor, pointing to a Picture'[1]

A family transported

The twentieth century inaugurated a new phase in journalism, a new chapter in the history of looking. The education of the population turned from *democratization* to *domestication*. The editors of the day went in for popular instruction, reconfiguring their mass readership from class to family. They wrote not for their peers, as the organic intellectuals of the pauper press had done; now, readerships were divided along class, not community lines, with the new generation of literates produced by the establishment of universal elementary schooling in 1870 forming a new market for simple, home truths. Journalists themselves were taught that they were 'writing for the meanest intelligence', as Kennedy Jones, one of Lord Northcliffe's senior editors, reminded his staff in 1919.[2]

Jones also wrote that the *Daily Mail*'s services to imperialism could be compared with Kipling's, a claim clearly designed to add lustre to the *Mail*, but which equally clearly shows how important to the idea of empire was the fact of readership; common readers on a global scale united imaginatively and politically by what they read, with literature and the popular picture press aligned in the same cause. Thus twentieth-century reading is not best understood as a solitary, individual, critical-rational, aesthetic, appreciative act; the traditional implied reader of literary criticism is not typical and does not describe what twentieth-century reading was for. Instead, reading may better be understood as a means for communalization, and both journalism and literature as technologies of society, bringing back together the classical attributes of politics – drama (performance), didactics (pedagogy), and democracy (participation) – on a global scale, and for the 'meanest intelligence', bearing in mind that literary Nobel laureates (Kipling, and later Churchill too) could and did reach that same constituency as the picture papers. The politics of participation and persuasion, of popular instruction and social drama, moved decisively into the realms of readership, and readers participated in the imaginary agora, the place of publicity, whenever they looked at the paper. The public domain was relocated into the place of reading – the 'hearth and home' of family, which in turn became the sustaining metaphor of larger sociopolitical unity.

The 'imperial services' performed by the *Daily Mail* (and its ilk) were simply this; the empire existed for its citizens by the act of reading the *Daily Mail*, an act which was consciously organized around hearth and home. Kennedy Jones sought to provide 'family reading' in the *Mail*, but the empire itself was also family – 'kith and kin':

> It was the policy on which we worked throughout the whole of my journalistic career – one Flag, one Empire, one Home. We are a single family. . . . I have always found the British public deeply interested in Imperial affairs. There is a personal bond, a domestic tie, but in Foreign affairs these were absent and, provided there did not happen to be a serious international crisis, it was well-nigh impossible to awaken a lively concern in Continental politics outside a limited circle.[3]

And so popular journalism could make a distinction between imperial and foreign, where the empire was home, despite being on the other side of the planet, and continental Europe was foreign, despite being 21 miles from the English coast, close enough to hear the thump of the big guns on the Western Front. This dismembered political body was united by metaphor: no longer Hobbes's single 'artificiall man' of Leviathan, where the body politic is united in the figure of the sovereign, nor the Aristotelian 'single view' of the assembled citizens, but the 'single family', imagined as coterminous with the global empire upon which the sun was said never to set. This geopolitical fantasy remained active long after the sun had in fact set on the empire, for instance in the Thatcherite world view which could go to war on behalf of 'our' Falkland Islands in the South Atlantic but resist to the last any move to integrate the United Kingdom more closely with the European Community.

Modern popular journalism, reckoning from the foundation of the picture press in the 1890s, located the public domain not in the practice of democratic politics, but in the personal bonds and domestic ties of the populace, as guided by the privatized media of popular instruction themselves. And the 'kith and kin' who settled those far-flung continents returned the compliment. Long before the *Daily Mail*'s populist jingoism came on the scene, the home-grown English adversarial-universal model of journalism had been exported to the colonies:

> In the great struggle of parties, neutrality is folly, and indifference is criminal, a bold and decided advocacy is demanded, that the struggle

may quickly cease, and truth more rapidly prevail. We are not the slave of a party. Nor shall we ever prostrate our principles at the shrine of faction. . . . We lend our energies and bow to no authority, however great, but that of truth.[4]

The great struggle of parties in question here is that between Whig and Tory (Liberal and Conservative), and the writer is John Fairfax of the county of Warwick, whose *Leamington Chronicle* espoused the cause of truth v. faction when it dropped its price from 7d. to 4½d. on the abolition of stamp duty in 1836. Armed with such sentiments and skills, Fairfax emigrated to New South Wales in 1838, and within five years was co-proprietor of the *Sydney Herald*, changing its name in 1842 to the *Sydney Morning Herald*. He thereby founded a family press dynasty which was to last until 1991, when the John Fairfax group, under the control of Warwick Fairfax, went into receivership after the disastrous failure of an ambitious bid to privatize its shareholdings, that is, to take them out of the Stock Exchange and concentrate them in the hands of young Warwick and his mother, Lady Mary Fairfax. The resulting debt bankrupted the company, which was thus forced to put the still-flourishing prestige titles of the *Sydney Morning Herald*, the Melbourne *Age* and the *Financial Review*, up for auction, eventually to be bought by a Canadian-backed group.

The 1836 *Leamington Chronicle*'s brand of universalist truth was 'respectable', i.e. diametrically opposed to that of the Painite and Hetheringtonian pauper press. Theirs was militantly factional, and it gave shape and ideology to an entirely new 'common reader', neither Whig nor Tory, but working class. So Fairfax's appeal to truth over the heads of party, struggle, faction and authority is not an appeal to 'the people' over the heads of 'the politicians', but an attempt to regulate the respectable classes, or, as Fairfax's *Sydney Morning Herald* put it in 1842, on the occasion of the first elections held in New South Wales after convict transportation had ended in 1840:

> Much, very much, depends upon this one question – whether the respectable classes – by which we mean professional gentlemen, merchants, bankers, shopkeepers, and master tradesmen – will come forward . . . or whether, from a sordid devotion to their private affairs, or from cowardly aversion to trouble, they will hold back, and leave the City [Sydney] in the hands of the working classes?[5]

Lest there should be any doubt about it, this truth is based not on common readers, but on property and 'proper influence'. Property, in turn, is based on common sense, and the common sense in question is that which dispossessed Australia's first inhabitants:

> The whites, by their improvements, though they arrived second in point of time, have acquired a right to the soil where they have

185

improved it, which is good in law, equity and common sense, against the whole fraternity of prior black wanderers.[6]

The hands of the working classes, and the lands of the Aborigines, were not part of this commonwealth, and neither were women: in 1837 the (pre-Fairfax) *Sydney Herald* had opposed 'an increase in female immigration, intended to correct the colony's gross imbalance of sexes, on the ground that more women would not ease the shortage of agricultural labour but merely "fill our streets with prostitutes or provide wives for the transported population, bond and free!"'[7]

Just as Dr Johnson's essay 'On the Duty of the Journalist' was being republished for the edification of readers of the *European Magazine* in February 1788 (see Chapter 6), the colonists of Botany Bay were establishing a community which saw its survival as militantly adversarial, dependent upon excluding Johnson's demography of 'women, shopkeepers and artisans', and now Aboriginal people as well, from society, never mind readership. Journalism of this stamp split Johnsonian 'duty' into two: accepting his rhetoric about truth, but forgetting his strictures about the need for journalists to communicate with the common reader, the 'lower orders of mankind', on 'easy terms'. Fairfax's philosophy of journalism, to bow only to the 'authority of truth', as opposed to party, sounds very fine and large, especially if you're trying to attract advertisements and readers from Whigs and Tories alike. But this partisan truth aspired to no higher social unity than a commonwealth of the two parties, and was transported in this form to the farthest reaches of English-speaking colonization. It was an adversarial truth, dedicated explicitly to the political interests of those for whom class, race and gender were *our* class, *our* race, *our* gender, but claiming to speak with the authority of the community as a whole. That is what is meant by 'one Flag, one Empire, one Home'. It's the journalistic equivalent of the eighteenth-century political philosophy that drove the American colonies to rebellion and the pauper press to sedition; the idea that a governing regime, whether of press or parliament, does not need the active participation and consent of those it claims to *represent*. Politically this idea had had its day long before the First World War, but journalistically it has lasted much longer.

Outrages by Apaches

This baggage is still weighing down the institutional juggernaut of contemporary journalism. But since the establishment and globalization of universalist-adversarial, domesticated-imperial journalism, one new element has loomed large – pictures. Now order and its negatives can literally be visualized. Journalism is, in Derrida's terms, a heliological profession, writing the history of the world in terms of metaphors of light, but by the twentieth century heliology had been joined by something much more imperative: *heliography*. Before William Henry Fox Talbot perfected the negative–positive Calotype technique in 1839, the process of obtaining a permanent image by means of the action of light on a prepared surface was known by various names. According to the *Penny Cyclopaedia of the Society for the Diffusion of Useful Knowledge* of 1840, the 'apparatus is named, after its inventor, the Daguerreotype, and the process itself either photogeny, photography, or heliography (sun-drawing)'.[8] It took another fifty years (and the invention of the half-tone) before the press became fully heliographical (and it is noteworthy how many newspapers have named themselves after the sun, as they follow its daily rhythm and vie with it to enlighten the world). The first fully commercial mass circulation popular daily press was also the first picture press: the *Daily Mail, Daily Mirror*, and *Daily Sketch* of the 1890s.

An early opportunity for 'sun drawing' to make its mark in the popular truth media was in connection with an event which has some claim to be the most single newsworthy story of the twentieth century – the Bolshevik Revolution, Wednesday, 7 November 1917.

REVOLT IN PETROGRAD.

Maximalists Seize Telegraph Office, Bank, And Palace.

Civil war is again threatened in Petrograd through the Maximalists' attempt to seize the supreme power.

An armed naval detachment acting under Maximalist orders has occupied the offices of the official Petrograd Telegraph Agency. The Maximalists have also occupied the Central Telegraph Office, the State Bank, and the Marie Palace, where the Preliminary Parliament—the proceedings of which have been suspended in view of the situation—had been sitting.

Street traffic and the general life of the city are practically normal, but outrages by Apaches are reported. The capital is guarded by troops faithful to the Government, but so far no collisions with the Maximalists are reported.

M. Kerensky told the Preliminary Parliament that the Maximalists had clandestinely distributed arms and cartridges to workmen. He considered part of Petrograd's population in revolt and had ordered an inquiry and necessary arrests. "The Government will be killed rather than cease to defend the honour, security and independence of the State."

Australia is to have another conscription referendum.

Figure 8.1 Revolt in Petrograd (*Daily Sketch*)

Here's how it appeared in the family reading of the popular (or more accurately populist) heliographic press: a four-paragraph inside-page story: And so began ten days that shook the world, as seen by the London *Daily Sketch* on 8 November 1917. The (Tory) *Daily Sketch* styled itself 'the premier picture paper', and its lead story that day was appropriately

187

No. 2,704.   LONDON, THURSDAY, NOVEMBER 8, 1917.   [Registered as a Newspaper.]   ONE PENNY.

Telephones:
London—Holborn 691.
Manchester—City 660l.

BOY SCOUTS' LAST HONOURS TO AIR RAID BUGLER.

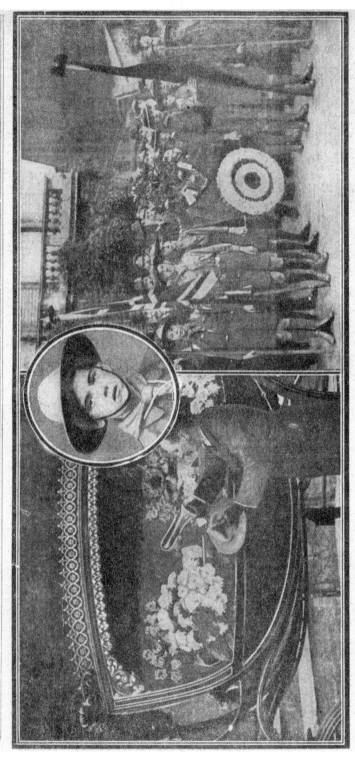

The funeral of Alfred Page, the Boy Scout, who was killed in the recent London air-raid while waiting to report himself on duty as a bugler to sound the "All Clear!" took place yesterday. On the flag-draped coffin lay the young hero's Scout's hat and a bugle, while Boy Scouts followed with floral tributes.—(*Daily Sketch*.)

Figure 8.2 Boy scout's funeral (*Daily Sketch*)

pictorial, if not world-shaking: 'BOY SCOUTS' LAST HONOURS TO AIR RAID BUGLER'.

> The funeral of Alfred Page, the Boy Scout, who was killed in the recent London air-raid while waiting to report himself on duty as a bugler to sound the 'All Clear!' took place yesterday. On the flag-draped coffin lay the young hero's Scout's hat and a bugle, while Boy Scouts followed with floral tributes.

Here then is the imperial family – one flag, one empire, one home – in the convincing guise of the flag-draped coffin of a boy whose family becomes the nation; a much more *significant* story than that of the exotic 'outrages by Apaches' reported from far-off Petrograd.

This was Thursday. By Saturday the 'Echoes of the Town' column by 'Mr Gossip' felt confident enough about the truth of the situation in Petrograd to deliver itself of this:

Bolo.—Of course, it's Boloism that has done the Russian trick, and anyway, it is topical to give you a few facts about these Boli. I find, by the way, that a vast amount of totally incorrect information is being ladled out concerning them.

"Saviours" Of Russia.—To show how completely Russia has been undermined by men of German-Jewish origin, here are some more prominent members of the Soviet:—

Lenin is Zederbaum.
Trotzky is Braunstein.
Kameneff is Rozenfeldt.
Zinowjeff is Apfelbaum.
Suchanoff is Zimmerstein.
Miesskowski is Goldenberg.
Lunotcharski is Piltzer.

This last-named is a most notorious person. The New York police know plenty about him, and he haunted the darkest dens of the Tenderloin district and the East Side.

The Red Guards.—Finally, the famous Red Guards of the Soviet are recruited from tramps known in Russia as "Bestiakee" (barefooted) and "Zolotovstcy" (hooligans). Among them, too, are plenty of a low class of boatmen, who drag barges up the river to the tune of "The Song of the Boatmen on the Volga," which the Balalaika orchestra made popular in London. Picturesque if you like, but as governors of Russia—hopeless, terrible

Figure 8.3 'Mr. Gossip'
(*Daily Sketch*)

So now you know; boatmen, tramps, hooligans, gangsters, pacifists, Jews, Germans, Apaches – these 'facts' (all lies) may not describe the actuality of the new Russian regime, but that hardly matters, for such qualities are drawn from a lexicon of adversarial terms with which the readership of the *Daily Sketch* may already be familiar. The 'facts' of the situation are that the new 'governors of Russia' should be visualized as foreign, unlike 'us', for obvious domestic reasons.

In the service of such a cause truth is not so much the first casualty as a non-combatant; by Monday the *Daily Sketch* was following to the letter Dr Johnson's strictures on how *not* to write the news. In 1758 (it will be recalled from Chapter 6) Dr Johnson had described his 'indignation' when 'writers of the news'

> know, by experience, however destitute of reason, that what is desired will be credited without nice examination: they do not therefore always limit their narratives by possibility, but slaughter armies without battles, and conquer countries without invasions.[9]

And so, on Monday, 12 November 1917, the *Daily Sketch*'s lead foreign story was headlined 'KERENSKY'S 200,000 ARMY AT THE GATES OF PETROGRAD', with a subhead announcing the 'Impending Fall of Short-Lived Leninist Regime'. Wishful thinking as banner headline; a long-lived journalistic regime.

Partisan pictures

A fortnight after the Revolution, on Tuesday, 20 November 1917, the *Daily Sketch* was unable to report the fall of the Leninist regime, but as the 'premier picture paper' it was at last ready to publish some photographs. Two of them purport to show 'MOSCOW'S REIGN OF TERROR' – 'Cathedral of St. Basil gutted by fire', and 'The Church of the Assumption in the Kremlin, another Moscow gem destroyed'. The pictures actually show these two buildings looking hale and hearty and upstanding (so they're not news but library pictures), a condition they have enjoyed to this day (i.e. the captions are lies). More interesting, perhaps, are two large photographs of what the *Daily Sketch* reckons to be the cause of the Russian Revolution. Their interest consists not so much in their subject matter as in their status: they are presented as news photographs, illustrating a world-shattering event, but they're entirely fictional, and what's more the *Daily Sketch* (Figure 8.5) seems to be quite proud of that fact:

> Rasputin, whose treacherous villainy provoked the Russian Revolution, figures in a remarkable film shortly to be seen on the cinematograph screen. These scenes depict the evil genius of Tsardom at a Court reception and trapped in Prince Yusupof's house, where Rasputin was slain by those he would have betrayed.

Unfortunately for posterity the title of the 'remarkable' film is not given; unfortunately for the readers of the *Daily Sketch*, no further analysis of the Revolution's causes was given.

By 23 November 1917 the *Daily Sketch*'s combination of racist gossip, wishful thinking, fabrication, and pictures that did not show what they purported to, had combined into hard news. Under the subheading 'LENIN

MOSCOW'S REIGN OF TERROR.—
Cathedral of St. Basil gutted by fire.

The Church of the Assumption in the
Kremlin, another Moscow gem destroyed

Figure 8.4 Moscow's reign of
terror (*Daily Sketch*)

Figure 8.5 Remarkable cinematograph (*Daily Sketch*)

RUSSIA'S ARMY NOW
LED BY SUBALTERN.

Commander-In-Chief Refuses To Negotiate With The Enemy.

LENIN UNMASKED.

Soldiers Called Upon To Arrest And Detain Loyal Generals.

Lenin, alias Zederblum, a German Jew, has struck a snag in ordering General Dukhonin, Commander-in-Chief, to open peace negotiations. The general has flatly refused to become a traitor, and he has been superseded in office by Ensign Krylenko.

Quick to see the effect of General Dukhonin's loyal action, Lenin has sent another manifesto to

Lenin (left) and Trotsky, the Russian pacifist leaders.

the troops, in which he advises them to arrest, but not to lynch, generals who are opposed to peace overtures being made.

France has conclusive proof that immediately before Lenin issued his peace-at-any-price manifesto, he received a mission of German spies which had come direct from Berlin!

Bolschevism On Its Last Legs.

M. Saies, Kerensky's private secretary, who has arrived in Stockholm, says that the anarchist regime will collapse within a month, as the majority of Russians is against them. In all probability a Socialist Government will be formed, he says, with Kerensky as Foreign Minister. Saies is convinced that Kerensky is on the way to Petrograd at the head of a great army.

According to messages from Finland, Kerensky, with a large army, is again advancing on Petrograd, while Korniloff, also with plenty of men behind him, has entered Moscow.

Britain's latest victories in Artois and Palestine are having a good effect upon the Russian nation.

Figure 8.6 Lenin unmasked (*Daily Sketch*)

THE PICTURES OF POLITICS

UNMASKED' the story opens with: 'Lenin, alias Zederblum, a German Jew, has struck a snag . . .'. It tells the readers that 'France has conclusive proof' that Lenin had 'received a mission of German spies which had come directly from Berlin!' Then, under the subheading, 'Bolschevism On Its Last Legs', it reports that 'the anarchist regime will collapse within a month', that 'Kerensky . . . is again marching on Petrograd' (again!), and that 'Britain's latest victories in Artois and Palestine are having a good effect upon the Russian nation'. The accompanying pictures of Lenin and Trotsky are the first portraits of 'the Russian pacifist leaders'. Needless to say, their ideological function far outpaces their accuracy (and note that Zederbaum has become Zederblum). For the *Daily Sketch*, it seems, all anarchists look the same; the purpose of these portraits is to lend credibility to its racist foe creation, not to acquaint curious Britons as to the true identity of the revolutionaries. These two photos don't illustrate Lenin and Trotsky, but they do work to *verify* the *Sketch*'s story by the simple means of giving its readers something to look at.

Foe creation is one thing, family is another. Three weeks after the Revolution, on Tuesday, 27 November 1917, the *Daily Sketch* found a (safe) way to associate Russian politics with British domestic affairs, using the time-honoured mechanism of a royal marriage to make family a metaphor for nation, and appealing to the political desires of the populace by the now-familiar means of visualizing an attractive woman's body. The front page shows two portraits of 'The Grand Duchess Tatiana, the ex-Tsar's second daughter', who is reported to have escaped from Russia by means of a 'mock marriage' with her father's former chamberlain.

> Beautiful and talented, 20 years old, Tatiana was wealthy, for when she was only a week old her father placed £1,000,000 to her credit. A year or so ago her name was much canvassed as that of the future bride of the Prince of Wales.

The Prince of Wales in question eventually married an American person called Mrs Simpson, at the cost of his throne, so the fairytale princess Tatiana is 'our' family only in suitability, not in fact. As if this 'if only' is not enough, however, the young, beautiful, talented, rich, royal, eligible Grand Duchess is also (unlike tsars in general) a democrat:

> [She] does not care whether the Romanoffs ever regain the Imperial throne, and has at heart rather the creation of a strong democratic government in Russia, or its transformation into a confederation of united states.

In the cause of this early version of perestroika, the Grand Duchess is said to be willing to work 'in any capacity', including lecturing and dancing in the (other) United States. This pleasant fantasy – an all-singing, all-dancing, real-life, fairytale princess – is printed over a second story which

194

EX-TSAR'S DAUGHTER ESCAPES FROM RUSSIA.

Flight From Siberia Via Japan To America.

MOCK MARRIAGE TRICK.

To Lecture And Dance In The States For Russian Relief.

According to reports from New York, the Grand Duchess Tatiana, second daughter of the ex-Tsar, has escaped from Siberia, and will reach New York in a few days.

A mock marriage is said to have been gone through between the Grand Duchess and the son of the ex-Tsar's former Chamberlain (Baron Fredericks), and by this means she obtained greater freedom from espionage, and was able to escape from Tobolsk to Harbin. Thence she took ship for Japan and America.

Officials of the Russian Civilian Relief Society say the Grand Duchess "does not care whether the Romanoffs ever regain the Imperial throne, and has at heart rather the creation of a strong democratic Government in Russia, or its transformation into a confederation of united states."

It is stated that the Grand Duchess will work "in any capacity" for Russian relief. She will write and lecture on her experiences and give folk dances.

Beautiful and talented, 20 years old, Tatiana was wealthy, for when she was only a week old her father placed £1,000,000 to her credit.

A year or so ago her name was much canvassed as that of the future bride of the Prince of Wales.

On inquiry of the family of the Grand Duke Michael of Russia, the *Daily Sketch* was informed that no news of the escape of the Grand Duchess had been received.

The Grand Duchess Tatiana, the ex-Tsar's second daughter, has escaped from Siberia—like many other Russian exiles before her. Arranging a mock marriage with the son of her father's ex-Chamberlain, she evaded strict surveillance at Tobolsk.

Figure 8.7 Grand Duchess Tatiana (*Daily Sketch*)

195

Trotsky, Lenin's right hand in the Bolshevik "Government," addressing the crowd at a Revolutionary demonstration in the st of Petrograd.

Lenin, who has betrayed Russia to the enemy, watching his dupes.

A Russian parlementaire being taken by motor-car to the German headquarters on the Ea front to arrange the armistice terms. He was blindfolded according to custom.

Figure 8.8 Traitorous deal with the Huns (*Daily Sketch*)

give the necessary contrast of darkness and shadow to the sparkling image of Tatiana: it describes both 'hunger mutinies' and mass desertions from the front by Russian soldiers, while 'monarchist ideas are again widely prevailing among the huge peasant population'.

The photographs of Tatiana Romanoff are not political but fashion portraits, on the cusp between high society and show business, and the job that they do is not to tell the truth but provoke desire; she is personalized to render the 'monarchist idea' both credible and desirable, despite the obvious fact that Russia had decisively turned its back on all that months before in the first revolution in February. Tatiana's personal, bodily qualities are politicized in *opposition* to Leninism; look at her youth, beauty (etc.) and the assertion that 'every day makes it more evident that the Bolshevik regime is nearing its end' begins to seem quite normal. And her body is politicized in *favour* of British constitutional monarchy; a democratic duchess who's a match for 'our' Prince Charming because like the British royal family she's willing to work, to dance for her daddy, and harbours no political aspirations of her own – she's 'family'.

Well, none of these people lived happily ever after, but meanwhile the 'premier picture paper' did get hold of some news photographs. Exactly one month after its report of the Revolution, on 8 December 1917, the *Daily Sketch* published as its front-page lead the first photographs of the event itself. Captioned 'Bolshevik Pacifists Rush Their Countrymen Into A Traitorous Deal With The Huns', the main picture, an early instance of photomontage in news journalism, shows a crowd, with a superimposed cut-out placed over the general area where the crowd's attention is focused, as a kind of close-up of what they can be seen looking towards: 'Trotsky, Lenin's right hand in the Bolshevik "Government", addressing the crowd at a Revolutionary demonstration in the streets of Petrograd'. The cut-out portrait does not in fact show Trotsky (it appears to be a picture of Lenin). Meanwhile, underneath, we see 'Lenin, who has betrayed Russia to the enemy, watching his dupes', but again the picture doesn't live up to its caption – it's not of Lenin. Two further news pictures complete the set, over a caption which tells us what they mean: 'Unhappy Russia, thrown into anarchy by the counter-revolution, stands humiliated before her allies and the civilized world'.

Finally, on 28 December 1917, the *Daily Sketch* got something right. It released 'A new portrait of Lenin', entitled 'A FRIEND OF GERMANY', whose novelty consisted in the fact that this time it actually was a picture of Lenin, though it didn't rate the prominence of a portrait of a peer's (pretty) daughter.

A place in the sun

In these early news photos the connection between politics and pictures is clear enough, but the commitment to an abstract or universal truth is

A new portrait of Lenin, the Bolshevik leader of Russia's counter-revolution.

Figure 8.9 A friend of Germany (*Daily Sketch*)

altogether absent. These are partisan pictures, dedicated to popular political edification. They are not unusual; perhaps with hindsight the *Daily Sketch* appears a little hasty in its predictions, a little clumsy in its manipulation of words and images, and not altogether trustworthy in its visualization of the facts. But its heliographical methodology is still standard professional practice – its treatment of pictures, captions, headlines and stories is commonplace in popular journalism from that day to this. Twentieth-century journalism established a kind of impartial-but-partisan truth alongside a concept of illustration where the function of pictures is to make any truth-impression of the stories not just visible but imperative. Press photographs are still playing the role developed by the proto-photo in nineteenth-century popular literature: to render (fictional) stories unarguably real (visual), and to entice the reader to keep looking.

During the eighteenth and nineteenth centuries, as has been chronicled in the previous two chapters, an increasing ascendancy occurred for adversarialism as opposed to universalism, resulting in both adversarial truth and an adversarial community, i.e. a 'we' identity for the common reader *as opposed to* the identity of 'them', whether foreigners or political antagonists, whose identity, inexorably, is visualized as 'foreign'. But at the same time each combatant in these wars of representation was apt to claim universal status for their own adversarial truth, and universal identity for their own 'we' community. The function of (photo)journalism has been

198

not only to visualize this partisan order, but to proclaim its reality and universality – in the teeth of evidence to the contrary. The *Daily Sketch*'s vision of the Russian Revolution may have had little to do with the naked truth, but it was as close fitting as a body stocking against the contours of domestic politics.

Foreign news is never foreign meaning; the Russian Revolution meant insurrection to the *Daily Sketch*, but the ferment it feared was a home brew. News of popular participation in the October Revolution reached Britain in the form of that cryptic reference to 'outrages by Apaches' in Petrograd (*Daily Sketch*, 8 November 1917). At that very moment, a debate was taking place in the British House of Lords. It was reported at much greater length in the *Sketch* than the enigmatic revolt in Petrograd, but it was substantially about the same subject: REMARKABLE SPEECHES ON LABOUR'S CLAIM TO 'PLACE IN SUN' proclaimed the main domestic headline of the day (Figure 8.10), over this:

> The Archbishop of York, during a debate last night on industrial unrest, regretted that the working classes had no representative in the Upper House. . . .
>
> Lord Salisbury, who opened the debate, said the workers distrusted employers, the Government, and trade union officials themselves. There was distrust of the whole social system.
>
> The employers, said Lord Salisbury, must be prepared to take the workers into partnership, treating them no longer as human machines.

And so on. Of course any connection between Bolshevism and the ·'disquieting unrest' among those of our own community who 'distrust the whole social system' and who desire a place in the sun, is not stated by the *Daily Sketch* (or the Peers), but the subsequent campaign of opposition to Bolshevism cannot be understood without reference to the possibility that socialism and sovietism would spread from Petrograd to the British 'working man', whom 'the ruling classes have too often been inclined to regard . . . as a dangerous animal' (Lord Salisbury, 8 November 1917).

A place in the *Sun* is of course just what the working classes eventually got. It is still being debated whether basking in it is wise, without the use of some form of blockout to protect the democratic body politic from its most harmful rays. But long-term trends do indicate that the heliographical composition of modern popular journalism, from the *Sketch* to the *Sun*, is designed more to domesticate than to illuminate that supposedly dangerous animal.

Sunny explosions of horror

After the election of 1842 that so concerned the *Sydney Morning Herald*, fearful lest the 'respectable classes' should be outdone by the working

PRIMATE AND PEER
PLEAD FOR WORKERS.

Remarkable Speeches On Labour's Claim To "Place In Sun."

PROFITEERING.

Government Arranging Better Distribution Of Food.

Will Lord Bryce's Committee on House of Lords reform advocate the election of Labour peers?

The Archbishop of York, during a debate last night on industrial unrest, regretted that the working classes had no representative in the Upper House.

All the speakers emphasised the part of profiteering in fomenting suspicion. Lord Salisbury, who opened the debate, said the workers distrusted employers, the Government, and trade union officials themselves. There was distrust of the whole social system.

The employers, said Lord Salisbury, must be prepared to take the workers into partnership, treating them no longer as human machines.

The Archbishop of York (Dr. Lang) stated that, while there was much disquieting unrest, he was surprised that there had been so little. He attributed much of the unrest to profiteering, the manner in which people had been harassed and harried in regard to recruiting, the suspension of trade union regulations, and so on.

DR. COSMO LANG
(Archbishop of York).

Pre-war conditions could not be restored. It must be put bluntly that those who had borne the greater portion of the strain and the sacrifice of the war were determined to see that the conditions after the war were adequate to the sacrifice they had made.

The Archbishop pleaded for a more equal distribution of the rewards of industry. The workers would not tolerate the scientific management imported from America or elsewhere as "Prussianising" industry, and they would resist it.

Figure 8.10 Place in the sun (*Daily Sketch*)

classes, the colony of New South Wales settled into the routine of self-government and the building of a suitably respectable community. From the start it was clear that this community was adversarial, and its journalism contributed to the public rationalization of the most extreme 'us v. them' ideology. In 1844, for instance, the *Sydney Morning Herald* reported this speech to the Legislative Council by William Charles Wentworth:

> He could not see if the whites in this colony were to go out into the land and possess it, that the Government had much to do with them. No doubt there would be battles between the settlers and the border tribes; but they might be settled without the aid of the Government. The civilized people had come in and the savage must go back. They must go on progressing until their dominancy was established, and therefore he could think that no measure was wise or merciful to the blacks which clothed them with a degree of seeming protection, which their position would not allow them to maintain. . . . It was not the policy of a wise Government to attempt the perpetuation of the aboriginal race of New South Wales. . . . They must give way before the arms, aye! even the diseases of civilized nations – they must give way before they attain the power of those nations.[10]

This argument is founded on the opposition of 'civilized people' and 'nations' against not only Aboriginal people but – if necessary – against their own government; the community is building itself, and government 'protection' of its adversary is the immediate concern of this speech. Siding with what was seen as historic, even natural, inevitability , i.e. common sense, *against* one's own government, made such exterminatory politics attractive to universalist-adversarial journalism – it could have its cake and eat it too, by supporting a vision of a universalist insider community (the whites), and simultaneously adhering to an adversarialist model of journalism *within* that community (opposition to colonial policy).

It so happens that, despite its unspeakable ideology, the exterminationist policy publicized by the *Sydney Morning Herald* was not only a form of popular common sense among the settlers of New South Wales and Van Dieman's Land,[11] it was also, like Painite common sense in America, one of the first and most pronounced manifestations of *independent* thinking, a marking of the boundary not only between whites and Aboriginal people but also between colonists and the home government in London. In other words it was the specifically Australian 'national identity' in the making, an uneasy tension between democratic aspirations among the 'we' community, and the Final Solution for those with whom we shared the continent. The boundary between 'we' and 'they' as it stood in the mid-nineteenth century has been described by Robert Hughes thus:

> The typical form of frontier skirmish was ambush and small, indiscriminate massacre. . . . Whites laid for blacks and shot them in

the back. Blacks crept into the hut and crushed the skulls of a settler and his woman with their waddies. 'The normal condition of life was an armed, watchful, wary, nervous calm,' slow in tempo but punctuated by sunny explosions of horror that soon settled again on the indifferent skin of the land.[12]

Hughes comments that the pattern of black resistance, answered by white retaliation and murder, along an ever-expanding frontier, 'ensured that convict attitudes towards Aborigines were carried and transmitted from generation to generation, from bond parents to free children. . . . In some parts of Australia, as any traveller can verify for himself, this attitude has never died.'[13] Australian racism was, says Hughes, 'the first Australian trait to percolate upward from the lower class'.[14] But it was not only an experiential, demotic ideology; it was also tutored, not least in the columns of the colonial press.

The formal colonial governing apparatus, however, was bound by ideas that were at least as old as Hobbes, whose philosophy of transportation (as noted in Chapter 5), was that:

'The multitude of poor, and yet strong people still encreasing, they are to be transplanted into Countries not sufficiently inhabited: where neverthelesse, they are not to exterminate those they find there; but constrain them to inhabit closer together.'[15]

The imperial authorities tried from the very start, both from the Governor's office in Sydney,[16] and from the Colonial Office in London, to adhere to such a policy as this. Hence we find imperial schoolchildren being taught, in a book whose avowed purpose was to make them 'good citizens' by means of reading, an explanation of what the Colonial Office was for:

When you look at the map and see what great countries *Canada* and *Australia* and *New Zealand* are, and when you remember that the people who live in them are countrymen of our own, with all our English love of liberty and fair play, you will understand how important it is that the Colonial Secretary should be both friendly and wise in all that he has to do with the people of these great countries.

And there is another very important thing which the Colonial Secretary has to do sometimes. . . . It has been found that whenever Englishmen and black men live together in the same country, there is a great danger of the English or white men acting cruelly or unfairly to the natives or blacks, unless great care is taken to prevent their so acting. But it would be very wrong if, under the rule of England, people were made to suffer merely because their skins were black, or were treated unfairly by the law because they were weak, and could not protect themselves.

SOME OF THE KING'S COLOURED SUBJECTS.

1. ZULU.
2. NORTH AMERICAN INDIAN.
3. INDIAN.
4. AUSTRAL ABORIGINAL
5. MAORI.

Figure 8.11 The King's coloured subjects (*Citizen Reader*)

As I told you, everyone, whether he be black or white, is equal before the law. But it is often necessary for the Colonial Secretary to watch very closely and carefully what is being done by Englishmen to the natives and black people in our colonies. It is his business to try to give equal justice to all, and we at home ought to try to support him in doing what is sometimes very difficult.[17]

The *Citizen Reader*, from which this advice is quoted, was first published in 1886, a century after the first Australian colony was implanted. Its purpose was 'to instruct boys and girls in our Elementary Schools with regard to their rights, duties, and privileges as British Citizens'. Its preface was written by W.E. Forster, who had been responsible for the 1870 Education Act, which set up universal elementary state schooling; he commented on the 'special fitness in the appearance of a book of this kind at a time when we have just added millions to the citizens who have the right of electing representatives'.[18] The link between citizenship and reading, between voting and education, is explicitly forged here, and part of its purpose was to temper the excesses of those who, despite their 'English love of liberty and fair play', are also the 'English or white men' who act 'cruelly or unfairly to the natives or blacks'.

From fair play to fair go

I don't know how influential the *Citizen Reader* may have been, beyond the fact that it stayed in print for decades and sold hundreds of thousands of copies. However, its *rhetoric* was very persistent, even among those whose racism it opposed. Here for example is *The Great Jubilee Book: The Story of the Australian Nation in Pictures*, issued in 1951 on the fiftieth anniversary of Australian Federation. This book is interesting because it is in the 'citizen reader' genre, but it was published by the *Herald and Weekly Times* newspaper group; it is a popular pedagogy, teaching the public the identity of their nation, but the teacher is *journalism* and the medium of instruction is heliographic. Its account of the Australian nation's origins makes no mention whatever of Aborigines, apart from this: 'The old stock jokes about Australia which once riled Australians are hopelessly naive today. People no longer come to the country expecting to find Sydney and Melbourne crowded with roaming aborigines, or boundary riders gaily shooting up the streets.'[19]

So in answer to its own founding question, 'Who are the Australians?', Aborigines are invisible in *The Great Jubilee Book*. It tells of the 'basic British heritage', of a nation made up from 'the common people' who have 'given Australia her basic traditions, her basic culture', upon which 'Australians have built their own concepts often more advanced than those held in Britain'. Thus, 'the "British" nations built Australia. But the "foreigners" who came to Australia gave something of their own to the Australian mixture.' These foreigners are listed as Germans, Scandinavians (Swedes, Danes, Norwegians), Mediterraneans (Italians, Greeks, Maltese, Albanians), and Jews. There follows a brief list, 'for the record', of the few 'full-blooded non-Europeans in the country', namely Chinese, Afghans and Indians. It is only at this point that Aboriginal people are allowed into the '*story of the Australian nation*':

Figure 8.12 '"Read that then," said the Governor . . .' (*The Great Jubilee Book*)

It is also worth recording the paradox that while Australians are adamant about 'White Australia', they are not prejudiced against colored peoples. The doctrine of 'a fair go', an Australian principle, is too strong.

Aborigines – a Dying Race

Nevertheless on the debit side of the paradox there is an uneasy conscience about the aborigines. The impact of white settlers upon these people has reduced them to remnants. Today they hold their own only in the far north of Arnhem Land, in the centre and in reaches of the Northern Territory. Thinking Australians have long realised that 'a fair go' must be given to our aboriginal peoples while there is still time.[20]

So by now everyone is agreed: English 'fair play' and Australian 'fair go' are combined, in education, media, history and nationhood, *against* the percolation of genocidal tendencies from the community which is not, paradoxically, racially prejudiced in its own egalitarian eyes. These paradoxes extend to time: 'thinking Australians' have '*long* realised' that 'a *dying* race' needs justice 'while there is *still time*' – a collection of incommensurate tenses that cannot be narrated into a 'story' of the nation, especially one whose chronology fixes 1788 as year zero, and whose 'foreigners' are therefore not the non-Aboriginal but non-British inhabitants. And the notion of Aborigines 'holding their own', albeit in the far north, the centre and 'reaches' of the continent, is paradoxical too, for the only thing they held in 1951 was their lives; they had no vote, no land, no rights, no representation, not even family, given the assimilationist policy of forcibly taking Aboriginal children away from their parents to be brought up in missions and white foster homes.

In this context, where 'home' might mean London or Melbourne, but not Arnhem Land, and where education into citizenship teaches about a home community of white Europeans, but not Aborigines, it is hardly surprising to find that Aboriginality is still 'foreign' to journalism, even that of 'thinking' Australians. The 'truth' of their situation cannot be pronounced in a lexicon of nationhood which is glossed as 'our family', and from which contemporary journalism constructs visions of order for its citizen readers. In the heliography of journalism, the only place in the sun reserved for Aborigines is still Hughes's 'sunny explosions of horror' in a landscape of indifference.

Wedom and Theydom

'Why Massa Gubernor said Black Jack – You Proflamation, all gammon – how blackfellow read him? eh! He no learn him read Book.'
'Read that then, said the Governor pointing to a Picture.'[21]

In modern, complex, fragmented societies, no one can hope to know the other members of their community directly.[22] The only *real* contact with others is, paradoxically, *symbolic*, and rendered in the form of stories, both factual and fictional, in the electronic and print media. The news media function, at the most general level, to create a sense of belonging for the population of a given city, state or country. Their readers and audiences are an 'imagined community'; in the case of popular (or monopoly) outlets these readers or viewers are assumed to be coterminous with the nation or state, and they are encouraged by each newspaper or TV channel to see the news as part of their own identity, while the news strives to identify with them. So news includes stories on a daily basis which enable everyone to recognize a larger unity or community than their own immediate contacts, and to identify with the news outlet as 'our' storyteller.

The news is organized around strategies of inclusion and exclusion from 'our' community; strategies which not only distinguish our nation and its leaders or representatives from others, but which separate out various values, types of action or classes of persons who, although they may be in the home community, are treated as 'foreign' to it. I shall dub the two domains as 'Wedom' and 'Theydom' respectively. The boundaries of Theydom are not coterminous with national boundaries; certain foreign countries, principally the USA, Britain and former dominions like Canada and New Zealand, are in Australia's Wedom, while certain nearby countries like Indonesia, Malaysia and Japan are in its Theydom. Similarly, not all Australian citizens are in its Wedom; there are people and actions which cannot be rendered in the news as 'we' and 'ours', but which instead are only intelligible as 'they'. Such persons include criminals, political extremists, drug traffickers, paedophiles, juvenile offenders and, in certain circumstances, immigrants.

The heliographic news media have inherited from adversarial-universalist, community-building journalism the habit of categorizing Aboriginal people and their actions in this way: as 'foreign' to the community values and goals of Australian society, as 'they' in news stories, as 'outside' the community. Australia's Theydom is its Aboriginality, which is itself already polarized by the heliographical metaphor into the opposites of light, before any story is written.

People from Theydom, such as Aboriginals in news stories, tend to be treated in routine ways. They are exempted from the established systems of balance which apply to Wedom's own adversarial politics; there are not 'two sides' to an Aboriginal story – not two *Aboriginal* sides, that is, only an Aboriginal side and a 'balance' supplied by, for instance, police, welfare, legal or governmental authorities. Further down the line, pictures of Aboriginal people are routinely printed without name captions; they are representative of their race, not of their persons, even in so-called

PLAYBOY ON THE SCENE

What's happening where and who's making it happen.
Compiled by Peter Olszewski

GETTING WARM

Okay gang, armed with the knowledge that it's cool for southerners to be warm in winter, be informed that it's now also cool to holiday in the Northern Territory. Darwin and environs offer all the tropical delights usually promised by the tourist brochures, but there's more for the discerning traveller.

For example, you might stumble across a sight like this — two Darwinites enjoying themselves in a crocodile-proof lake. Leaping out of the water for the sheer hell of it is model Simone Campbell, 24. Her ''bloodline'' is a bit of a mix: Aboriginal, Afghan and Scottish. When her mother was born to an Aboriginal woman and an Afghan camel driver, the tribe put her on an antheap to die because she was half-caste. But other Aboriginals took her to an orphanage which is fortunate because otherwise we would not have been blessed with Simone.

There's more to the North than *Crocodile Dundee*, and if you want to follow the sun this summer, ring the Northern Territory Government Tourist Bureau in your State. They're continually organising new deals to get you a cheaper, more interesting holiday.

Figure 8.13 'Two Darwinites' as tourist attraction for Australian *Playboy* – but only one of them has a name (*Australian Playboy*)

positive human interest stories. People from Wedom are scrupulously named.

Individuals in Theydom are treated as being all the same; their identity consists in being 'unlike us', so they are 'like each other'. The news often has difficulty in recognizing internal differences in the overall Aboriginal community, not distinguishing between traditional and urban Aborigines, or between different geographical, political and other positions among them. This is contrary to one of the most fundamental news values within 'our' community: that differences *must* be recognized by giving 'both sides of a story'. Aboriginals are only 'all the same' with reference to one unifying feature – they are 'unlike us'. To give this negative identity some positive attributes there is a routine tendency to characterize all Aboriginals in relation to traditional tribal stereotypes, despite the fact that more than half the people identifying themselves as Aboriginal in the most recent census were city-dwellers.

Aborigines who are stereotyped as outsiders or as tribal cannot be seen as citizens with rights. More often they are treated as subjects of welfare, or in connection with crime stories. Groups like Aborigines who are routinely covered in news stories where the emphasis is on welfare or correction are rarely asked to speak for themselves; as outsiders with a 'they' identity they are newsworthy for their economic, security or welfare impact on 'our' community. So routine has the strategy of inclusion and exclusion become that it is now 'natural', a part of common sense. One serious result is that it is hard for an Aboriginal spokesperson or eyewitness, or a story told from an Aboriginal perspective, to be seen as *true*. In other words, truth is not an absolute value in the news media; it is 'what *we* know to be true'. Aboriginal perspectives may be so foreign to 'our' notions of truth that they come across not as a point of view with its own validity but as literally untrue, biased, distorted or propaganda.

Hence a spokesperson who insists on the citizenship or the rights of Aborigines, as opposed to conforming to welfare or corrective stereotypes, is likely to be represented in the news as an extremist. As far as Aboriginal Australia is concerned, the function of general intellectual, wise elder for the whole community, is performed by white authorities or sympathetic interpreters, by anonymous vox-pops, or by individuals who are caught in the limelight of a particular story, looming into ephemeral social visibility, only to disappear again once the story is covered. Australian journalism doesn't make use of Aboriginal knowledge for its own getting of wisdom; often it doesn't even use Aboriginal spokespeople to under-stand Aboriginality. Aboriginals are not routinely asked for their own opinion on a given news story, nor, more importantly, are they able to represent themselves in the media with their own agenda of newsworthy issues or their own debates about possible solutions to problems they can identify for themselves. When they are accessed, either by quotation or picture, it is to give verisimilitude to the 'line' of the story which is already determined.

However, open, offensive prejudice is rare. Racial malice on the part of individual journalists or editors may occur, but it is just as irrelevant to the routine production of news as are the voting habits of journalists who interview politicians. Racial stereotyping and racism in the media is institutional not individual. That is, it results from news values, from editorial policies, and from routines of newsgathering that are not in themselves racist or consciously prejudicial. It results from the fact that most news stories are 'already written' before an individual journalist is assigned to them, even before the event has taken place. A story featuring Aboriginals is simply more likely to be covered, or more likely to survive subeditorial revision or 'spiking', if it fits existing 'definitions of the situation' – that is, if the story represents Aborigines as 'they' rather than as 'we', and makes sense of them as in need of protection, correction or welfare, and not in terms of what they may wish to say and do for themselves.

From fair go to fair game

Newspaper editors are inclined to assert that a prime reason for running a story as the page one lead is when it is, in the words of the *West Australian*'s editor Paul Murray, 'of wider appeal to all our readers'.[23] This was Murray's rationale for the lead story of 28 February 1990, headlined 'ABORIGINAL GANGS TERRORISE SUBURBS' (Figure 8.14). In this case the formula cannot include Aboriginal people among 'all our readers'. It is only possible for the headline to be read as '*They* terrorise suburbs', not '*We*' or '*our gangs* terrorise suburbs' – such a statement is so contrary to common sense as to seem ungrammatical, an implausible use of language. Given the *West Australian*'s central role in sustaining a sense of community identity for the whole of Western Australia, it is clear that if Aboriginal people are not recognizable as 'we', as part of 'our readers' for the *West*, then they are being excluded by every such story from membership of the community of Western Australia itself.

But there was more to this particular story than a headline. The story itself was not about terrorism in the usual sense; there was no political motivation, no cohesive activist group, no attempt to destabilize the political or civil apparatus, and none of the standard terrorist weapons or tactics. Instead, there was juvenile and teenage petty crime – shoplifting, vandalism and assault – centred on one suburb and involving mostly theft from bottle shops. Routine, low-grade stuff; urban and social, not Aboriginal. In the same day's paper there are further straightforwardly anti-Aboriginal news stories on page 2, a political cartoon that manages to combine the themes of Aboriginal crime with state handouts, and a

The West Australian

ESTABLISHED 1833   PERTH WEDNESDAY FEBRUARY 28 1990   168 PAGES 50c'

Telephone 482 3111 (Classified 420 1111)

GES 90,91

KHMER ROUGE
SHOW A
SWEETER FACE

WIN a $160,000 home
96fm
The West. Australian

REVUE   TOMORROW
Nicole Kidman
FAST TRACK
TO SUCCESS

Aboriginal gangs terrorise suburbs

By HELEN WINTERTON

ORIGINAL gangs with mbers as young as seven are rorising Bayswater residents d police fear the situation is ting out of control.

With racial tension rising in the a, police have launched a big kdown in an effort to identify g leaders.

ocal hoteliers, who met senior ice officers and Bayswater city uncillors this week, have threat-d to take matters into their own nds if the gangs are not stopped.

The hoteliers claim the area has n targetted by about 30 origines who continually damage ir premises and steal goods and ney. Anyone who tries to stand in ir way is assaulted.

In recent weeks there has been a spate of window smashings and house break-ins. In the most serious instance of violence a couple were viciously assaulted by a gang of stone-throwing Aboriginal youths.

Senior police officers and the hoteliers yesterday accused adult Aborigines of organising child crime gangs which have been responsible for the numerous thefts and break-ins.

Chief-Supt. Harry Riseborough said the Aborigines refused to obey the law.

"I don't like picking on the Aborigines, but they are creating the problems in this area," he said.

"All we can do is present the offenders to the courts and after that it is up to the courts to decide what happens to them. The assaults have been violent, they were deliberate and intended to cause harm to people."

The manager of the Maylands Peninsula Hotel, Mr Brian Bannon, said staff members were terrified of the gangs and he blamed WA's legal system for being too soft on Aboriginal offenders.

"It's not justice," he said. "These people are getting away with blue murder because they are black."

"About two or three adults and six kids under the age of 10 come into the bottle shop and the adults divert our attention while the kids steal the top-shelf liquor," he said of a typical gang operation.

"We caught one eight-year-old with three bottles of scotch hidden in his tracksuit pants. But what can we do? Because the kids are under the age of 10, the law says they are not responsible for their actions."

Mr Bannon said he was assaulted last week when a teenager tried to hit him with a bottle of claret.

He said the tavern had also been under siege by a group of six teenagers who pelted the windows with rocks.

"We asked them to leave after they came into the main bar and tried to pick a fight. Then they went across the road and came back with stones and a pole. They smashed three front windows and rammed the front door with the pole," he said.

A senior Ashfield Tavern staff member said the gangs had become a living nightmare after weeks of constant harassment and thefts. The tavern was robbed on Monday night when three Aborigines stole a till and money from the bottle shop.

"They pulled up in a stolen car, they walked into the shop and they grabbed the till — it was that quick," he said.

The licensee of another tavern in the area, who did not want to be named, said a number of ... Aborigines had been harassing staff and customers since Christmas.

● More reports, page 2;
Alston, page 10

Figure 8.14 Aboriginal gangs (*West Australian*)

Woman, 19, scarred by gang attack

A BAYSWATER woman has been emotionally and physically scarred by an attack in which she was repeatedly stoned and punched by a gang of young Aborigines.

Ms Leanne Clark, 19, says she often wakes up shouting "leave me alone, please stop".

Ms Clark and 33-year-old Rob Harvey were attacked last Wednesday night.

They believe the attack was provoked by nothing more than the fact that they were white.

"We were walking under the Bayswater subway when about 10 Aborigines appeared from nowhere and started calling us whities," Ms Clark said.

"They threw stones at us and one of them had a steel bar which he threw at Rob, hitting him in the neck.

"Rob grabbed the bar and told me to run, so I ran for my life.

"When Rob got the bar the gang backed off, so he threw it on the ground and ran after me.

"But some of them caught him in the laneway and started throwing stones at him and punching him.

"The other half ran after me and found me hiding

By HELEN WINTERTON

behind some air-conditioning units at the back of shops in King William Street.

"They stood over me and threw rocks at my head and punched me, and they kept saying 'where's your whitre boyfriend now?'.

"I pleaded with them to stop, please stop, but they kept hitting and stoning me.

"I have never pleaded so much in my life, for my life."

Ms Clark believes her life was saved when two women who lived nearby yelled at the group that they had called the police.

"After that the whole lot of them ran off."

One of her ears was ripped from her scalp during the attack and she required stitches in two large cuts in her head.

Mr Harvey was cut on the neck where the steel pole hit him and has bruises where he was punched.

"I have nightmares about that night all the time," Ms Clark said. "I would like to stone them so they would know how it felt."

● News Extra, page 11

Figure 8.15 (a) Woman scarred (*West Australian*)

full-page feature about Aboriginal petrol and glue sniffing that opens with a standard visualization of deviance: 'a generation of Aboriginal children are stumbling into oblivion' with 'glazed eyes and numb brains'. Why do they do this? 'They sniff to get away from their heritage: they sniff to get away from the boredom of unemployment and racial hatred: and, most importantly, they sniff because they want to.'

Why does the *West Australian* do this? Tucked away at the bottom of page 4, that day, was a story that even a vigilant reader might have missed. Its headline is in two decks, and the top deck reads 'BELL BREAKS RECORD . . .'. Intrigued locals may not have needed to be told that Bell is not only an object whose clanger may be dropped but also the name of the

212

Figure 8.15 (b) Alston cartoon (*West Australian*)

company, Bell Resources, which owned the *West Australian* newspaper, and was itself part of the severely troubled Bond group. Enter the second deck of the headline '. . . WITH $862.5M LOSS'. Bell Resources had just announced the biggest loss in Australian corporate history. This story made the front page of the *Australian*, the *Sydney Morning Herald* and the *Age*, but not the *West*, house paper of the Bond group and newspaper of record for Bond's home state. But just to show that it was not prejudiced against financial stories appearing on its front page, the *West Australian* ran one the very next day, 1 March 1990, with a story that just happened to be in the Bond group's favour (Figure 8.17).

It is hard to resist the conclusion that the obvious lead story of 28 February was buried, to be replaced by a story about nothing at all – a beat-up. When a researcher from the Royal Commission into Aboriginal Deaths in Custody, Steve Mickler, to whom I am indebted for this section, approached the local police in the suburbs named in the *West*, he found that the officers stationed there reported no increase in incidents, no 'rising' racial tension, and a normal arrest and charge rate for Aboriginal juveniles or adults, around the time of this story. On the contrary, one officer asserted that crime was not as serious in the suburbs in question as people think, and that most offenders are white. Another officer said that 'We've never had a call from the *West Australian*' and that her first reaction on reading the 'Aboriginal gangs' story was: 'I thought . . . you've got to be joking! They [the *West*]'re in it for a headline.'[24]

213

Aboriginal children sniff their lives away

WITH glazed eyes and numb brains, a generation of Aboriginal children are stumbling into oblivion.

They are children who have become dependent on the fumes of petrol and glue. They sniff to get away from their heritage; they sniff to get away from the boredom of unemployment and racial hatred; and, most importantly, they sniff because they want to.

Aboriginal worker Marian Kickett believes an entire generation of Aborigines could be crippled by this deadly craze which began when American servicemen showed Aborigines in the Top End how to get high during World War II.

She says the craze then filtered down through the Northern Territory and into WA.

It has now reached epidemic proportions in WA and is slowly taking a stranglehold on a youth already devastated by crime, poverty and unemployment.

"Research seems to indicate that it was a problem initially for American servicemen who did not have access to drugs or alcohol," Mrs Kickett says.

"They got an immediate high by sniffing petrol. Aborigines are very quick to pick these things up. They then passed it on to any others willing to watch."

In the five years to 1986, eight young Aboriginal men died from the effects of sniffing solvents in outback desert regions.

All of them were aged between 14 and 24 and came from communities in the Western desert region.

So what caused these youngsters to dip a rag in petrol, put it over their mouths and suck and inhale?

"There are many causes, but the number one cause would have to be boredom," Mrs Kickett says.

"There is a lack of sporting and recreational things for them to do in these areas. You must remember that we are talking about the outback and the facilities are limited.

"They also sniff because they feel neglected by their parents and this is one way out for them."

Another cause, according to Mrs Kickett, is cultural breakdown.

"Many of them are torn between their ways and the ways of the white man. Many of them have lost that respect for their elders.

"They have become rebellious and will do anything to buck the system.

"I also think the parents are the key to the whole problem being solved."

So what must they do?

"Well, what we can do is push for a massive community awareness program.

"We must tell the parents exactly what their kids are getting up to. When we travel to these outback areas, we get the whole community to come to our talk and give them some indication of the dangerous nature of this craze.

"We have developed a picture graph on how petrol affects the mind and tell these people how

□ **TONY BARRASS** encounters a deadly epidemic of petrol and glue addiction in WA among victims of outback boredom and parental neglect — a tragic craze that can only be stopped by the community getting together with the police and welfare agencies.

some of the kids are killing themselves.

"We are also attempting to make many of these people feel proud again. We have messages like how to be proud and strong and that you don't need these substances to have a good time.

"We are using role models like Stephen Michael and other sportsmen to let the kids know that they must be proud to be Aboriginal, it's not a crime to be one."

One of the main problem areas in Perth is Midland, where children as young as six are being pressured into glue sniffing.

Glue is freely available in many shops and, despite a joint move by the Health Department and the Aboriginal Affairs Planning Authority to warn shopkeepers of the epidemic, children are still able to get their hands on glue.

Snr Sgt Lou Dorsa, of Midland police, watches his junior officers attempting to control hysterical Aboriginal youths high on solvents at least three times a week.

"It is happening on a regular basis, too regular a basis for my liking," Sergeant Dorsa says.

"It really is becoming a problem in this area and, when you see it first hand, it is pathetically sad.

"I mean, what kind of future do these kids have? How are they going to get on with their lives and keep out of trouble if they continue to get plastered every night?"

Sergeant Dorsa says the hands of the police are tied when these youngsters, who average around 14, are arrested.

"We really can't do much with them. In most cases we can't prove that one of them stole some glue, although we know they have done so in the past.

"They have committed no offence, no offence we can prove anyway, so we have to get in contact with the Community Services Department.

"Once that happens, then it's out of our hands.

"But it's bloody sad, that's all I can say.

"Personally, I think a lot of the

blame must be put at the feet of the parents. I sometimes get the impression that many of them just don't care."

Sergeant Dorsa says one 12-year-old boy is arrested on an average of three times a week in Midland.

"When he comes in here he is completely gone, in no-man's land, doesn't have a clue what's going on. Sometimes he is hysterical and violent and uncontrollable.

"We have arrested some 10-year-olds too.

"Parents should put more effort into bringing up their children. And that's not just to stop this problem.

"I'm sure that if they did attempt to find out where their kids were or what they were doing, then we would see a general drop in all sorts of crime."

Community Services social worker Kevin McAllan agrees.

He believes that his department alone can't solve the problem, but a combined effort by all those trapped in the dirty web — police, health workers, Aboriginal leaders, social workers — can.

"And above all we need the help of the community," he says.

"The controls many Aborigines have over their children are different from white cultures. Sometimes they may give the appearance that they don't care.

"Society's attitude to this problem must change. This problem must be solved by groups of people getting together and figuring a solid, aggressive approach."

The number of Aborigines being admitted to hospital suffering the effects of solvent-sniffing has risen steadily — except in 1987 — for the past 10 years.

If the tide can't be held back, a white man's substance will have succeeded in putting yet another nail into the coffin of a race already struggling to survive in a white man's world.

Figure 8.15 (c) Children sniff lives away (*West Australian*)

Bell breaks record with $862.5m loss

BELL Resources yesterday secured an unenviable place in Australian corporate history when it posted a $862.5 million loss for the six months to December 31.

It also announced an investigation into more than 30 transactions involving the company under the control of Alan Bond and Robert Holmes à Court.

The big loss was the result of a clean-out of the accounts by the new independent directors who gained control of the company from the Bond group — its 58 per cent parent — last December as part of a Supreme Court deal involving the National Companies and Securities Commission.

The new board has slashed the value of loans which Bell Resources is owed by other Bond companies by $850 million, including a $504.4 million sum relating to the planned purchase of Bond Corp's Australian brewing assets.

Bell Resources now believes that the brewing deal will not eventuate and that it will recover just a fraction of outstandings from other Bond companies.

The company has made a full loss provision on a $604 million sum advanced to the failed petrochemical pro-

By JOHN McGLUE.

ject, an amount it will seek to recover by joining its estranged parent in a legal battle against the State Government.

But despite the big write-offs — $977.1 million in total — chairman Geoff Hill said he believed the company has a future as an independent corporation. At December 31, it retained net assets of $298.6 million.

As part of the company's move to prove its independence, Mr Hill said Bell Resources would investigate more than 30 transactions a task force of specially appointed lawyers and accountants had identified as requiring scrutiny.

The transactions stretch back three years and include deals carried out when the company was controlled by Mr Holmes à Court and later Mr Bond.

Copies of reports from lawyers Freehill Hollingdale & Page and accountants Deloitte Ross Tohmatsu have been sent to the NCSC. Mr Hill and another Bell Resources director Colin Henson have also personally briefed NCSC chairman Henry Bosch on the transactions.

● Full report, page 56.

Figure 8.16 Bell breaks record (*West Australian*)

The 'Aboriginal gangs' story caused immediate controversy. It was picked up by talk-back radio hosts on both metropolitan and country stations to solicit anti-Aboriginal sentiments from listeners. But it also elicited strong protest both from other journalists (forty-five of whom signed a letter that the *West*'s editor Paul Murray refused to publish) and from representatives of the Aboriginal community. One letter, from Rob Riley, was published, and Riley also made a formal complaint to the Australian Press Council (to no avail). The Royal Commission into Aboriginal Deaths in Custody roundly condemned the story (and so do I). Commissioner Dodson concluded that:

It is my Commission's belief that no reasonable case can be made for justifying such a headline, with its connotations of civil emergency and race riots, on the basis of the 'facts' offered in the accompanying article, and information relating to the circumstances of the writing of the article.[25]

The Royal Commission comments on the 'fundamental untruth' of this headline and article.

Unfortunately for the Aboriginal community – denizens of Theydom

Bond victory: court removes receivers

By JOHN McGLUE and LEONIE WOOD

THE Bond group yesterday scored a significant legal victory when the full bench of the Victorian Supreme Court ruled that the receivers of Bond Brewing Holdings should quit immediately.

The decision by Justices Kaye, Brooking and Murphy rescinds an order made by Justice Beach on December 29 on the application of an international banking syndicate led by the National Australia Bank.

It buys the Bond group more time to solve crippling debt problems, clears the way for plans to sell the Australian breweries and, at least temporarily, gives the group breathing space to make commercial decisions.

Bond Corp has already signalled its intention to sue the NAB syndicate for damages.

Legal sources in Perth indicated last night that the claim could run as high as $500 million.

The Bond group could claim damages for loss in reputation, loss of market share during the receivership, and damage caused by moves by US creditors to seek the winding-up of Bond Brewing after the receivers blocked interest payments due on debenture notes.

Receivers David Crawford and Charles Frar also face a multi-million-dollar damages suit.

The syndicate, owed $880 million by Bond Brewing Holdings, is considering whether to seek leave to appeal the decision in the High Court or to launch a new application for the appointment of a receiver, liquidator or provisional liquidator.

Last night, the Bond camp was adopting a conciliatory approach to the banks, hoping for a commercial settlement of their differences.

Bond Corp executive director Peter Lucas said that although the group had suffered "an extraordinary level of damage" from Justice Beach's decision on December 29, he believed efforts should now be directed towards negotiation rather than litigation.

Mr Lucas said the removal of the receivers "probably removes that cynicism and scepticism in the marketplace which happens if your major asset is tied up".

He doubted if the NAB syndicate would be granted leave to appeal such an emphatic decision.

But it is unlikely that yesterday's legal victory will prompt an easing of the attitude of Bond group bankers and creditors.

Aside from the NAB syndicate, Bond Brewing is also under threat from a group of US debenture holders owed more than $650 million. The group has petitioned the Victorian Supreme Court for the winding-up of Bond Brewing.

Preliminary procedural action continues today but the court has set a tentative timetable for a two-month trial beginning on May 1.

The trial is expected to argue the rights of the bank and bond holders as creditors.

Other Bond group companies are also facing big threats, including flagship Bond Corp which is facing a winding-up threat from its independently controlled subsidiary Bell Resources.

Yesterday, Justice Kaye said the bench had no doubt that the receivers should be removed immediately, and he set aside all orders made by Justice Beach.

"These companies (in the Bond Brewing group) should not have been placed in receivership," he said.

The reasons for the ruling would be published "as soon as possible" but he admitted the finding was "not complete" as questions of court costs and remuneration for the receivers would have to be dealt with.

But Justice Kaye said the bench believed the bank syndicate should bear the remuneration costs for the receivers.

In an affidavit which was partly read in the week-long court appeal, senior Bond group director Tony Oates said the group had lost about $2.5 million on a Euro-currency financing facility due to what he called "the non-management or inadequate management" of the facility.

Bond Corp has previously said the receivers' refusal to roll over foreign exchange contracts had caused losses.

Mr Oates' affidavit said that since the receivers and managers were installed, other funds had attracted interest penalties of about $26,301 a day, and losses on zero-coupon bonds financing amounted to $17,265 a day.

● Alston, page 10;
Attack on ABT, page 14
More reports, pages 46, 47

Figure 8.17 Bond victory (West Australian)

even in newspapers of record (among which the *West Australian* prides itself) – reason and truth are not the guiding principles of journalism, if they ever were. More fundamental than truth, more desirable than reason, are the adversarial visions which serve as common sense and civic education in the public domain of contemporary politics. And in this heliography, where politics is personalized and concepts are attached to people's bodies, the contrast between Wedom and Theydom is visualized as bodily opposition. Theydom is dark, threatening, glazed-eyed terror; even in the person of a seven-year-old boy, as in the first sentence of the 'Aboriginal gangs' story: 'Aboriginal gangs with members as young as seven are terrorising Bayswater residents and police fear the situation is getting out of control.' Certainly something is out of control when police can't control seven-year-olds, but of course that's not the point. The point is to create aliens out of people who've been 'residents' of the neighbourhood for up to 40,000 years.

Meanwhile, over the page as it were, Wedom is personified by a rhetorical and photogenic device that newspapers the world over will send their sons to death for – a pretty, young, white, heterosexual, naked woman.

Heliotroppo

The word *trope* comes from the Greek 'turn'; a trope in rhetoric is figurative language, the 'turning' of a word or phrase to a sense other than that which is proper to it. The sun, helios, also 'turns' at the solstices, i.e. the *tropics* of Capricorn and Cancer. A *heliotrope* is a plant whose flower turns to follow the sun. And *troppo* is an Australianism describing someone who's 'having a turn', going slightly crazy, 'going troppo' as those (Europeans) who spend too long in the tropics are reputed to do. Bearing all this in mind, and in the light of what follows, I think the term *heliotroppo* should be coined to describe journalism in a post-truth society.

'There are many challenges in journalism and the *Truth* is one of them.' So says Evan Whitton, one of those senior men who become known as doyens of their profession. Whitton's diverse and distinguished career as a journalist in Australia included a stint at the Melbourne *Truth*, a paper with a long history, that now operates as a bottom of the market weekly, somewhere between the *National Enquirer* and the *Sunday Sport*. Whitton's witty acknowledgement of the 'challenge' of the *Truth* comes from a tension between the *Truth*'s unabashed sexism and sensationalism, its populist unpretentiousness, on the one hand, and Whitton's own views on the social significance of journalism, on the other:

'Journalism is absolutely at the heart of democracy', he said. 'The press invented parliamentary democracy, not the politicians, not the lawyers, not anyone else. . . . If you believe in democracy, it appears

Outburst haunts Hawke

NUKE THE ARABS!

War reopens old ALP feud

★ HAWKE   ★ HARTLEY   ★ McMULLA

By RIC TURNER

AN outburst by Bob Hawke that nucle weapons be used against the Arabs has be revived as part of a campaign to discredit Prime Minister's stand on the Gulf War.

Mr Hawke made the comments during a heated La Party debate 17 years ago after Egypt had attacked Is in the 1973 Yom Kippur War.

Photocopies of a newspaper story wh appeared at the time — headlined "HAWKE: A-BOMB ARABS!" and quoting him as sa that if he were the Israeli Prime Ministe would drop an atomic bomb on invading Arab are now being circulated anonymously.

A copy was posted to *Truth* and a numbe phone calls about it have been received. anti-Hawke campaign has angered the A Kalgoorlie MHR Graeme Campbell describe as "mischief making".

Published on February 16, 1974, the s reported an outburst by Mr Hawke, then A president and federal president of the ALI Labor Federal Executive delegates Bill Ha and Bob McMullan.

The report said Mr Ha made the statement only b after Labor Party insiders tried to smooth over a between the then Prime M ter, Gough Whitlam, and Hawke over the governm neutral stance in the Mi East.

● CONTINUED. P

Figure 8.18 Nuke the Arabs! (*Truth*)

Truth joins the War

THE LAUGH'S ON SADDAM

THE first casualty of war may be the truth, but jokes thrive in the deadly atmosphere of combat.

By TIM BLAIR

Within hours of Iraq's first attack on Israel, a New Zealand joke surfaced: What does a Kiwi call a crater in Tel Aviv?

A SCUD mark.

And as pressure to blow the Iraqis away increased, we heard this weather forecast for Bagdad: early showers and overcast — with a top of 4000 degrees.

The Iraqi SCUD missiles were instant hits with US ground troops, who sang "Oh when the SCUDs come flying in" for the television cameras, and gags about the similarity between pantyhose and Saddam Hussein (they both aggravate Bush) began to circulate.

D-Generation jokester Tommy G awaits SCUDcam and has already developed a few lines of his own.

Duress

Tommy said the captured American airmen were obviously under duress during their appearance on Iraqi TV — "Every one of them used the phrase 'peace-loving Iraq'.

"Clearly there was someone nearby with a cattle prod.

"I've seen more convincing performances on Home And Away."

Kevin "Bloody" Wilson had a newsflash from the Gulf — "The Italians have surrendered."

And he's composed a tune about the anti-war protesters, with the lyrics: "Hell's Angels wouldn't root us. Said they're not that f...., sick."

"If you had somebody like those protesters at home, you'd start a bloody war to get away from them," Wilson said.

Veteran Los Angeles political comedian Mort Sahl said "after they defeat this guy Hussein, and the Iranians come back to reclaim the Ayatollah's home and holy resting place, and Hassad takes the part the Syrians want, and

the Turks take the northern provinces, President Bush can be known as the Thief of Baghdad."

Sahl is an avid Gulf newswatcher. "There was a funny thing today on CNN," he said.

"One of the reporters asked an Israeli major if he could name the neighborhood which the missile struck.

"And the major said: 'If you want to commit suicide, do it in another country'."

The Duke secret

TRUTH has discovered the secret of Saddam Hussein's military planning.

Saddam's a John Wayne fan who stores prints of The Duke's movies in 17 secret locations around Iraq and, two or three times a week, makes his generals watch the movie great in action.

Figure 8.19 Truth Gulf girl

to me there is no more important subject you can teach at a university than journalism. If the organs of the media don't work properly democracy doesn't exist.'[26]

I happen to think Whitton is right on all counts: journalism is at the heart of democracy, it is an important subject for tertiary teaching, and the *Truth* is certainly a challenge. As for the press 'inventing' parliamentary democracy, that is truth of a different order; it's strictly a political myth, a story of origins whose interest lies in the story, not the origins.[27]

As for the *Truth*, it's a celebration of fecundity, turning words, phrases and pictures to uses that are hardly proper at all, going troppo with the truth, telling stories that jangle the sensibilities of anyone looking for sense, common or otherwise. But it is also *representative* of journalism from Milton to Paine, the *Daily Sketch* to *Playboy*, synchronized swimmers to the *Sun*; it feminizes and sexualizes 'our' body politic.

On Australia Day, 26 January 1991, Australia was at war (though not with CNN; I don't think they ever mentioned the fact). The *Truth*'s headline for the day was 'NUKE THE ARABS!' Eyecatching and foe creating, the headline actually refers to a seventeen-year-old newspaper story about how, after the Yom Kippur War in 1973, Bob Hawke had said to Bill Hartley (no relation) that 'if he were the Israeli Prime Minister he would drop an atomic bomb on invading Arabs'. Of course Bob Hawke subsequently became the Australian Prime Minister, and sent HMAS *Sydney*, *Brisbane* and *Westralian* to the Persian Gulf. The *Truth* arranged to have itself sent to these ships, along with messages from home. 'With Valentine's Day just around the corner, what better way to get in touch . . .?' The *Truth*'s own message to 'our Gulf boys' is of course a '*Truth* Gulf Girl', Christine Peake, whose page-3 pin-up appears alongside this: 'The first casualty of war may be the truth, but jokes thrive in the deadly atmosphere of combat.' True to its word the *Truth* 'joins the Gulf War' on the home front with this, which is not in fact a joke:

Our boffins kill Arab pest

AUSTRALIA has turned to biological warfare to crush an Iraqi invasion.

Boffins have unleashed a deadly fungus to wipe out the enemy.

They warn that the blitz will cover the whole of Australia.

But no lives will be lost in this battle — against a native Iraqi weed, the common heliotrope.

The weed costs Australia a staggering $46 million a year by poisoning livestock and killing off crops.

Its flowers cause liver damage to grazing animals. The weed also sucks the goodness out of soil, starving crops.

Because there is nothing native to Australia which can control the spread of the weed, experts searched for a cure overseas.

After 10 years of research, they believe a fungus from Turkey holds the key to fighting off the Iraqi attack.

The fungus has just been released in the New South Wales rural town of Jugiong.

Spores from the fungus will infiltrate the weed through the soil and kill it.

Large areas of New South Wales and Western Australia will be treated with the fungus.

Spores from fungus released in the two states are expected to spread throughout Australia.

Dr Ernest Delfosse, of the CSIRO, in Canberra, said scientists were convinced the fungus would not harm other plants or native grasses in Australia.

"There was the most detailed testing program of any biological control agent ever undertaken," Dr Delfosse said.

The weed thrives in semi-desert areas.

It has small dark-green leaves and tiny white flowers.

Figure 8.20 Boffins kill pest (*Truth*)

USSIE SEX SPIES SNARE ARABS

AUSTRALIAN secret service agencies are using three sexy women to try to trap suspected Arab terrorists.

The daring move is part of a major domestic security crackdown accompanying the Gulf War.

Australian intelligence agencies are using the glamorous undercover agents to tighten the net on known pro-Saddam Hussein agitators in Melbourne and Sydney.

Two highly-placed Arab agents have already had their covers blown by the Aussie "sex squad".

Government sources say the two men, and a woman, are now under

By a STAFF REPORTER

24-hour surveillance as the war escalates.

The three women secret agents have been working as security operatives over the past three months and, according to secret service sources, were recruited because of their glamorous looks.

They report daily to their security chiefs in Canberra and have already infiltrated the tight ranks of four separate groups of Australian Arabs.

One of the women is believed to be an exotic dancer who has worked in clubs all over Australia. Recently, she has been a popular belly-dancer in Melbourne and Sydney.

Only one of the three women in the sex squad is a trained spy. She is also a part-time aerobics instructor believed to have worked for the feared Israeli Mossad spy agency in London, Paris and Cairo.

The three women have cultivated relationships with a number of Arab men and mingle socially with them.

Intelligence sources say the information gathered by the women agents — who have targeted nearly 50 Arabs living in Victoria and New South Wales — has been invaluable.

The undercover move follows Federal Government warnings to Australians to take seriously the threat of terrorism.

Figure 8.21 Sex spies (*Truth*)

The common heliotrope as trope for war with Iraq is a marvel of rhetoric, quite outshining the story itself, turning the release of a fungus as a biological control agent in the New South Wales rural town of Jugiong into 'fighting off the Iraqi attack', and so fulfilling on the same page an expectation expressed by the Minister for Defence, Senator Robert Ray, who is reported as saying '"I'm certain that all our Navy personnel in the Gulf will enjoy receiving news and messages from home – especially presented so colorfully by *Truth*".'

As with fungus, so with journalism; after release its spores are 'expected to spread throughout Australia', to 'infiltrate' the opposition without doing harm to the natives. Thus, on the next page, under the headline AUSSIE SEX SPIES SNARE ARABS, *Truth* reports that 'Australian secret service agencies are using three sexy women to try to trap suspected Arab terrorists.' The three women, one a 'popular belly dancer', another a 'part-time aerobics instructor', were 'recruited because of their glamorous looks'. They are reported to have 'already infiltrated the tight ranks of four separate groups of Australian Arabs'. Their mission is to 'tighten the net on known pro-Saddam Hussein agitators', and already two 'highly placed Arab agents' are 'under 24-hour surveillance' after having 'their covers blown by the Aussie "sex squad"'. This story is about setting up a boundary where there was none before, making a binary distinction

221

Figure 8.22 Stars back our men (*Truth*)

between the traditionally hostile domains of Wedom and Theydom. *Truth* conjures up an enemy out of nothing: Australian Arab becomes Arab, Arab becomes agitator, agitator becomes terrorist. At the same time *Truth* fakes a desirable identity for Wedom by sexualizing surveillance: women security operatives become glamorous sex spies whose qualifications are exotic dancing; mingling socially makes them a sex squad. None of the information is credited to named sources, and some of it is only 'believed to be' the case.

In this politics of knowledge Wedom is pretty as a picture, and to prove

222

it *Truth* completes its Gulf War coverage on Australia's national day by parading its symbolic community in support of the war effort. A middle-page spread combines a feature on how SEX REALLY DOES KEEP YOU HEALTHY with a banner that proclaims STARS BACK OUR MEN IN THE GULF. *Truth* lines up sportsmen and soap-opera stars from *Neighbours, E Street, The Flying Doctors* and *A Country Practice* to send cheerios to the sailors. One of them in fact 'backs' our men by saying 'even though I disapprove of the war I hope you all come back in one piece and soon'. Readers are reminded to send Valentine messages, and the circuit between the community, its symbolic media representatives, sex and politics is complete. The smiling professions have gone heliotroppo to advance Australia by fair means or foul, fair sex or fakes.

This, then, is the politics of pictures, journalism in a post-truth society, where the body politic is naked and smiling, and the public is turning towards the sun. What they may see there is anyone's guess, but it may include an image of themselves that is even more ancient than Leviathan, even more dazzling than synchronized swimming. For, as Borges reports in his *Book of Imaginary Beings*, in ancient Egypt the heliological sun was guarded by identical synchronized swimmers:

> As all Egyptians knew, Abtu and Anet were two life-sized fishes, identical and holy, that swam on the lookout for danger before the prow of the sun god's ship. Their course was endless; by day the craft sailed the sky from east to west, from dawn to dusk, and by night made its way underground in the opposite direction.[28]

And so we return to the place from which we started; the public as an imaginary being, its safety in the keeping of something very fishy indeed.

Of The Right Writing Of Our English Tung

Richard Mulcaster concludes the *First Part of the Elementarie* of 1582, the first attempt to teach the vernacular English tongue to its own speakers and readers, by saying:

> We should then know what we both write and speak. . . . Whereas at this daie: we be skillfull abode [abroad] and ignorant at home, wondring at others not waing [weighing] our own. Thus much at this time concerning these things, now must I to my table.[29]

Me too.

NOTES

1 Popular reality: a (hair)brush with cultural studies

1 John Katz, 'Anchor monster', *Rolling Stone* (US edn), 10 January 1991: 61–76.
2 *Australian Vogue*, January 1991: 40.
3 Graeme Turner (1990) *British Cultural Studies*, New York: Unwin Hyman.
4 Stuart Hall (1959) 'Absolute beginnings', *Universities & Left Review* 7: 16–25; this quotation p. 19.
5 ibid., p. 21.
6 ibid., p. 24.
7 ibid., p. 23.
8 Stuart Hall (1959) 'The big swipe: some comments on the "classlessness controversy"', *Universities & Left Review* 7: 50–2.
9 ibid., p. 51.
10 Source: *The Australian*, 21 November 1990.
11 Jeff Giles, 'The Milli Vanilli wars', *Rolling Stone* (US edn), 10 January 1991: 24.
12 See Hans Magnus Enzensberger (1970) 'Constituents of a theory of the media', *New Left Review* 64. All my quotations come from the same essay as republished in Enzensberger's (1976) *Raids and Reconstructions: Essays on Politics, Crime and Culture*, London: Pluto Press, pp. 20–53.
13 ibid., p. 34.
14 ibid., p. 32.
15 ibid., p. 34.
16 Hall, 'The big swipe', p. 52.
17 Stuart Hall himself is credited with the first published use of the very term 'Thatcherism', so astute and convincing was his analysis, in a 1979 issue of *Marxism Today*, i.e. *before* her election victory.
18 Hall, 'The big swipe', p. 50.

2 Agoraphilia: the politics of pictures

1 Walter A. McDougall (1985) . . . *The Heavens and The Earth: a Political History of the Space Age*, New York: Basic Books, p. 20 (my emphasis).
2 Quoted ibid., p. 20.
3 Aristotle, *Politics*, vii. 4–14, trans. B. Jowett, cited in Louis Wirth (1938) 'Urbanism as a way of life', in Richard Sennett (ed.) (1969) *Classic Essays on the Culture of Cities*, Englewood Cliffs, NJ: Prentice-Hall, pp. 143–64; this citation, p. 151. See also Chapter 4, below.

4 In the media, 'the public domain' does have specific meaning, referring to words and pictures that may freely be reproduced by other media because they are not copyright. Here the public domain is intellectual property without an owner, common property to be plundered at will for private, usually corporate, gain. It includes 'the public record'; for instance statements made in or to a parliament, and it encompasses 'the public interest'. Statements in the public interest, on the public record, may circulate in the public domain, and avoid litigation for piracy if not defamation.

5 See the excellent essay on 'Postmodernism' in Martin Coyle, Peter Garside, Malcolm Kelsall and John Peck (eds) (1990) *Encyclopedia of Literature and Criticism*, London: Routledge.

6 Charles Jencks (1973) *Modern Movements in Architecture*, Harmondsworth: Penguin, p. 375.

7 ibid.

8 ibid., p. 376.

9 See I.F. Stone (1989) *The Trial of Socrates*, London: Picador.

10 Jencks, op. cit., pp. 204–5.

11 ibid., p. 185.

12 See Henry Tudor (1972) *Political Myth*, London: Macmillan, Chapter 3.

13 Jencks, op. cit., p. 15.

14 ibid., p. 31.

15 ibid., p. 373.

3 No picnic: for all flesh *is* as grass

1 I Peter, 1:24, Authorized Version; Isaiah, 40:6–7; Johannes Brahms, *Ein Deutsches Requiem*, op. 45. (St Peter continues, incidentally, with an early statement of the power of *discourse*: 'But the *word* . . . endureth for ever.')

2 Terry Eagleton (1988) 'The critic as clown', in Cary Nelson and Lawrence Grossberg (eds) *Marxism and the Interpretation of Culture*, Urbana and Chicago: University of Illinois Press, pp. 619–31; this quotation p. 625. The paper is concerned with the work of William Empson.

3 ibid., p. 619.

4 ibid., p. 620.

5 ibid., p. 627.

6 ibid., p. 626.

7 Bede Morris (1986) *Images: Illusion and Reality*, Canberra: Australian Academy of Science, pp. 18–19.

8 Kodak Consumer Markets Division (n.d.) *Home Movies Made Easy: An Idea Book From Kodak*, Rochester, NY: Eastman Kodak. Although not dated, this handbook contains internal evidence that it was compiled and published between 1968 and 1970.

9 Hans Magnus Enzensberger (1970) 'Constituents of a theory of the media', in *Raids and Reconstructions: Essays on Politics, Crime and Culture* (1976), London: Pluto Press, pp. 20–53.

10 See Chapter 1, note 12.

11 Edwin Hodder (n.d.) *Heroes of Britain in Peace and War*, London, Paris and Melbourne: Cassell, pp. 264–5.

12 ibid., p. 262. 'Victoria Nyanza' is Lake Victoria, whose south-eastern corner is still called Speke Gulf.

13 ibid., p. 267. This region would be what is now Uganda, Tanzania and Kenya, all former British colonies.

14 Truth depends on how you look at it: 'Speke was the discoverer of the source of the Nile, though not of its remotest source': ibid., p. 267. The story is nearly as complicated as the Nile's headwaters, but it is unravelled, along with a rather different account of King Mutesa, in Alan Moorehead (1971) *The White Nile*, revised edn, London: Hamish Hamilton.

15 Bede Morris, op. cit., p. 27.

16 ibid., pp. 3–4.

17 G.M. Trevelyan, OM (1942–4) *English Social History*, London: Longmans, Green, pp. 571–2.

18 See Walter J. Ong, SJ (1958) *Ramus: Method, and the Decay of Dialogue: From the Art of Discourse to the Art of Reason*, Cambridge, Mass., Harvard University Press; or Walter J. Ong (1982) *Orality and Literacy: The Technologizing of the Word*, London and New York, Methuen, pp. 134 and 168.

19 Advertisement for Continental Gravy, *Australian Women's Weekly*, April 1990. An ad for gravy which teaches art theory may be the place to acknowledge that picnics also have a food content, and that interested readers may follow the history of the diet of an entire continent in Michael Symons (1980) *One Continuous Picnic*, Adelaide: Duck Press.

20 Jacques Donzelot (1980) *The Policing of Families*, trans. Robert Hurley, London: Hutchinson.

21 *Hero* (July–August 1986), Numero [*sic*] 6: 24–9.

22 The opening editorial ('Hello Again') by Robin Powell introduces the fashion spread thus: 'Pip and Don and a hoard of models went up to the Blue Mountains to do a shoot about picnics and walking through parks and fabulous clothes with a retro feel. They camped out overnight and saw Halley's Comet on the best night of all' (ibid., p. 3).

23 But see Kay Schaffer (1988) *Women and the Bush: Forces of Desire in the Australian Cultural Tradition*, Melbourne: Cambridge University Press; and her article 'Landscape, Representation and Australian National Identity,' *Australian Journal of Cultural Studies* (4) 2: 47–60, 1987.

24 Advertisement for Brooke Bond Tea, *Illustrated* (London), 31 August 1957, back cover. See also 'Jimmy Edwards entertains the picnic girls' (Figure 3.13), which is the front cover of the same magazine.

25 *The Face*, October 1981, p. 41.

26 ibid.

27 Larry Gross (June 1990) 'The right to privacy vs. the duty of sexual secrecy: battlefield sketches from the sexual counter-revolution', paper presented to ICA Conference, Dublin.

28 *Illustrated* XIX (28), 31 August 1957.

29 'Heroine addicts', *West Australian Magazine*, 21 March 1991: 19–22.

30 'Tally Ho, Toff They Go: Canada Di dresses up to meet the Mounties' by Sue Evison, *The Sun*, London, 17 October 1991, p. 3.

31 'Gee, don't they look cute: Britain's best export packaged to conquer the Canadian Market' by Sandra Parsons, *Daily Mail*, London, 17 October 1991, pp. 32–3.

32 'Portrait of a Princely Picnic: By Lord Snowdon . . . with a little help from Gainsborough' by Jane Moore. *Today*, London, 17 October 1991, pp. 12–13.

33 'Nice Picnic (Shame about the price . . .): Royals made a meal of it when they forked out on summer snaps for the family album' by Sue Blackhall and Liz Duxbury, *Daily Star*, London, 17 October 1991, pp. 24–5.

34 'I Say! One's forgotten the sandwiches: Royal Picnickers make a real meal of it' by James Whitaker, *Daily Mirror*, London, 17 October 1991, p. 13.

35 'Growing up so fast: Lord Snowdon captures the princes' new maturity', *Evening Standard*, London, 17 October 1991, p. 18.
36 'Thatcher girl to defence of royal film muckrakers' by Mike Graham, *Today*, London, 17 October 1991, p. 14.
37 News Ltd., News International and Fox TV are all part of the Murdoch media empire.
38 'Wanted – real dad for Di's two' by Mary Keenan, *The Sunday Times*, Perth, W.A., 23 February 1992, 'Sunday' section p. 6.
39 'Ideas by Jung, hamper by Harrods' [Leader editorial], *The Independent on Sunday*, London, 20 October 1991, p. 24.
40 'A princess and her princes', *Vogue*, London, vol. 155, no. 11, November 1991, pp. 222–5.
41 *Vogue*, London, vol. 155, no. 12, December 1991, cover.

4 Power viewing: a glance at pervasion in the postmodern perplex

1 John Hartley (1992) *Tele-ology: Studies in Television*, London and New York: Routledge, Chapter 2.
2 Marshall Sahlins (1976) *Culture and Practical Reason*, Chicago: University of Chicago Press.
3 Karl Marx (1961) *Economic and Philosophical Manuscripts of 1844 [The Paris Manuscripts]* (1844), Moscow: Foreign Languages Publishing Service, p. 105.
4 Nick Brown (1987) 'The political economy of the television (super) text', in Horace Newcomb (ed.) *Television: The Critical View*, 4th edn, New York: Oxford University Press, pp. 585–99.
5 Karl Popper (1967) 'Knowledge: subjective versus objective', in David Miller (ed.) (1983) *A Pocket Popper*, London: Fontana, pp. 58–77; this reference p. 72.
6 R. Buckminster Fuller, with Jerome Agel and Quentin Fiore (1970) *I Seem to be a Verb*, New York: Bantam Books. The Emerson quotation is taken from 'The compilers to the reader', in (1941) *The Oxford Dictionary of Quotations*, 1st edn, Oxford: Oxford University Press, p. xii.
7 Michel Foucault (1977) *Discipline and Punish: the Birth of the Prison*, trans. Alan Sheridan, Harmondsworth: Penguin.
8 Jacques Derrida (1987) *The Postcard: from Socrates to Freud and Beyond*, Chicago: University of Chicago Press.
9 Hartley, op. cit., Chapter 3. Kurt Vonnegut (1981) *Palm Sunday: An Autobiographical Collage*, London, Cape, p. 14.
10 Sahlins, op. cit., p. 217.
11 John Fiske (1990) 'Ethnosemiotics: some personal and theoretical reflections', *Cultural Studies* 4 (1): 85–99.
12 Edward Said (1978) *Orientalism*, London: Routledge & Kegan Paul.
13 Sahlins, op. cit., p. 203.
14 ibid., pp. 203–4.
15 Hartley, op. cit., Chapter 12.
16 John Hartley (1987) 'Been there – done that: on academic tourism', *Communication Research* 14 (2): 251–61; this quotation p. 256.
17 This refers to the 'Toward a Comprehensive Theory of the Audience' conference at the University of Illinois, for which the paper on which this chapter is based was written.
18 *Australian Magazine, Weekend Australian* 10–11 March 1990.

19 Robert Park (1916) 'The city: suggestions for the investigation of human behaviour in the urban environment', *American Journal of Sociology* 20, reprinted in Richard Sennett (ed.) (1969) *Classic Essays on the Culture of Cities*, Englewood Cliffs, NJ: Prentice-Hall, pp. 91–130; these references pp. 121–4.

20 Ien Ang and David Morley (1989) 'Mayonnaise culture and other European follies', *Cultural Studies* 3 (2): 133–44; this quotation p. 137.

21 John Ellis (1982) *Visible Fictions: Cinema, Television, Video*, London: Routledge & Kegan Paul.

22 Thorstein Veblen (1953) *The Theory of the Leisure Class: an Economic Study of Institutions* (1899), New York: New American Library.

23 Aristotle, *Politics*, vii. 4–14, trans. B. Jowett, cited in Louis Wirth (1938) 'Urbanism as a way of life', in Richard Sennett (ed.) (1969) *Classic Essays on the Culture of Cities*, Englewood Cliffs, NJ: Prentice-Hall, pp. 143–64; this citation p. 151, my italics, and see Chapter 2.

24 Thomas Hobbes (1968) *Leviathan* (1651), ed. C.B. Macpherson, Harmondsworth: Penguin, p. 683.

25 ibid., p. 684.

26 ibid.

27 ibid., p. 685.

28 *Washingtoon, Village Voice*, New York, April 1990.

29 Veblen, op. cit., p. 252.

30 John Hartley (November 1991), 'Show Piece: The personalization of television', in David Watson and Denise Corrigan (eds) *TV Times*, Sydney: Museum of Contemporary Art.

31 'I was terribly worried during those first six months (1956–7) because the public were still watching television in shop windows. But once we came in with *Disneyland* and *I Love Lucy*, the sets started to sell and we were away with a gallop.' From 'Ken G. Hall and Australia's Fledgling TV: An Interview with Graham Shirley', in Denise Corrigan and David Watson (eds) (1991) *TV Times*, Sydney: Museum of Contemporary Art, pp. 41–3. [Ken Hall was hired by Sir Frank Packer to 'sort things out' at TCN–9 in Sydney after a poor start.]

5 The smiling professions: from a sea monster to synchronized swimming

1 Mary Dejevsky (1991) 'Soviets in search of heroes to lift morale', *Weekend Australian* (from *The Times*), 20–1 April.

2 For an extended and definitive account of various constructions of the TV audience, as market, public, and as object of both critical and empirical research, see Ien Ang (1991) *Desperately Seeking the Audience*, London and New York: Routledge.

3 Thomas Hobbes (1968) *Leviathan* (1651) ed. C.B. Macpherson, Harmondsworth: Penguin, p. 227.

4 C.B. Macpherson (1973) *Democratic Theory: Essays in Retrieval*, Oxford: Oxford University Press, p. 242.

5 ibid., pp. 40–1 and 64ff.

6 Hobbes, op. cit., p. 81.

7 The idea of total transfer of sovereignty did not endear Hobbes to the newly ascendant class of propertied men, who had to wait for John Locke before a political philosophy based on Hobbesianism could be seen to coincide with their interests. Locke allowed that civil power is class power, and that the propertied class retains its power even while assenting to representative government. The historic manifestation of this compromise was the Glorious Revolution of 1688,

228

which established a 'Constitutional monarchy', i.e. a government which was sovereign but subject to class power.

8 Hobbes, op. cit., p. 379.
9 ibid.
10 ibid., pp. 380–3.
11 ibid., p. 381.
12 Macpherson has shown that despite his acuity, Hobbes's political philosophy was deficient in not recognizing the possibility of cohesive class action within possessive individualism; a theoretical weakness which was corrected in the liberal individualism of John Locke, whose version of Hobbesianism allowed for class power, and 'rationalized' the political arrangements of the Glorious Revolution. See Macpherson, op. cit., and especially his (1962) *The Political Theory of Possessive Individualism: Hobbes to Locke*, Oxford: Oxford University Press.
13 Hobbes, op. cit., p. 384.
14 ibid., pp. 725–8.
15 ibid., pp. 383–5.
16 ibid., p. 688.
17 John Locke, *The Reasonableness of Christianity*, cited in Macpherson (1962), p. 224.
18 Cited ibid., p. 225.
19 Hobbes, op. cit., p. 387.
20 Robert Hughes (1988) *The Fatal Shore: a History of the Transportation of Convicts to Australia 1787–1868*, London: Pan Books, p. 141.
21 ibid., p. 140.
22 Thorstein Veblen (1953) *The Theory of the Leisure Class: An Economic Study of Institutions* (1899), New York: New American Library, p. 248.
23 ibid., p. 250.
24 ibid., p. 249.
25 Hobbes, op. cit., p. 82.
26 Veblen, op. cit., p. 249.
27 Peter Kropotkin (1974) *Fields, Factories and Workshops Tomorrow* (1899), ed. Colin Ward, London: Allen & Unwin, Chapter 4.
28 Fredric Jameson (1988) 'Cognitive mapping', in Cary Nelson and Lawrence Grossberg (eds) *Marxism and the Interpretation of Culture*, Urbana and Chicago: University of Illinois Press, pp. 347–57.
29 Umberto Eco (1987) *Travels in Hyperreality*, trans. W. Weaver. London: Picador, p. 83.
30 Henry Tudor (1972) *Political Myth*, London: Macmillan.

6 Heliography: journalism and the visualization of truth

1 Jacques Derrida (1978) *Writing and Difference*, trans. Alan Bass, London: Routledge & Kegan Paul, p. 92. The internal quotations are from J.L. Borges, *La Sphère de Pascal*.
2 ibid. See also Chapter 8, note 8.
3 Richard V. Ericson, Patricia M. Baranek and Janet B.L. Chan (1987) *Visualizing Deviance: a Study of News Organization*, Milton Keynes: Open University Press, p. 3.
4 ibid., p. 4.
5 R.M. Ballantyne (1882) *Saved by the Lifeboat: a Tale of Wreck and Rescue on the Coast*, London: James Nisbet. This quotation from the introductory note, p. iii.

6 Ericson *et al.*, op. cit., p. 339.
7 ibid.
8 ibid., pp. 340–2.
9 'Numbering a newspaper', *The Times* (no. 50,000) 25 November 1944.
10 John Milton (1644) 'Areopagitica', in C.A. Patrides (ed.) (1974) *John Milton: Selected Prose*, Harmondsworth: Penguin, pp. 234–5.
11 ibid., p. 236.
12 ibid., p. 241.
13 ibid., pp. 226–7.
14 ibid., pp. 218–19.
15 ibid., p. 220.
16 ibid., pp. 239–41.
17 *The Spectator, Corrected from the Originals . . . by N. Ogle, Esq., in Eight Volumes*, London: Geo. B. Whittaker, 1827; Volume VIII, p. 112.
18 ibid., p. 115.
19 ibid., p. 117.
20 Samuel Johnson (1788), 'Of the Duty of a Journalist' (1758), *The European Magazine, and London Review: Containing the Literature, History, Politics, Arts, Manners & Amusements of the Age* (London: Philological Society of London) XIII: 77–8. Originally published (according to a headnote) as 'the Preface to Payne's Universal Chronicle, in which the Idler originally was printed, in April 1758'.
21 ibid.
22 ibid.
23 Cited in the editor's introduction to Christopher Hibbert (ed.) (1979) *James Boswell: The Life of Johnson*, Harmondsworth: Penguin, p. 25. (The wording differs from the cleaned-up version to be found in the *Life* itself.)
24 Patrick Cruttwell (ed.) (1968) *Samuel Johnson: Selected Writings*, Harmondsworth: Penguin. This quotation from Cruttwell's introduction, p. 21.
25 ibid., p. 22.
26 ibid.
27 ibid., p. 17.
28 ibid., p. 18.
29 From, Johnson's *Journal of a Tour to the Hebrides*, cited ibid., p. 17.
30 Hibbert (ed.), op. cit., p. 66.
31 Johnson, 'Of the Duty of a Journalist', op. cit.

7 Common sense: universal v. adversarial journalism

1 Winston S. Churchill (1956) *A History of the English-speaking Peoples*, 4 vols, London, Melbourne, Sydney, Toronto, Johannesburg, Cape Town and Auckland: Cassell.
2 Quoted on the blurb to my paperback edition.
3 Churchill, op. cit., Preface to vol. I, pp. vii and xvii.
4 ibid., p. viii.
5 See Chapter 6 for Johnson's remarks on the duty of a journalist in detail.
6 Malcolm Thomson (1965) *Churchill: His Life and Times*, London: Odhams Books, pp. 41–51.
7 Thomas Paine (1976) *Common Sense* (1776), ed. Isaac Krammick, Harmondsworth: Penguin.
8 Quoted in Editor's Introduction, ibid., p. 10.
9 The quotations and figures cited in this paragraph are from ibid., pp. 7–59.
10 Thomas Paine (1937) *Rights of Man: Being an Answer to Mr. Burke's Attack*

on the French Revolution (1791–2) ed. Hypatia Bradlaugh Bonner, London: Watts, p. 196, footnote by Paine.

11 From Trevelyan's *History of the American Revolution*, quoted in Krammick, op. cit., p. 29.

12 ibid., p. 30.

13 The Declaration of Independence, quoted from Churchill, op. cit., vol. III, p. 154.

14 Paine (1976), op. cit., pp. 82, 91, 89.

15 ibid., pp. 99–100.

16 Cited in Krammick, op. cit., p. 23. See also Pauline Maier (1974) *From Resistance to Revolution*, New York, p. 270.

17 The Declaration of Independence, op. cit.

18 Paine (1976), op. cit., pp. 65–6.

19 *The Times*, 25 November 1944.

20 Stanley Harrison (1974) *Poor Men's Guardians: A Record of the Struggles for a Democratic Newspaper Press, 1763–1973*, London: Lawrence & Wishart, p. 30. I am indebted to Harrison's book for many of the original statements and statistics used in this chapter. I have also drawn on, and am equally indebted to, George Boyce, James Curran and Pauline Wingate (eds) (1978) *Newspaper History: From the Seventeenth Century to the Present Day*, London, Constable; Beverly Hills, Sage; and to Louis James (1976) *Print and the People 1819–1851*, Harmondsworth, Penguin.

21 In his *Reflections on the Revolution in France*, published in 1792.

22 See Krammick, op. cit., pp. 36–7.

23 Churchill, op. cit., vol. IV, p. 41.

24 Quoted in Krammick, op. cit., pp. 14–15. Lord Mansfield's 1766 figure for the number of electors (one million) is much too high if Churchill's estimate of 800,000 voters *after* the Reform Act of 1832 is correct.

25 Churchill, op. cit., vol. IV, p. 36.

26 Philip Elliott (1978) 'Professional ideology and organisational change: the journalist since 1800', in Boyce *et al.* (eds), op. cit., pp. 172–91. This quotation, pp. 178–9.

27 The (London) *Sunday Times* Colour Magazine, April 1977, reproduces this photograph. It was first published in a book in Harold Evans (1978) *Pictures on a Page: Photo-Journalism, Graphics and Picture Editing*, London: Heinemann, p. 324.

28 Source: *Sunday Times*, April 1977.

29 James Curran (1978) 'The press as an agency of social control: an historical perspective', in Boyce *et al.* (eds), op. cit., pp. 51–75. This citation, p. 70.

30 Thomson, op. cit., p. 61.

31 George Boyce (1978) 'The fourth estate: the reappraisal of a concept', in Boyce *et al.* (eds), op. cit., pp. 19–40. This citation, p. 31.

32 *The Times*, 25 November 1944.

8 Journalism in a post-truth society: the sexualization of the body politic

1 Caption to 'Governor Davey's proclamation to the Aborigines, 1816'; see note 21.

2 Kennedy Jones (1919) *Fleet Street and Downing Street*, London: Hutchinson, pp. 149–50. Jones was editor of the London *Evening News* in the 1890s. See Michael Palmer (1978) 'The British press and international news, 1851–99: of agencies and papers', in George Boyce, James Curran and Pauline Wingate

(eds) *Newspaper History: From the Seventeenth Century to the Present Day*, London, Constable; Beverly Hills, Sage, pp. 205–19.

3 Kennedy Jones, op. cit.

4 *The Leamington Chronicle*, 15 September 1836, cited in Gavin Souter (1981) *Company of Heralds*, Melbourne: Melbourne University Press, p. 10.

5 *Sydney Morning Herald*, 1842, quoted in Souter, op. cit., p. 34.

6 *Sydney Morning Herald*, quoted ibid., p. 35.

7 Souter, op. cit., p. 17.

8 Cited under 'heliography' in the *OED*. See also John Moynihan (1988) *All the News in a Flash*, Perth: Australian Telecom and the Australian Institution of Engineers' WA Branch, which has a chapter on heliographic signalling from Rottnest Island to the Australian mainland in the nineteenth century – a technology of news visualization which was indeed all done with mirrors.

9 Samuel Johnson (1788) 'Of the Duty of a Journalist' (1758), *The European Magazine and London Review: Containing the Literature, History Politics, Arts, Manners & Amusements of the Age* XIII: London: Philological Society of London, 77–8.

10 *Sydney Morning Herald*, 21 June 1844, quoted in Robert Hughes (1987) *The Fatal Shore: A History of the Transportation of Convicts to Australia 1787–1868*, London: Pan Books, p. 281.

11 See ibid., pp. 272–81.

12 ibid., p. 280.

13 ibid.

14 ibid., p. 95.

15 Thomas Hobbes (1968) *Leviathan* (1651), ed. C.B. Macpherson, Harmondsworth: Penguin, p. 387.

16 Hughes, op. cit., pp. 91–4.

17 The Right Hon. H.O. Arnold-Forster, MP (1904) *The Citizen Reader* (1886), London, Paris, New York, Melbourne: Cassell, pp. 58–62.

18 ibid., preface by the Right Hon. W.E. Forster.

19 Jules Feldmann (1951) *The Great Jubilee Book: The Story of the Australian Nation in Pictures*, Melbourne: Colorgravure Publications (The *Herald & Weekly Times*), p. 7. My thanks to Roger Simms for this.

20 ibid., p. 16.

21 Caption to 'Governor Davey's proclamation to the Aborigines, 1816', reproduced ibid., p. 17, from the Mitchell Library. Another version of this celebrated Van Demonian notice is reproduced in Hughes, op. cit., where it is credited to Governor Arthur (1828), not Davey (1816), from the Tasmanian Museum and Art Gallery.

22 The following section draws substantially on my submission to the Royal Commission into Aboriginal Deaths in Custody (1987–91), hearing on Underlying Issues (the press), by Commissioner Patrick Dodson, Perth, Western Australia, 30 May 1990.

23 Letter from Murray to Doug Spencer and other journalists of the ABC in Perth, who had written to complain about the story. Murray's letter is dated 6 March 1990. The correspondence is in the Royal Commission's transcripts, and was published in *Scoop*, the journal of the Australian Journalist's Association (WA Branch), no. 41990.

24 Royal Commission into Aboriginal Deaths in Custody (May 1991) Regional Report of Inquiry into Underlying Issues in Western Australia, vol. 2, pp. 714–15. See also Steve Mickler (1992) 'Visions of disorder: media, police, Aboriginal people and the politics of youth crime reporting', *Cultural Studies* 6 (3).

25 ibid., p. 715.
26 *University of Queensland News*, October 1990.
27 Cf. Henry Tudor (1972) *Political Myth*, London: Macmillan.
28 Jorge Luis Borges with Margarita Guerrero (1974 [1967]) *The Book of Imaginary Beings*, trans. and revised by Norman Thomas di Giovanni, Harmondsworth: Penguin, p. 16.
29 Richard Mulcaster (1582) *The First Part of the Elementarie which entreateth chefelie of the right writing of our English tung*, facsimile edition (1970), Menston, Yorks.: Scolar Press, p. 169.

BIBLIOGRAPHY

Ang, Ien (1991) *Desperately Seeking the Audience*, London and New York: Routledge.

Ang, Ien and Morley, David (1989) 'Mayonnaise culture and other European follies', *Cultural Studies* 3 (2): 133–44.

Boswell, James (1979) *James Boswell: The Life of Johnson*, ed. Christopher Hibbert, Harmondsworth: Penguin.

Boyce, George, Curran, James and Wingate, Pauline (eds) (1978) *Newspaper History, From the Seventeenth Century to the Present Day*, London: Constable.

Brown, Nick (1987) 'The political economy of the television (super)text', in Horace Newcomb (ed.) *Television: The Critical View*, 4th edn, New York: Oxford University Press, pp. 585–99.

Buckminster Fuller, R., with Agel, Jerome, and Fiore, Quentin (1970) *I Seem To Be a Verb*, New York: Bantam Books.

Churchill, W.S. (1956) *A History of the English-speaking Peoples*, 4 vols, London, Melbourne, Sydney, Toronto, Johannesburg, Cape Town, Auckland: Cassell.

Corrigan, Denise and Watson, David (eds) (1991) *TV Times: 35 Years of Watching Television in Australia*, Sydney: Museum of Contemporary Art.

Coyle, Martin, Garside, Peter, Kelsall, Malcolm and Peck, John (eds) (1990) *Encyclopedia of Literature and Criticism*, London: Routledge.

Derrida, Jacques (1978) *Writing and Difference*, trans. Alan Bass, London: Routledge & Kegan Paul.

Derrida, Jacques (1987) *The Postcard: from Socrates to Freud and Beyond*, Chicago: University of Chicago Press.

Donzelot, Jacques (1980) *The Policing of Families*, trans. Robert Hurley, London: Hutchinson.

Eagleton, Terence (1988) 'The critic as clown', in Cary Nelson and Lawrence Grossberg (eds) *Marxism and the Interpretation of Culture*, Urbana and Chicago: University of Illinois Press, pp. 619–31.

Eco, Umberto (1987) *Travels in Hyperreality*, trans. W. Weaver, London: Picador.

Ellis, John (1982) *Visible Fictions: Cinema, Television, Video*, London: Routledge & Kegan Paul.

Enzensberger, Hans Magnus (1970) 'Constituents of a theory of the media', in *Raids and Reconstructions: Essays on Politics, Crime and Culture* (1976), London: Pluto Press, pp. 20–53.

Ericson, Richard V., Baranek, Patricia M. and Chan, Janet B.L. (1987) *Visualizing Deviance: a Study of News Orrganization*, Milton-Keynes: Open University Press.

234

Evans, Harold (1978) *Pictures on a Page: Photo-Journalism, Graphics and Picture Editing*, London: Heinemann.

Fiske, John (1990) 'Ethnosemiotics: some personal and theoretical reflections', *Cultural Studies* 4 (1): 85–99.

Foucault, Michel (1977) *Discipline and Punish: the Birth of the Prison*, trans. Alan Sheridan, Harmondsworth: Penguin.

Gross, Larry (1990) 'The right to privacy vs. the duty of sexual secrecy: battle-field sketches from the sexual counter-revolution', paper presented to ICA Conference, Dublin, June.

Hall, Stuart (1959a), 'Absolute beginnings', *Universities & Left Review* 7: 16–25.

Hall, Stuart (1959b) 'The big swipe: some comments on the "classlessness controversy"', *Universities & Left Review* 7: 50–2.

Harrison, Stanley (1974) *Poor Men's Guardians: A Record of the Struggles for a Democratic Newspaper Press, 1763–1973*, London: Lawrence & Wishart.

Hartley, John (1987) 'Been there – done that: on academic tourism', *Communication Research* 14 (2): 251–61.

Hartley, John (1992) *Tele-ology: Studies in Television*, London and New York, Routledge.

Hobbes, Thomas (1968) *Leviathan* (1651) ed. C.B. Macpherson, Harmondsworth: Penguin.

Hughes, Robert (1988) *The Fatal Shore: a History of the Transportation of Convicts to Australia 1787–1868*, London: Pan Books.

James, Louis (1976) *Print and the People, 1819–1851*, Harmondsworth: Penguin.

Jameson, Fredric (1988) 'Cognitive mapping', in Cary Nelson & Lawrence Grossberg (eds) *Marxism and the Interpretation of Culture*, Urbana and Chicago: University of Illinois Press.

Jencks, Charles (1973) *Modern Movements in Architecture*, Harmondsworth: Penguin.

Johnson, Samuel (1788), 'Of the Duty of a Journalist' (1758) *The European Magazine* 13: 77–8 (London: Philological Society of London).

Johnson, Samuel (1968) *Samuel Johnson: Selected Writings*, ed. Patrick Cruttwell, Harmondsworth: Penguin.

Kropotkin, Peter (1974) *Fields, Factories and Workshops Tomorrow* (1899), ed. Colin Ward, London: Allen & Unwin.

McDougall, Walter A. (1985) . . . *The Heavens and The Earth: a Political History of the Space Age*, New York: Basic Books.

Macpherson, C.B. (1962) *The Political Theory of Possessive Individualism: Hobbes to Locke*, Oxford: Oxford University Press.

Macpherson, C.B. (1973) *Democratic Theory: Essays in Retrieval*, Oxford: Oxford University Press.

Marx, Karl (1961) *Economic and Philosophical Manuscripts of 1844*, Moscow: Foreign Languages Publishing Service.

Mickler, Steve (1992) 'Visions of disorder: media, police, Aboriginal people and the politics of youth crime reporting', *Cultural Studies* 6 (3).

Milton, John (1974) *John Milton: Selected Prose*, ed. C.A. Patrides, Harmondsworth: Penguin.

Moorehead, Alan (1971) *The White Nile*, revised edn, London: Hamish Hamilton.

Morris, Bede (1986) *Images: Illusion and Reality*, Canberra: Australian Academy of Science.

Moynihan, John (1988) *All the News in a Flash: Rottnest Communications 1829–1979*, Perth: Australian Telecom & the Australian Institution of Engineers' WA Branch.

Mulcaster, Richard (1970) *The First Part of the Elementarie which entreateth chefelie of the right writing of our English tung* (1582), facsimile edition, Menston, Yorks: Scolar Press.

Nelson, Cary and Grossberg, Lawrence (eds) (1988) *Marxism and the Interpretation of Culture*, Urbana and Chicago: University of Illinois Press.

Newcomb, Horace (ed.) *Television: The Critical View*, 4th edn, New York: Oxford University Press.

Paine, Thomas (1937) *Rights of Man: Being an Answer to Mr. Burke's Attack on the French Revolution* (1791), ed. Hypatia Bradlaugh Bonner, London: Watts.

Paine, Thomas (1976) *Thomas Paine: Common Sense* (1776), ed. Isaac Krammick, Harmondsworth: Penguin.

Park, Robert (1916) 'The city: suggestions for the investigation of human behaviour in the urban environment', in Richard Sennett (ed.) (1969) *Classic Essays on the Culture of Cities*, Englewood Cliffs, NJ: Prentice-Hall, pp. 91–130.

Popper, Karl (1967) 'Knowledge: subjective versus objective', in David Miller (ed.) (1983) *A Pocket Popper*, London: Fontana, pp. 58–77.

Royal Commission into Aboriginal Deaths in Custody (1991) Regional Report of Inquiry into Underlying Issues in Western Australia, by Commissioner Patrick Dodson, 2 vols, Canberra: Australian Government Publishing Service.

Sahlins, Marshall (1976) *Culture and Practical Reason*, Chicago: University of Chicago Press.

Said, Edward (1978) *Orientalism*, London: Routledge & Kegan Paul.

Schaffer, Kay (1987) 'Landscape, representation and Australian national identity', *Australian Journal of Cultural Studies* 4 (2): 47–60.

Schaffer, Kay (1988) *Women in the Bush: Forces of Desire in the Australian Cultural Tradition*, Melbourne: Cambridge University Press.

Sennett, Richard (ed.) (1969) *Classic Essays on the Culture of Cities*, Englewood Cliffs, NJ: Prentice-Hall.

Souter, Gavin (1981) *Company of Heralds*, Melbourne: Melbourne University Press.

Stone, I.F. (1989) *The Trial of Socrates*, London: Picador.

Symons, Michael (1980) *One Continuous Picnic*, Adelaide: Duck Press.

Trevelyan, G.M. (1942–4) *English Social History*, London: Longmans, Green.

Tudor, Henry (1972) *Political Myth*, London: Macmillan.

Turner, Graeme (1990) *British Cultural Studies*, New York: Unwin Hyman.

Veblen, Thorstein (1953) *The Theory of the Leisure Class: an Economic Study of Institutions* (1899), New York: New American Library.

Wirth, Louis (1938) 'Urbanism as a way of life', in Richard Sennett (ed.) (1969) *Classic Essays on the Culture of Cities*, Englewood Cliffs, NJ: Prentice-Hall, pp. 143–64.

INDEX

237